MW01280071

FROMMER'S

GUIDE TO MINNEAPOLIS AND ST. PAUL

by Lucille Johnsen Stelling

Copyright © 1988
Simon & Schuster, Inc.

All rights reserved
including the right of reproduction
in whole or in part in any form

Published by Prentice Hall Press
A Division of Simon & Schuster, Inc.
Gulf + Western Building
One Gulf + Western Plaza
New York, NY 10023

ISBN 0-13-331554-1

Manufactured in the United States of America

*Although every effort was made to ensure the accuracy
of price information appearing in this book,
it should be kept in mind that prices
can and do fluctuate in the course of time.*

CONTENTS

MAPS

ACKNOWLEDGMENTS

Many Minnesotans offered valuable suggestions and information for this book, and I thank them all, particularly Judy Hohmann of the Minnesota Office of Tourism, Eileen McMahon of the St. Paul Convention Bureau, and Lynn Casey, who works with the Minneapolis Convention and Visitors Commission. I benefited too from the enthusiasm of my students and colleagues at Normandale Community College and from that of many other present, past, and potential Minnesotans, including Dan and Marcie Johnsen, Amy and Mark Johnsen-Harris, Carol Johnsen, and Bruce Bryant.

Finally, my very special thanks to Marilyn Wood, who first recognized the promise in this terra incognita, and to Edie Jarolim, who provided such gracious guidance along the way.

To Del,
who helped so much
in so many ways.

INFLATION ALERT: I don't have to tell you that costs will rise regardless of the level of inflation. For that reason it is quite possible that prices may be higher at a given establishment when you read this book than they were at the time this information was collected. As we go to press, I believe I have obtained the most reliable data possible. Nonetheless, in the lifetime of this edition—particularly its second year (1989)—the wise traveler might add 15% to 20% to the prices quoted throughout these pages.

INTRODUCING MINNEAPOLIS AND ST. PAUL

IF ALL YOU'VE SEEN of Minneapolis and St. Paul are the scenes that flashed by behind the credits of the ever-popular "Mary Tyler Moore Show," you're in for a real treat. It's no accident that the Twin Cities were chosen as the backdrop for Mary Richards' weekly adventures: the sleek downtown skyscrapers, the lush parks and lakes, and the comfortable old residential neighborhoods reflect the same intriguing blend of big-city sophistication and innocent, small-town charm that endeared the TV characters to millions of viewers.

Until recently, though, the attractions of this area were generally a well-kept secret, pretty much the private preserve of home-grown Twin Citians—and of transplants from other parts of the country. Many residents had arrived originally for what was to have been a short stay and just remained. It's not that they couldn't go home again; it's just that home was never like this.

Although every Minnesota license plate declares this the land of 10,000 lakes, there are really more than 12,000 in all—and that's only counting the ones that measure ten acres or more. It shouldn't be surprising then that 31 large lakes lie within the metropolitan area of Minneapolis and St. Paul, making outdoor recreation an important part of Twin Cities life throughout the year. Boating, fishing, and swimming in the summertime—ice skating, ice fishing, skiing, snowmobiling, and ice sailing during the winter—are all just a few minutes away by foot or by car from wherever you happen to be.

With one acre of city parkland for every 43 Twin Citians,

joggers, walkers, skaters, and bikers can do their thing in picturesque settings that are intersected by two sets of lakeside routes. Public parks here maintain separate but equal paths for those on foot and those on wheels.

The suburbs offer outdoor attractions of their own: for example, in Apple Valley, cross-country skiers glide past elk, bison, and moose on authentically landscaped terrain at the Minnesota Zoo. And whether you're enjoying outdoor life in the suburbs or the cities, it's nice to know there's no cleaner, fresher air anywhere in the country. This is the only metropolitan area that's never had a single pollution-alert day.

Should you neglect to pack your skates or your bike or your boat while you're getting ready for your visit to the Twin Cities, not to worry. Just about anything you might need for outdoor fun can be rented hereabouts, even if your exercise of choice is strictly hand-to-mouth. At downtown Loring Park in Minneapolis, you can even rent a basket and a blanket to go with the picnic lunch or supper that you buy.

St. Paul has its own popular picnic settings, including a luxuriant fourth-floor, glass-enclosed city park atop the shops and offices of downtown Town Square. Here, among trees and shrubs and cascading waterfalls, you'll find noontime diners enjoying the finger foods they've brought from home or from one of the fast-food stands in the courtyard four levels below. A welcome added touch to the pleasure of passing time in this unique retreat are the organ recitals that take place in Town Square Park every weekday at noon.

Musical performances play a prominent role in much Twin Cities entertainment, most notably at two world-class symphony halls, the elegant old-world Ordway Music Theatre in St. Paul and the modern Orchestra Hall in Minneapolis. And there's music for the eye as well as the ear in downtown Minneapolis where 32 windows of the Schmitt Music Center were bricked up on the parking-lot side of the building to accommodate a mammoth mural of a segment from the score of Maurice Ravel's *Gaspard de la Nuit.* Van Cliburn, in town for an appearance at Orchestra Hall, was so intrigued by the mural that he agreed to perform portions of the piece on a nine-foot Steinway that was pushed out into the parking lot for the occasion. (Pictures of that event appeared in hundreds of newspapers, including *My Weekly Reader,* so your children may already know more about the Twin Cities than you do!)

Perhaps, though, it's theater that has provided the Twin Cities' most significant contribution to culture. *Time* evidently thought so back in the '70s when it highlighted the Tyrone

Guthrie Theater in a cover story called "The Good Life in Minnesota," an article that told the whole world about the remarkably rich quality of life in an area of superb natural beauty, where first-rate sports and recreation coexist amiably with some of the finest art, music, and theater to be found anywhere.

Since its opening performance in 1962, the Guthrie Theater has staged dozens of exciting productions, none more acclaimed, though, than the recent record-shattering *Gospel at Colonus*, which daringly transformed Sophocles' ancient tragedy into an exhilarating musical play set in a contemporary black church. But the Guthrie is only one of more than 90 playhouses in and around Minneapolis and St. Paul. No city in the country outside of New York has more theaters per capita than you'll find here, and no city except New York spends more on the performing arts than Minneapolis and St. Paul do.

Theater in the Round, near the University of Minnesota main campus, is one of the oldest continuously operating community theaters in the country; the Old Log, on the banks of Lake Minnetonka, houses the longest-lived theatrical stock company; and the Minneapolis Children's, adjoining the Institute of Art, is the largest of all American theaters for children; Great North American History Theater offers original historical plays based on actual Minnesota events and people.

Art fanciers can find more than 130 galleries throughout Minneapolis and St. Paul and several major museums as well. The Minneapolis Institute of Art and the Walker Art Center are widely known, not only for their local holdings, but for the successful touring exhibitions that both have originated. More than a quarter of a million people visited the Walker in early 1980 to see 160 Picasso paintings, sculptures, collages, and drawings which the artist had kept for his own collection; later these works were sent to New York City for incorporation into the Picasso retrospective at the Museum of Modern Art.

The hands-on Children's Museum in St. Paul's Bandana Square has an appreciative public of its own, as tomorrow's doctors and dentists, engineers and crane operators, service-station attendants, computer scientists, and TV personnel get to practice their future professions here.

And the Science Museum of Minnesota attracts audiences of all ages to attend films at their unusual Omnitheater, where panoramic adventures are displayed on a huge curved screen by the world's largest (72-mm) movie projector. First, though, you have to get by that giant iguana at the museum's front door. A 16-year-old artist created this remarkable reptile that's become a local celebrity, serving sometimes as an extended bench for young museum-goers. Popular as he is, though, no one has tried taking Iggy home, maybe because at 40 feet in length and 3,900 pounds in weight, this one-of-a-kind iguana is far from portable. Lighter but no less popular are the dinosaurs you'll find inside the Science Museum, where, in the fascinating "dinosaur lab," visitors can watch the step-by-step reconstruction of one of these extinct mammals.

For those who prefer competition to culture, four professional major-league teams call Minnesota home. At the Hubert H. Humphrey Metrodome, 55,000 fans can watch the world-champion Minnesota Twins in action. When the Minnesota Vikings are in town, the Dome becomes a stadium, with seats for 62,000 football enthusiasts.

Metropolitan Sports Center in suburban Bloomington draws large crowds for North Stars hockey and Minnesota Strikers soccer games. And out in Shakopee, you can bet your bottom dollar at Canterbury Downs where thoroughbreds and quarter horses race six days each week from April through October.

If you prefer spending your money on a sure thing, you need look no farther than the suburbs: shopping history was made there in 1956 when Southdale, the nation's first enclosed two-story regional shopping mall, was born. By now suburban malls have become so integral a part of people's lives that many people go there on doctor's orders. Long before shops open each day, fitness fans are walking and jogging in the malls' climate-controlled comfort, giving only sidelong glances at the tempting window displays on all sides. And now, one step ahead as usual, the Twin Cities are in the process of bringing shopping malls right into the heart of town, in handsome centrally located downtown skyscrapers.

Maybe the greatest strides in the Twin Cities during the past decade have been architectural. Prize-winning skyscrapers like the World Trade Center in St. Paul and the IDS Building in Minneapolis tower above older, more familiar structures. The Investors Diversified Services Tower, centrally located on Minneapolis' Nicollet pedestrian mall, was designed by famed architect Philip Johnson, who said of its glass expanses, "God changes my wallpaper four times each year." And, in fact, for the benefit of passersby the outer appearance of this handsome reflective structure changes several times each day. Along with the creation of new Twin Cities landmarks, there's a healthy respect here for distinguished old buildings, many of which are listed on the National Register of Historic Places.

In Minneapolis, the shops, restaurants, and galleries of St. Anthony Main and Riverplace reside in restored brick and limestone warehouses and mills on the banks of the Mississippi, not far from the waterfalls that powered Minneapolis' early industries.

At the historic World Theatre in St. Paul, where Garrison Keillor used to host the phenomenally popular "Prairie Home Companion," you can now enjoy an incredible array of entertainment from the Eastman Brass Quintet to harpsichordist Edward Parmentier to rock-singer Donovan. This grand old building continues as a very vital part of downtown St. Paul.

In both cities, at any time of year you can walk from one end of downtown to the other without any regard for rain or snow or anything else the weather forecaster might dream up: the skyways are absolutely weatherproof. In Minneapolis, the network of glassed-in second-story thoroughfares extends for 21 blocks, making it the world's longest privately owned skyway system. Measuring three miles, St. Paul's Skyway system is the world's largest publicly owned one.

Certainly mobility is one of the prime perks offered by these enclosed second-story glassed-in walkways. Another is the view they provide. In Minneapolis you'll be able to look down on the busy Nicollet Mall, surrounded by striking new skyscrapers like the Conservatory, the IDS Tower, and City Center. St. Paul has some skyscrapers of its own for skyway viewing: the new World Trade Center and Town Square, among others. But nothing here or anywhere can beat your St. Paul Skyway view of the magnificent Minnesota State Capitol.

In both downtowns, architectural beauty is complemented by the natural beauty of the Mississippi, just a short walk away. In fact, it was this mighty river that first brought white men to these shores as they searched for a water route to fabulous wealth in the mysterious Orient.

How It All Began

French explorers, traveling south from Canada, thought the Mississippi River might be their Northwest Passage toward the opulent East of which Marco Polo had written such tantalizing accounts. During the 17th century at least one of these adventurous souls, the self-confident Jean Nicollet, brought along on his expedition a change of clothes that he must have considered appropriate for the pomp and circumstance of his arrival in China. Imagine his chagrin and the open-mouthed astonishment of passing Dakota Indians when Nicollet stepped ashore in an intricately decorated robe "all strewn with flowers and birds of many colors."

Disappointed in their search for a new continent, these explorers may have found some consolation in the abundance of valuable furs that awaited them much closer to home. Also waiting were Indians who were more than willing to exchange their beaver and muskrat pelts for blankets, knives, tobacco, tools, and other unfamiliar and intriguing items.

In time the Ojibwa tribes from the East Coast joined the Dakotas, moving into this area in advance of white men who had given them rifles, liquor, and other trappings of civilization. The name "Ojibwa" sounded like "Chippewa" to white men's ears, and that's the name by which the tribe is still known today. In turn, these advancing Indians disparaged the Dakotas, calling them "Nadouessioux" or "little vipers," a name the white men shortened to "Sioux." Different from each other in language and customs, the Sioux and the Chippewas waged fierce and bloody warfare which threatened not only the white men's fur trade, but their settlements as well.

French dominion over this area came to an end in 1763, at the conclusion of the French and Indian War, when France surrendered to Great Britain all the land east of the Mississippi River. British rule was short-lived, however. Just 20 years later Britain relinquished this land to the newly formed United States of America, and in 1803, by terms of the Louisiana Purchase, Napoleon sold to the United States the territory that would one day include the state of Minnesota.

Now it was time to establish a permanent official presence here, and President Thomas Jefferson sent army troops out to prepare for the construction of a "center of civilization" at the juncture of the Mississippi and Minnesota Rivers. Fort Snelling became a refuge for traders, explorers, missionaries, and settlers, among them several Swiss families that had earlier been lured by promises of a bright future in Canada. Essentially squatters on land that had been ceded to the military by the Sioux, these families made their homes and livelihood in the protective shadow of the fort until a treaty with the Indians in 1837 officially opened new lands for settlement. The families then crossed the Mississippi to live and work on land that has since become St. Paul.

Awaiting the settlers when they arrived was an unsavory Canadian voyageur, Pierre "Pig's Eye" Parrant, who did a brisk business bootlegging rum to soldiers. The new settlement was known as "Pig's Eye" until 1841, when Fr. Lucien Galtier named his recently constructed log chapel in honor of St. Paul. Townspeople made that the name of their community as well.

Until as late as 1848 many of the inhabitants of this area spoke only French, but when Minnesota became an American territory in 1848, settlers from the eastern United States began to arrive in large numbers. And then came immigrants from elsewhere in Europe. During the decades between 1860 and the turn of the century, thousands of newcomers arrived from northern European countries, including Sweden, Norway, Denmark, and Germany, along with some from Great Britain, particularly Ireland. Pamphlets printed in a variety of languages and distributed abroad had borne offers that were impossible to refuse—reduced ship and railway rates and reduced costs for food, clothing, and shelter while the newcomers searched for land.

St. Paul, now the port of entry to the frontier beyond, was also the acknowledged center of business and culture in the new territory. Incorporated as a city in 1854, St. Paul became the state capital in 1858.

Minneapolis, off to a somewhat slower start, didn't become a city until 1867, but in 1872 it absorbed the village of St. Anthony, whose waterfall powered the sawmills and flour mills that would make the "Mill City" a prosperous industrial center. By the end of the decade, Minneapolis was declaring itself superior to St. Paul in numbers as well as importance. Competition grew more and more intense, and finally, in 1890, sibling rivalry erupted into internecine warfare when census results showed the population of Minneapolis to be 40,386 greater than that of St. Paul. Amid cries of foul play, a recount showed that both cities had substantially inflated their numbers. The results: while Minneapolis was in fact the more populous of the two, its original total had been padded by 18,386 votes, with St. Paul's initial claim 9,425 over the recounted figure. Mutually embarrassed, the cities were mutually forgiving. Angry headlines gradually faded away, and so, too, did the free-swinging antagonism that had marked the recount of 1890.

The Twin Cities Today

Through the years, Minneapolis and St. Paul have developed individual styles that complement rather than conflict with each other. More traditional than her younger sister, St. Paul is often called "the last city of the East." And if St. Paul reminds you a bit of New England, Minneapolis, "the first city of the West," may make you think of fast-paced Los Angeles.

Which of the two will you prefer? That's a question that needn't be answered—or even asked. One of the best things about the Twin Cities is that you don't have to choose between them. With their downtown areas only ten minutes apart, they combine to offer a remarkable diversity of activities and attractions, and that's what makes them such an extraordinary vacation value. It's two great destinations for the price of one when you visit Minneapolis and St. Paul.

Chapter II

GETTING THERE AND GETTING ACQUAINTED

SITUATED MIDWAY BETWEEN the Atlantic and the Pacific, Minneapolis and St. Paul are readily accessible from anywhere in the world.

Northwest Airlines brings international visitors here daily from Europe, Asia, Mexico, and the Caribbean, with non-stop flights from London and Hawaii. Eastern Airlines flies passengers to the Twin Cities every day from the Caribbean as well as from South America. And Continental Airlines arrives daily with travelers from Australia and Tahiti.

Domestic visitors often arrive by rail and by road. Amtrak maintains a large Twin Cities terminal in the Midway District between Minneapolis and St. Paul. Greyhound Bus Lines and Trailways Bus Lines have terminals in both St. Paul and Minneapolis as part of their coast-to-coast service. And for travelers who prefer to do their own driving, major Interstate highways converge in the Twin Cities, making this area easy to reach and easy to get around in after you've arrived.

Getting There

BY AIR: Because nearly two dozen international, national, and regional airlines serve the Minneapolis–St. Paul airport, it should be possible to make specific recommendations concerning rates and schedules. Unfortunately, that's not the case. At this writing, conditions could hardly be more chaotic, with fares on the selfsame plane varying wildly, depending on the day of the week that you'll be traveling, the length of your stay, and the advance notice you can provide. And if the present

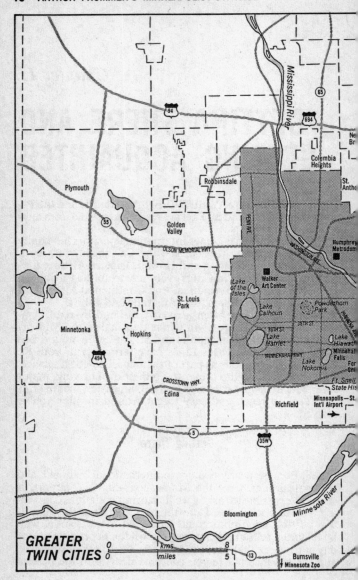

GREATER TWIN CITIES

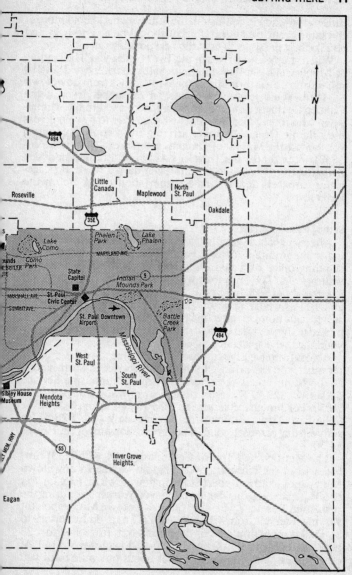

prices are a study in confusion, the future seems to hold more of the same. Your trusty travel agent should be able to help find you the best possible flight at the best possible rate.

When your plane arrives in the Twin Cities, you'll be landing at **Minneapolis–St. Paul International Airport,** located just 10 miles from downtown Minneapolis, 8½ miles from downtown St. Paul. You'll leave your plane on the upper level of the Charles Lindberg Terminal Building, dedicated to the Minnesotan who in 1927 became the first man ever to fly solo across the Atlantic Ocean. If you're arriving from another country, you can use the Mutual-of-Omaha currency exchange (tel. 726-5848), located near the Traveler's Aid and Information desks; it's open from 6 a.m. to 6 p.m. seven days a week. Baggage-claim carousels and ground-transportation desks are on the lower level.

Getting from the Airport

After you collect your luggage and leave the terminal building on the ground-floor level, you'll see across the street the free-standing office of a taxi dispatcher at the head of a line of waiting cabs. Taxi fares to downtown Minneapolis and St. Paul average about $15, but at this writing, a 20% discount is available from Airport Taxi (tel. 721-6566) if you phone for an assigned cab number after picking up your luggage. You'll be picked up by your designated taxi near the phone booth just beyond the taxi dispatcher's office.

Across from baggage carousel no. 10 on the lower level of the terminal, you can arrange for **limousine service** to Minneapolis at the Minneapolis & Suburban Airport Limousine Service desk (tel. 827-7777). Service to downtown Minneapolis is $6.50. For limousine service to St. Paul, go to the St. Paul & Suburban Airport Limousine Service desk (tel. 726-5479) across from carousel no. 6. The fare to downtown St. Paul is $4.50.

The Metropolitan Transit Commission (tel. 827-7733) runs **buses** from the airport to Washington Avenue in downtown Minneapolis and to Robert Street in downtown St. Paul for 75¢ or 90¢, depending on whether or not you're traveling during the rush hour. Bus no. 7 will take you to downtown Minneapolis at varying intervals from 4:18 a.m. to 12:17 a.m. daily. Service to St. Paul is more limited. For nearly an hour, from 3:43 to 4:33 p.m., you can get a no. 62 bus directly to downtown St. Paul. At other times, take the no. 7 bus for about one mile until you

reach the Federal Building, where you transfer to a no. 9 bus
that will take you to downtown St. Paul. These no. 9 buses leave
the Federal Building from 4:32 a.m. through 11:35 p.m. each
day. (You'll know the large MTC buses by their color. Newer
ones are white; older ones are red. All are marked with a large
"T" on the side.)

BY TRAIN: Amtrak passengers to the Twin Cities arrive in St.
Paul at the St. Paul / Minneapolis Minnesota Midway Station,
730 Transfer Rd., St. Paul (tel. 612/339-2382), located about 10
minutes from downtown St. Paul, 20 minutes from downtown
Min-neapolis. Present round-trip Amtrak fares to Minneapolis
and St. Paul from New York are $223; from Chicago, $104;
from Los Angeles and Miami, $200. Cab service from the Am-
trak terminal is $1.10 per mile.

BY BUS: Both Greyhound and Trailways Bus Companies serve
the Twin Cities. In Minneapolis, the **Greyhound Bus Terminal** is
at 29 N. 9th St. (tel. 371-3320); Greyhound's St. Paul address is
9th Street at St. Peter Street (tel. 222-0509). The **Trailways Bus
Terminal** in Minneapolis is at 400 S. 3rd St. (tel. 332-3273); in
St. Paul, at 469 St. Peter St. (tel. 228-0681). Greyhound's current round-trip rate from New York is $238, from Chicago it's
$88, from Los Angeles, $160, and from Miami, $169, with a
bargain fare to customers who order their tickets 30 days in
advance—$118 round trip to anywhere Greyhound goes.
Trailways' round-trip rate from New York is $226; from Chica-
go, $76; from Los Angeles and from Miami, $226.

BY CAR: As for highway accessibility, Interstate 35, which extends from the Canadian border to Mexico, and Interstate 94,
which extends from the Atlantic to the Pacific, intersect in
downtown Minneapolis about ten miles from downtown St.
Paul. Within the Twin Cities, I-35 divides, becoming I-35E in
St. Paul and I-35W in Minneapolis: I-35E goes nearly all the
way through St. Paul, except for about one mile which remains
to be completed, while I-35W goes north to south through Minneapolis. Interstate 94 goes through both cities in an east-west
direction. A Belt Line freeway system encircles the Twin Cities
area, with I-494 extending through the southern and western
suburbs and I-694 traveling through the eastern and northern
suburbs. The Belt Line has interchanges with all the major
highway routes.

Getting to Know Minneapolis and St. Paul

Although they share many miles of common border, Minneapolis and St. Paul are not Siamese twins: they're separated here and there by the Mississippi River, which saw the cities' earliest settlements on its banks. To this day, parts of downtown Minneapolis and downtown St. Paul overlook the majestic Mississippi. A more modern, man-made form of transportation has also become dominant in the Twin Cities during the past couple of decades—those glass-walled skyway systems, heated in the winter and air-conditioned in the summer, which connect miles of downtown shops, offices, restaurants, and entertainment areas. By now, these second-story walkways are an important part of life in the cities. In fact, it's said that the skyways are to Minneapolis and St. Paul what the canals are to Venice.

The creation of the skyway systems was the first move in a continuing crusade by local community leaders to prevent in the Twin Cities the kind of deterioration that has plagued downtown areas elsewhere. One measure of their success is a recent building boom unprecedented in Twin Cities history, adding dozens of handsome office buildings, high-rise condominiums, and enclosed shopping centers to the downtown areas. Returnees to the Twin Cities are astonished at the way the skylines have changed during the past several years. First-timers are impressed by the dramatic beauty of gleaming glass-and-steel structures, many of them designed by internationally recognized architects.

I'll choose the tallest, most centrally located building in each city as the focal point for your Twin Cities orientations. In each case, the focal point is set squarely in the center of the city's downtown area—not surprising, for in this part of the country each city's downtown begins on the banks of the Mississippi River and then extends from there into clearly definable sections and neighborhoods.

MEET MINNEAPOLIS: One of the first things you'll notice about downtown Minneapolis is the **Nicollet Mall,** with its trees, flowers, decorative street lamps, and—weather permitting—dancing fountains. This is the nation's longest major pedestrian mall, with heated bus shelters, a farmer's market on Fridays during the summer, extending about one mile down fashionable Nicollet Avenue. Halfway down the mall, between 7th Street and 8th Street South, stands one of the city's most imposing buildings, the 57-story **Investors Diversified Services (IDS) Tower,** which rises from the midst of the bustling **Crystal Court,**

a three-story center of shops and eating places. You'll also find in the Crystal Court a **tourist information desk** with maps, brochures, and specific answers to any questions you might have about the city.

Two major department stores, Dayton's and Donaldsons, stand on either side of 7th Street South, across the mall from the IDS Tower connected via a skyway. Dayton's is freestanding; Donaldsons is part of a large enclosed complex known as **City Center,** which contains three stories of smart shops, fine restaurants, and assorted fast-food stands. Among the most famous tenants of City Center are an elegant Marriott Hotel and a charming Laura Ashley boutique, with its fine line of British apparel and accessories. City Center occupies one square city block between 7th and 6th Streets and between Nicollet and Hennepin Avenues.

The Warehouse District

If you follow 7th Street past City Center and across Hennepin Avenue, you'll find, one block beyond, on 7th Street and First Avenue North, **Butler Square,** the start of the first neighborhood on our tour, the historic Warehouse District. Butler Square is a handsome office and commercial complex that started life in 1906 as a sprawling warehouse. Now it stands at the edge of several blocks of carefully restored turn-of-the-century structures that house restaurants, bars, nightclubs, shops, and galleries.

The Warehouse District is a popular gathering place for nearby office workers and, in fact, for Twin Citians in general. Toward the eastern edge of the district you'll find antiquers, in shops that are beginning to establish their own niche here.

St. Anthony Falls, the cities' earliest source of water power, still function at their original site on the Mississippi River, their size surprisingly modest considering the monumental part they played in the development of this area.

St. Anthony Main and Riverplace

Before there was a city of Minneapolis or a city of St. Paul, there was the village of St. Anthony with its cobblestone Main Street. When the business district moved across the Mississippi and beyond toward the end of the 19th century, Main Street fell into disrepair. During the 1970s, though, its cobblestone surface was restored, and it has since become the site of a major center, **St. Anthony Main,** with specialty shops, restaurants, and galleries all housed in vast river-view warehouses that once stored grain and other locally manufactured products.

DOWNTOWN MINNEAPOLIS

More recently, an upscale mall called **Riverplace** opened nearby with its own mix of restaurants, bars, and shops. This area's blend of the historic and the contemporary has made it popular with home folks and visitors alike. (If you visit the Twin Cities during the Christmas season, be advised that the gloriously decorated courtyards at Riverplace rank high among holiday must-sees here.)

A block beyond the historic riverfront district, you'll find University Avenue. Follow it east, and you'll pass by fraternity and sorority houses on your way to the main campus of the University of Minnesota, which has buildings on both the east and west banks of the Mississippi River.

The University of Minnesota Area

A hub of activity in any university town is the local campus, where interesting people gather to share their knowledge and their talent. Imagine, then, the variety and vitality to be found here in the Twin Cities, home of the largest university on one campus in the entire United States.

There's an assortment of architecture to be admired on the campus of the **University of Minnesota,** extending from venerable old buildings like Eddy Hall on the east bank of the Mississippi to sleek new complexes like the west-bank Humphrey Institute of Public Affairs. Particularly interesting to visitors is the Civil and Mineral Engineering Building, which extends six stories underground, tunneled out of natural bedrock.

University-related shopping and entertainment draw students and their elders to two stimulating areas on opposite sides of the Mississippi, **Dinkytown** on the east bank and Seven Corners on the west. At **Seven Corners,** you'll find a particularly lively atmosphere in an area that's recently been designated the West Bank Theater District. Popular after-hours hangouts abound, and you'll find here some of the best theater, music, and stand-up comedy in town.

Between Seven Corners and the downtown Nicollet Mall stands the **Hubert H. Humphrey Metrodome,** a sports facility which is beloved by some, bemoaned by others. It's not the prettiest part of the Minneapolis scene, but the Dome does draw large crowds to games played by the Minnesota Vikings, the Minnesota Twins, and the University of Minnesota Golden Gophers. Out-of-towners, here for a brief stay, seem to like the Dome, if only because they can be sure their game won't be rained out. Don't worry about being unable to find the Metrodome; you can't miss it—a huge white mushroom planted on the eastern edge of downtown Minneapolis.

A Cultural Corner of Downtown Minneapolis

Returning now to the IDS Building and proceeding south-ward on the mall to 12th Street South, you'll pass the sleek, modernistic **Orchestra Hall**, home of the internationally fa-mous Minnesota Orchestra. Just a few blocks farther ahead, lovely **Loring Park,** named for the founder of Minneapolis' ex-tensive park system, provides a beautiful border to the southern edge of downtown. If present plans materialize, Loring Park will also be the site of a new pedestrian bridge, due to open in the spring of 1988. It'll provide passage over Hennepin and Lyndale Avenues to the **Minneapolis Sculpture Gardens,** a brand-new area of outdoor statuary facing the **Tyrone Guthrie Theater,** with its famous repertory company, and the **Walker Art Center,** with its renowned collection of modern art. (A more traditional collection can be found at the Minneapolis In-stitute of Art, still farther to the south.)

On the hilly terrain behind the Walker-Guthrie complex, overlooking downtown, are two of the city's prime residential areas, Lowry Hill and Kenwood Parkway. **Lowry Hill** is famous for its 19th-century mansions, many of which had third-story ballrooms because in those days people entertained at home. The homes in nearby **Kenwood** are lovely, but less elaborate. Still, one of them has gained a bit of fame as the place where Mary Richards (a.k.a. Mary Tyler Moore) used to live. (By the way, it was at the IDS Tower Crystal Court that Mary threw her hat up in the air week after week!)

Uptown and the Lake District

Following Hennepin Avenue southward through about two tidy miles of stores, restaurants, and multiple dwellings, you'll find yourself in the heart of a smart residential and commercial neighborhood long known as **Uptown** and more recently dubbed "Yuptown." The well-heeled young urban profession-als who now live and work here spend a lot of time in local clas-sic movie houses, ethnic restaurants, and trendy bars. **Calhoun Square,** at the corner of Hennepin Avenue and Lake Street, is a fashionable shopping mall that adds further to the magnetic charm of Uptown. Another major draw is the annual outdoor Uptown Art Fair, which attracts craftsmen each summer from throughout the country.

Hennepin Avenue ends a few blocks farther south at **Lake-wood Cemetery,** where a large and memorable graveside plaque marks the burial place of Hubert H. Humphrey, formerly mayor of Minneapolis, U.S. senator from Minnesota, and vice-president of the United States. And a few blocks farther to the west, in one of the most picturesque parts of the city, you'll find the start of a chain of popular neighborhood lakes: **Lake Calhoun, Lake Harriet,** and **Lake of the Isles.** On the north side of Lake of the Isles, Kenwood Parkway will take you back to the vicinity of the Guthrie Theater, and then, via Hennepin Avenue, you're on your way back to downtown Minneapolis.

A VIEW OF ST. PAUL: And now for your introduction to St. Paul. Like other older "river towns," downtown St. Paul defies directions based strictly on north, east, south, and west designations because its streets and avenues were originally set up to run parallel with and perpendicular to the meandering Mississippi.

An appropriate focal point for your St. Paul orientation is the striking, centrally located **World Trade Center,** a towering complex of offices at 8th Street between Cedar and Wabasha Avenues. Standing on the Wabasha Avenue side of the World Trade Center, whether you're looking north toward the State Capitol or south toward the Mississippi, you'll see the series of second-story skyways that link one side of this busy avenue to the other.

The 40-story World Trade Center, opened in late summer of 1987, is expected to promote and extend trade between the Upper Midwest and foreign markets throughout Europe, Asia, and Central and South America. The Twin Cities, known widely as the "computer capital of the country," already does a brisk business with overseas markets. The fact that so many major corporations headquarter here—Honeywell, Control Data, 3M, Northwest Airlines, and Pillsbury, among others—makes Minneapolis–St. Paul an especially appropriate headquarters for international trade.

Toward the State Capitol

One block north of the World Trade Center, at the corner of Wabasha Avenue and Exchange Street, stands the **Science Museum of Minnesota,** home of Iggy, the giant iguana, among other impressive creatures and exhibits. Diagonally across the street you'll find the exquisite **World Theatre,** where Garrison Keillor's "Prairie Home Companion" used to be broadcast live each week to radio fans throughout the nation. From this corner, looking north, you've got a picture-perfect view of the superb **State Capitol** of Minnesota and of its famous dome, the largest unsupported marble dome in the entire world. At the base of the dome, a group of graceful gilded figures represent *The Progress of the State:* a charioteer holds up a horn of plenty, prancing horses represent the power of nature, and two majestic women embody the spirit of civilization.

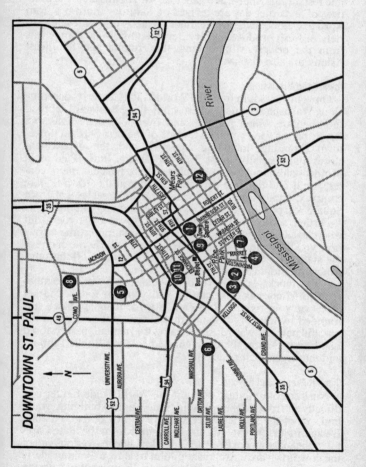

DOWNTOWN ST. PAUL

1. Minnesota Office of Tourism
2. Ordway Music Hall
3. Civic Center
4. St. Paul Public Library
5. State Capitol
6. St. Paul Cathedral
7. Minnesota Museum of Art
8. Minnesota State Fairgrounds
9. Minnesota World Trade Center
10. Science Museum of Minnesota
11. 3M William L. McKnight Omnitheatre
12. Union Depot Place

Historic Lowertown

To the east of the World Trade Center, the past and the present blend harmoniously in a restored area known as Lowertown. Venerable buildings like the old **Union Depot, Galtier Plaza,** and the **Park Square Court Building,** all of which played an important role in St. Paul's earlier history, now house fine restaurants, shops, and galleries. And in this area, the practices of an earlier day are revived on Saturday mornings from April to October, when the **Farmer's Market** offers for sale a variety of fresh produce, bakery items, and flowers. Handcrafts from the newest Minnesotans, the Hmong and Southeast Asians, are also displayed.

Toward the Mississippi

On your way south from the World Trade Center, proceeding along Wabasha Avenue you'll reach **Kellogg Boulevard,** a broad thoroughfare which parallels and overlooks the Mississippi River; on the way, you'll pass some of the best St. Paul downtown shopping, including Dayton's and the department stores and specialty shops at **Town Square.** In St. Paul as in Minneapolis, Donaldsons has chosen to be part of a major center; you'll find this fine department store in the Town Square complex. A tourist-information desk on the street level of Town Square will provide answers to your questions about the city.

Farther south on **Wabasha Avenue,** toward the riverfront where excursion-boat tours are a popular summertime attraction, you'll see the **St. Paul City Hall.** This is the home of one of the state's most beloved statues, a 36-foot-high, 60-ton onyx American Indian called *The God of Peace.*

A few blocks west on Kellogg Boulevard, beyond the modernistic **Minnesota Museum of Art,** you can follow Market Street on your right to **Rice Park,** a verdant square block surrounded by four of St. Paul's most important structures: the graceful new Ordway Music Theatre, the meticulously restored Landmark Center, the distinguished St. Paul Public Library, and the elegant Saint Paul Hotel.

Summit Avenue and Beyond

North of our vantage point at the World Trade Center and directly in front of the splendid State Capitol building, you'll find one of the shortest streets in this or any other city. **John Ireland Boulevard** extends just half a mile from the State Capitol to the magnificent **St. Paul Cathedral,** which overlooks all of the downtown area. Archbishop John Ireland, a dynamic cleric who used his considerable influence and powers of persuasion to create a stately cathedral modeled after St. Peter's in Rome, dedicated it in 1915 to the people of St. Paul. In front of the cathedral, John Ireland Boulevard runs into Summit Avenue, one of two designated Monumental Residential Boulevards in the United States.

Extending for five miles until it ends at the Mississippi River, **Summit Avenue** is the address of some of the nation's stateliest Victorian mansions, among them the home of James J. Hill, founder of the Great Northern Railroad, and the more modest digs of F. Scott Fitzgerald, who wrote parts of *This Side of Paradise* while living here. The official residence of the governor of Minnesota is also on Summit Avenue, and farther on you'll find the campuses of two famous Midwestern colleges, Macalester and the College of St. Thomas.

Running parallel to and south of Summit is **Grand Avenue,** St. Paul's version of Minneapolis' Uptown, a trendy neighborhood that's popular for its distinctive dining, shopping, and entertainment and for its annual summertime festival, Grand Old Day.

Farther to the northwest is **Como Park,** with its popular lake, zoo, and conservatory, and nearby there's the **Bandana Square Complex** with the Children's Museum for kids of all ages. (The complex formerly housed Northern Pacific Railroad's trains, which were painted and refurbished there.) Kids of all ages also enjoy the 17 scale miles of tracks, trains, and landscaping set up by members of the Twin City Model Railroad Club in the nearby Bandana Square Shopping Mall.

The **State Fairgrounds** lie in this area too, not far from I-94, which will take you back to downtown St. Paul.

A FEW WORDS ABOUT THE WEATHER: If you want to start an animated conversation with one of the locals during your stay in the Twin Cities, just ask about the winter of 1986–1987. Through much of January and February, while folks in other parts were digging out from under record-breaking snowfalls or slipping and sliding on icy roads, we were basking in mid-40s sunshine. There was plenty of man-made snow on city and suburban ski slopes, but little sign of winter white anywhere else. Visitors must have been astonished by the balminess of it all, particularly since the common perception of Twin Cities' winters is that they're comparable to what you'd find in outer Siberia or, closer to home, at International Falls, the northernmost Minnesota town whose bone-chilling temperatures regularly make national news. Actually, weather in Minneapolis and St. Paul tends to be similar to that in other northern American cities, except that for most of the year there's relatively little humidity in these parts, so you probably won't feel as warm or as cold as the thermometer might indicate.

WHAT TO BRING ALONG: Casual clothing is appropriate for most activities throughout the year, but if you're planning an extraspecial evening out, you'll want something a bit more formal. Some restaurants do require that men wear jacket and tie for dinner. Remember to bring a pair of shorts for your summertime stay and a light sweater or jacket for those cool summer evenings. Whatever the winter weather, many Twin Citians go through the entire season hatless and scarfless. A warm coat's a necessity, though, and so are gloves and boots—unless the winter of 1986–1987 plays a return engagement. Finally, of course, for this and every other trip, a pair of comfortable walking shoes can make all the difference.

Getting Around

BY CAR: Unless you plan to spend all your time downtown, you'll want to rent a car for at least part of your visit to the Twin Cities. Otherwise you'll miss some of the many attractions and activities hereabouts. Metropolitan Transit Commission buses are the only form of mass transportation, and although they're efficient and reliable, their schedule may not coincide with yours.

Local car-rental companies include **National Car Rental,** Minneapolis–St. Paul International Airport (tel. 726-5600); **Dollar Rent-a-Car,** Minneapolis–St. Paul International Airport (tel. 726-9494); **Hertz Rent-A-Car,** Minneapolis–St. Paul International Airport (tel. 726-1600); and **Avis Rent-A-Car,** Minneapolis–St. Paul International Airport (tel. 726-1526).

BY BUS: If you're going to spend the day or the evening downtown, one thin dime will take you to most offices, restaurants, and businesses, thanks to the Metropolitan Transit Commission's **"Dime Zone."** You don't even need to remember route numbers, just the direction in which you want to travel the cities' major streets.

For longer MTC expeditions, you can get **maps,** pocket schedules, and tokens in St. Paul at Town Square, 7th Street and Cedar Avenue. In Minneapolis, you'll find them at the IDS Crystal Court, 7th Street and Nicollet Mall, or the MTC Transit Store, 719 Marquette Ave.

Fares range from 60¢ to $1.25, depending on the time of day and distance traveled. You'll need the exact change when you board the bus unless you've purchased a token or a Commuter Ticket. They don't reduce the cost of your MTC ride, but they might reduce the scrounging for change you'd otherwise face when you get on the bus.

For Metropolitan Transit Commission **information,** phone 827-7733.

BY CAB: Cab fares are $1.10 per mile. Cab companies include **Airport Taxi** (tel. 721-6566), **Suburban Taxi** (tel. 888-9199), and **St. Paul Yellow Cab** (tel. 222-4433).

Chapter III

WHERE TO STAY

THREE MAJOR AREAS and types of accommodations have developed in the Twin Cities over the years: large, expensive, rather formal hotels in downtown Minneapolis and downtown St. Paul, and smaller, more casual, more moderately priced motels elsewhere, particularly along the strip of I-494 (Bloomington) that links the southern and western suburbs to the Twin Cities International Airport. Generally hotels and motels on the "strip" are 15 minutes or less from the airport, 30 minutes or less from downtown Minneapolis and St. Paul.

Recently, larger and pricier hotels have begun making their appearance beyond the city limits, but in general it's safe to say that you'll pay more for accommodations downtown than in the suburbs and, according to recent studies, you'll pay more in Minneapolis than in St. Paul.

If you're going to be carless for most of your stay, you may be better off in one downtown or the other, where you can get around by foot or by bus to many of the most popular local attractions. Destinations that lie outside downtown areas are readily accessible by cab, and frequently by bus.

On the other hand, if you're going to have the use of a car during your stay, you might consider heading for the "strip," where hotels and motels offer free parking and easy access from I-494 to the network of beltlines, freeways, and Interstates that connect the cities and suburbs. If you're here on business, you'll find that many of the corporate offices in the Twin Cities are located in suburban rather than downtown areas.

I've selected hotels and motels in three price categories: expensive, moderate, and budget. Admittedly, one person's moderate is another person's expensive and a third one's budget, but let's use these dollar amounts, including tax, as guidelines: **expensive** hotels charge $85 and more per night,

budget lodgings run $50 and less, and **moderate** choices cover anything in between.

Of course there are variables here and there. For example, at Embassy Suites, prices are pushed into the expensive category by the 11% **hotel tax** in Bloomington and St. Paul. (In Minneapolis, the hotel tax is 12%.) Certain amenities, though, combine to make the final cost very moderate indeed when you factor in those complimentary cooked-to-order Embassy breakfasts, nightly cocktail parties, and free parking. Free parking in the downtown area is a rarity.

By the way, don't hesitate to ask about discounts when you're making reservations, especially if you'll be here on vacation. Weekend rates, senior citizens' rates, and children's rates, among others, are widely available and can make a big difference in your total tab.

The **Minnesota Office of Tourism** (tel. 612/296-5029, or toll free 800/328-1461, 800/652-9747 in Minnesota) will prepare a customized printout for you of hotels and motels offering the kinds of amenities you're most interested in.

Expensive Hotels ($85 and up, Double)

Luxury abounds at the downtown **Hyatt Regency Minneapolis**, 1300 Nicollet Mall, Minneapolis, MN 55403 (tel. 612/370-1234, or toll free 800/228-9000). A handsome fountain sculpture is the focal point of a large, decorative lobby where there's plenty of comfortable seating for prime people-watching. This is a hotel that's as popular with the home folks as with guests to the city. Two of the finest restaurants in town adjoin the main lobby of the Hyatt Regency. The Willows, an elegant contemporary dining room with mirrored pillars and ceilings, is famous for its daily smörgåsbord, a dazzling array of pâtés, seafood and vegetable marinades, mousses, salads, and more—a best buy at $7.25. And the Terrace is one of the more popular casual dining spots in town.

But for visitors to the Twin Cities, one of the major attractions at the Hyatt Regency may be the guest membership in the excellent Greenway Athletic Club, located on the 6th floor of this 24-story building. Local members enjoy the finest of fitness facilities here, including weight-lifting, racquetball, tennis, squash, a running track, sauna, and Jacuzzi; the price for all this is $8 per visit. There's also a large swimming pool available to all Hyatt Regency guests.

Nonsmokers have the 16th floor all to themselves, and women travelers often ask for the rooms outfitted with hair dryers, lighted cosmetic mirrors, and reel-out clotheslines. All rooms enjoy delightful views of the city and provide in-house pay movies, complimentary HBO and cable news, AM/FM clock-radios, and for that special homey touch, green plants. Rates are $99 single occupancy, $114 double. Senior citizens get a real bargain here: $75 for either single or double occupancy, subject to availability.

You'll find a beautiful blend of the old and the new at the downtown **Saint Paul Hotel**, 350 Market St., St. Paul, MN 55102 (tel. 612/292-9292). Back in 1910 this was St. Paul's première hotel. Now, after an extensive renovation in 1982, it has taken its place once more as a distinguished grand old hotel which offers superb accommodations and services to those who expect and appreciate the best. Looking across Rice Park at the Ordway Music Theatre, the Saint Paul Hotel is adjacent on one side to the beautiful St. Paul Public Library and on the other to Landmark Center, the restored Old Federal Courts Building which, after its dedication in 1896, became headquarters for all federal offices in the Upper Midwest.

But if the Saint Paul Hotel maintains close ties with the city's past, it's also an integral part of St. Paul's burgeoning present. Situated at one end of an extensive skyway system, it offers guests climate-controlled access to 38 downtown blocks of shops, banks, restaurants, and varied forms of entertainment.

Accommodations at the Saint Paul Hotel are appropriately elegant. Once past the lobby with its antique crystal chandeliers, its turn-of-the-century love seats and chairs, and its giant Oriental screen, you'll find that the rooms, decorated individually, contain either a king-size bed or two double beds, along with two comfortable chairs and an ample table. Superior rooms cost $89 single occupancy, $109 double. The standard rooms, slightly smaller and located adjacent to an elevator, go for $84 single occupancy, $99 double. Deluxe rooms, outfitted with a love seat in place of the two chairs, cost $94 single occupancy, $109 double. Executive rooms, at $109 single, $124 double, contain a king-size bed with sofa sleeper and love seat.

There are two fine restaurants here—the Café, an informal dining room, open from 6 a.m. to 10 p.m., serves three meals a day in a pleasant country-French setting. See Chapter IV for more information on the formal continental dining room called L'Étoile.

If you enjoy shopping, you'll be well located at the **Minneapolis Marriott**, 30 S. 7th St., Minneapolis, MN 55402, (tel. 612/349-4000, or toll free 800/228-9290). Rising above the three-level downtown City Center shopping mall, this luxury hotel is connected to Donaldsons, one of the city's best department stores, and is just skyway-steps away from perennially popular Dayton's and from the brand-new Conservatory fashion center. There's a diversity of fine specialty shops accessible by skyway as well. But that's only part of the fun of staying at this sleek, modernistic 32-story triangular tower.

The decor in the Marriott's public places is stunning throughout, starting—if you can believe it—in the infinitely mirrored, spacious elevators, which serve as conversation pieces as well as transportation.

Colors throughout the hotel have been keyed to the seasons of Minnesota: maroons for the autumn leaves, gray-beiges for the boulders, and greens for grass and shrubs and trees. Put them all together and they spell serenity—a truly relaxing atmosphere that blends with a light-hearted approach to hospitality.

Take, for example, the daily "Hungry Hour" that takes place on the fifth floor of the Marriott each weekday, not far from the hotel's two superb restaurants, Gustino's and the Fifth Season. Actually, it's the Fifth Season lounge that serves as setting for the long buffet table filled with salads, chips, pastas, chicken wings, and assorted items that can be piled high on plates at $1 for each trip. Hotel guests soon discover this unexpected pleasure. Locals at the end of a day's work or the start of an evening's fun often stop by as well.

The tunes of Gustino's singing servers add a musical touch from time to time, as do the strains of piano-bar melodies in the lobby lounge below.

Guest rooms here are luxurious, many of them with upholstered chairs and matching ottomans, built-in oak desks, and oversize beds. Also notable is the lighting provided by illuminated wall coves, casting a soft warmth over rooms that look out, day and night, on beautiful cityscapes. Rates here are $110 single occupancy, $125 double; senior citizens may pay as little as $55, depending on availability.

A long-standing Twin Cities tradition was renewed in March 1987 with the opening of the **Radisson Plaza Hotel Minneapolis,** 35 S. 7th St., Minneapolis, MN 55402 (tel. 612/339-4900, or toll-free 800/228-9822). Since 1909 there's always been a Radisson Hotel on the same site in downtown Minneapolis, so many a qualm was experienced by local folks when the decision was made in 1981 to tear down the familiar old structure and replace it with a bigger and better one—the flagship of what has by now become a Minneapolis-based chain of 131 Radisson hotels throughout the world.

The Radisson Plaza Minneapolis still occupies one of the most centrally located sites in the Twin Cities: across the street from City Center, half a block from the Nicollet Mall, and attached by skyway to downtown's shops, offices, restaurants, and more.

The first thing you'll notice as you approach the Radisson Plaza is its elegant recessed entryway; the second, in the main lobby, is a 1,200-pound marble pedestal, on which a huge, 2,750-pound marble ball floats on half an inch of water. (It's 65 pounds of water pressure that keeps the ball suspended, in case you wondered—I did.)

The effort here has been to contrast the elegance of the public spaces with the residential feeling of the guest rooms. How residential it feels will depend a lot on your own residence, of course. The colors throughout the hotel combine teal and mauve; the French provincial and Chippendale furnishings have the look of the Old World but offer the convenience of the New: for example, the mahogany armoires have color TV sets hidden inside. Each bathroom has a TV speaker and telephone.

Large desks are provided for business travelers, and maids switch the phones from the bedside table to the desk when they're making up the room each day.

A health club is available at no extra charge to guests. Rates are $98 single occupancy, $108 double.

Moderately Priced Accommodations ($50 to $85 Double)

A winning combination of downtown location and suburban rates is available at the three-story, 193-room **Regency Plaza Best Western**, 41 N. 10th St., Minneapolis, MN 55403 (tel. 612/339-9311, or toll free 800/523-4200 in the U.S., 800/423-4100 in Minnesota, or 800/633-4300 in Canada), located at the end of Hwy. 12 on the edge of downtown Minneapolis.

Wood paneling and marble give the lobby a classical look; so does the library beyond. The rooms are large and pleasant, many of them enhanced by the beautiful prints of Les Kouba, a popular Minnesota painter of nature. The raspberry and royal-blue color combination carries through all the rooms; so do the light-oak furnishings. There's a large indoor swimming pool, a children's wading pool, and a whirlpool, and in each room you'll find color TV and free in-house movies.

There are two attractive restaurants here—the Regency Café,

serving breakfast, lunch, and dinner from 6:30 a.m. to 8 p.m., and Harrigan's Dining Room, serving burgers, steaks, seafood, and other American fare from 5 to 10 p.m. The Hub Cap Pub is open from 11:30 a.m. to 1 a.m. Monday through Friday, 5 p.m. to 1 a.m. on Saturday, and 5 to 10 p.m. on Sunday. Soup and sandwiches are served there from 11:30 a.m. to 2 p.m. Monday through Friday.

There's free shuttle service in a 35-passenger van to any downtown destination within a three-mile radius—and that includes Riverplace and St. Anthony Main, the Metrodome, the Guthrie Theater, and the IDS Tower. Rates are $50 for a single, $56 for a double, and $85 for a suite. Special packages are available for Vikings and Twins games, and for certain holidays.

Late 1986 marked the arrival of the Twin Cities' first bed-and-breakfast hotel when **Bradbury Suites,** 7770 Johnson Ave., Bloomington, MN 55437 (tel. 612/893-9999), opened its canopied front doors to surprised and delighted travelers. What's different about this kind of accommodation? Well, for the price of a single room, you'll be staying in a two-room suite with a small refrigerator of your own and with two TV sets, one that's visible in both the bedroom and the sitting room, and a tiny one for the counter in the bathroom.

The suites, all done in shades of green and mauve, are comfortable and spacious enough for an evening "at home," with dinner delivered by nearby Mother Tucker's, the Lincoln Del, or T.G.I. Friday. And if you'd rather pass the time with cribbage or Trivial Pursuit than with TV, just check out the game of your choice from the Comfort Chest in the lobby. You'll find other useful items there as well—everything from hair dryers to throat lozenges. Consider yourself at home.

For those who prefer going out to dinner, there's a van to take you to any of the local restaurants, including the Camelot, Victoria Station, Rusty Scupper, and Kincaid's. And at $5 per visit, you're welcome to use all the facilities of the nearby U.S. Swim and Fitness Club.

A complimentary newspaper awaits you in the morning, along with the complimentary continental breakfast buffet that offers a variety of fruit, Danish pastries, cereal, bread, juice, and coffee or tea. And at other times of the day or night there are complimentary cookies and beverages—coffee, cider, hot chocolate, you choose!—in the lobby. All this, and complimentary airport shuttles too, will cost you $55 single occupancy, $63 double occupancy, in an executive suite; $55 single, $63 double, in a double suite; and $65 single, $73 double, in a theme suite. This bed-and-breakfast hotel clearly seems an idea whose time has come.

Like many other moderate and economy-priced motels, the **Dillon Airport Inn,** 4201 W. 80th St., Bloomington, MN 55437 (tel. 612/835-6643, or toll free 800/253-7503, 800/345-5661 in Minnesota), has no on-site restaurant of its own. Unlike others, though, it's only a few steps away from four of the area's most popular eating places and less than a mile away from a fifth. Denny's, open 24 hours a day, is attached to the Dillon Inn; Mother Tucker's, Rusty Scupper, and the Lincoln Del are less than a five-minute walk away; Victoria Station is just a bit farther down the I-494 service road. A complimentary continental breakfast and 24-hour-a-day complimentary coffee are offered at this comfortable inn which also provides shuttle service to the airport from 6 a.m. to midnight.

You'll feel welcome at once in the attractive lobby, with its sunken sitting room, brick-walled fireplace, and comfortable burgundy-and-beige seating. There's cable TV and complimentary Showtime in each of the 136 rooms here, and you can choose among a room with a king-size bed, a water bed, or two double beds. All rooms contain a pair of upholstered chairs and a small desk; some rooms have a balcony.

Rates are $45 single occupancy, $51 double occupancy; there's a $6 charge for a rollaway, but no charge for a crib. Local phone calls are free as well.

You'll find one of the largest swimming pools on the Bloomington "strip" at the **Holiday Inn Airport 2,** 5401 Green Valley Dr., Bloomington, MN 55437 (tel. 612/831-8000, or toll free 800/HOLIDAY). You'll also find a whirlpool and sauna in the new west wing of this sprawling six-story complex. Located 7½ miles from the Minneapolis–St. Paul International Airport, this Holiday Inn does a lot of fly-and-drive business: if they stay for at least one night, guests can leave their cars in the parking lot and take advantage of the free 24-hour airport shuttle service, thereby saving the cost of airport parking. Shuttle service is also available to nearby shopping malls and nearby restaurants.

There are two on-site restaurants here. Marti's serves moderately priced lunches daily from 11 a.m. to 1:30 p.m. and dinner from 5:30 to 10 p.m.; the Coffee Shop, serving three meals a day, is open from 7 a.m. to 10 p.m. And Partners, the cocktail lounge, is open from 11 a.m. to 1 a.m., with live entertainment from 8 p.m. until closing.

Standard rooms with two twin beds, a work table, and two chairs cost $62 single occupancy, $70 double. Nonsmoking

A Special-Value Chain Hotel

If you live in one of the 26 states with **Embassy Suites** hotels, you'll be glad to know that there are three of them here in the Twin Cities: one in downtown St. Paul at 175 E. 10th St., St. Paul, MN 55101 (tel. 612/224-5400); one near the airport at 7901 34th Ave. South, Bloomington, MN 55420 (tel. 612/854-1000); and one in suburban Bloomington at 2800 W. 80th St., Bloomington, MN 55431 (tel. 612/884-4811).

These value-packed hotels have effectively countered the old admonition: "If you want the comforts of home, stay home." Actually, the comforts awaiting you here may rival what you've left at home: not one but two handsomely furnished rooms with a TV set and a phone in each, a kitchenette whose facilities include a microwave oven, and decor to suit your individual preference, with whole floors devoted to rooms decorated in tones of mauve, green, and blue. Just choose your floor and you choose your color.

Choose your full cooked-to-order breakfast each morning too, and at the end of each day, choose your favorite drinks at the two-hour cocktail party, held in the attractive skylit indoor courtyard. Here brick pillars, tile floors, fountains, and even a waterfall will remind you of your last visit to the Mediterranean or of the Mediterranean visit you've yet to make.

The suite, breakfast, Happy Hour, and airport transportation, plus swimming pool, whirlpool, sauna, and steamroom, come to $79 single occupancy, $89 double, plus local tax. And if you're a senior citizen with an A.A.R.P. card on your person, your room rate will be reduced by 10%.

rooms cost $63 single occupancy, $71 double. The price of other accommodations is determined by their size and location.

You'll find a lot more than a comfortable and convenient place to stay at the **Thunderbird Motel,** 2201 E. 78th St., Bloomington, MN 55420 (tel. 612/854-3411). Located just five miles from the Minneapolis–St. Paul airport, with complimentary shuttle service to the airport 24 hours a day, the Thunderbird is one of dozens of motels on the Bloomington strip, but it has certain notable distinguishing features. A towering statue of an Indian chief dominates the front lawn, and a graceful Apache rides his steed atop a granite pedestal near the main entrance. These are an introduction to the kind of art that draws thousands of visitors from throughout this area each year to see the largest collection of authentic Indian artifacts and animal mountings in the Upper Midwest.

In addition to authentic likenesses of Native Americans, there are likenesses of many of the animals that shared the wilderness with them. In the Totem Pole Dining Room, for example, two stalwart braves paddle a birchbark canoe while a nearby wolf bays at the ceiling.

Throughout the complex is a dizzying array of Indian-related works of art—from a beautiful porcelain collection of figurines to the massive buffalo head mounted in the ballroom. The theme extends to guest rooms as well, where paintings, draperies, and even carpeting are consistent with the prevailing theme.

But there are 20th-century trappings at the Thunderbird too. This is the only motel on the strip with both an indoor and outdoor swimming pool. You'll have the use of a hot lamp, a whirlpool, a kiddie pool, and picnic tables in the vicinity of the spacious kidney-shaped swimming pool. And across the hall from these, a sauna and exercise room are available without extra charge to guests of the motel.

The Totem Pole dining room is open from 11 a.m. to 10 p.m. Monday through Friday, with weekend dinners served from 5 to 10:30 p.m. and all-you-can-eat brunches from 10:30 a.m. to 2:30 p.m. Room rates here are moderate: $60 for a single, $66 double.

The convenience of a motel and the appearance of a hotel are what you'll find at the **Rodeway Inn,** 1321 E. 78th St., Bloomington, MN 55420 (tel. 612/854-3400). Rooms are attractively furnished in a variety of decors, and if you order king-size accommodations, you'll find a leisure recliner waiting along with the standard furnishings. Each of the rooms in this five-story complex offers free HBO.

There's an indoor pool on the premises as well as a lounge that features live band music. And you'll be treated to free hors d'oeuvres at the nightly Happy Hour from 5 to 8 p.m.

Located on the Bloomington "strip" just five miles from the airport, the Rodeway Inn provides free transportation to and from the Minneapolis–St. Paul International Airport 24 hours a day. Rates range from $56 to $61 for single accommodations, $63 to $68 double.

You'll find attractive, moderately priced accommodations at the suburban **Hopkins House,** 1501 Hwy. 7, Hopkins, MN 55343 (tel. 612/935-7711). Located about ten miles from Lake

Minnetonka, the largest freshwater lake in Minnesota, and 20 minutes from downtown Minneapolis, this seven-floor, 164-room complex offers an indoor pool, sauna, exercise room and table tennis tables. The predominant color scheme throughout the complex features shades of rose and blue, starting with the deep-rose cushioned couches and soft-blue table lamps in the lobby. Oak end tables and a brass ceiling punctuated with modern open globe lights complete the bright, cheery decor. Your own room will doubtless be decorated in combinations of rose and blue as well, and if you like, it can also contain a heart-shaped waterbed; just ask for a "happy-tub room." You'll find basic cable color TV here plus free Showtime and ESPN sports. Rates are $49 single, $55 double, plus 11% hotel tax. The happy-tub room goes for $82.

One of the most central locations in the Twin Cities is offered by the **Holiday Inn Crowne Plaza Metrodome,** 1500 Washington Ave. South, Minneapolis, MN (tel. 612/333-4646, or toll free 800/HOLIDAY). Situated on the eastern edge of downtown Minneapolis, with the University of Minnesota campus on one side and the Metrodome on the other, the Crown Plaza stands right at the hub of the Seven Corners area with its top-notch ethnic restaurants and bars. Grandma's Restaurant is right next door, an exciting place famous for its hodgepodge of historical artifacts and its menu featuring a wide variety of basic American food and drink. You're right in the heart of the West Bank Theater District here, with the satiric productions of Dudley Riggs's Experimental Theatre Company (E.T.C.) right next door and a miscellany of shows by local troupes at the Southern Theatre just around the corner. Across the street, you'll find the famous Theater in the Round, and don't overlook the delightful entertainment that's available to you on the four stages of the nearby University Theatre and on their summertime bonus, the Centennial Showboat, docked on the east bank of the Mississippi River.

In the Crowne Plaza lobby as well as in the guest rooms, you'll find decor that's been described as "subtle art deco." Amenities include an indoor pool, whirlpool, sauna, and exercise room, all on the 14th floor with an exceptional view of the city. Rates are $65 to $75 single, $75 to $85 double.

There's the ambience of romantic Old Spain at the large and lovely **Seville Hotel,** 8151 Bridge Rd., Bloomington, MN (tel. 612/830-1300). Orange, brown, and yellow dominate the large lobby, while guest rooms are done in softer earth tones of beige and brown. A pool, sauna, and whirlpool are available here, as are a popular lounge and dining room. Located right on I-494, the Seville is about 20 minutes from the airport, 30 minutes from downtown Minneapolis and St. Paul. You're also close to fine suburban shopping at the nearby Southtown Center and just a bit farther away, at the legendary Southdale with its satellite centers, Galleria, Yorktown, and Southdale Square. Rates at the Seville are $55 single, $61 double.

The amenities are exceptional at the **Holiday Inn International,** 3 Appletree Square, Bloomington, MN 55420 (tel. 612/854-9000, or toll free 800/HOLIDAY). You won't have to forgo your fitness regimen here, thanks to an Olympic-size swimming pool, a superbly equipped fitness center complete with Nautilus equipment, and aerobic classes. There's no extra charge for these or for the use of the whirlpool and sauna, but if you decide on a suntan, the booth will cost $6 to $10, depending on how long you want to bask. (By the way, an on-site "hair design studio" can put your coiffure back in shape if all the foregoing proves too much for it.) Two restaurants, the moderately priced Applebutter and more elegant Pippins, are popular with hometown folks as well as with visitors. That's true of the Greenhouse lounge as well. The 13-story, 431-room building boasts a truly imposing lobby with two-story atrium and furnishings done in tones of rust and brown. These colors give an air of tranquility to the lobby and to the guest rooms too. There's free 24-hour shuttle service to the airport, leaving every half hour. Rates for a standard room with two double beds are $59 for one person, $67 for two people. Rooms with king-size beds are $64 for one person, $73 for two people.

The escalator that dominates the lobby of the **Holiday Inn Town Square,** 411 Minnesota St., St. Paul, MN (tel. 612/332-4000, or toll free 800/HOLIDAY), will take you right into the heart of one of the most fascinating shopping-dining-recreation complexes in the Twin Cities. Whatever the weather, you'll be able to luxuriate in the lush and lovely Town Square indoor park with its trees and waterfalls. And you'll have access through the skyway system not only to the square's department stores and specialty shops, but to virtually all of downtown St. Paul's shopping and entertainment. The Museum of Art, the Science Museum, the Civic Center, and the Ordway Music Theatre are just a short walk away from your room at Holiday Inn Town Square. Should you wish a honeymoon suite with a heart-shaped Jacuzzi, it's yours for $150 per night. There are other gala accommodations here too: one full floor of suites, some of them with fireplaces and stereos, that go for $150 to $200; but perfectly comfortable and attractive rooms are also available for considerably less. Rooms are decorated individually, some of them done in the attractive mauve-and-aqua combination that you'll find in the lobby. The large triangular solar panels on the exterior of this hotel demonstrate a unique claim to fame: Holiday Inn Town Square is the only local hotel that uses solar energy in its heating and cooling systems. Rates for standard rooms here are $58, with a $10 surcharge for each additional person. There's no charge for local phone calls.

For decades, visitors to the Twin Cities have been made welcome at the **Normandy Inn,** 405 S. 8th St., Minneapolis, MN 55405 (tel. 612/370-1400). The rustic, Swiss-chalet look to the exterior of this four-story building stands in sharp contrast these days to the high-rise structures that have grown up around it. The interior has a country look with dark woodwork, marble tile floors, and a graceful central fountain. Guest rooms are done in earth tones of rust and beige.

Among local folks, the Normandy is best known for its moderately priced restaurant, which features high-rise popovers at dinnertime, beer-cheese soup, and pecan pie, both afternoon and evening. Located four blocks from the Nicollet Mall, the Normandy is within walking distance of the Convention Center and Loring Park. Economy rooms are $44 single, $49 double; deluxe rooms run $60 single, $67 double.

Twin Citians out for a special evening or event are apt to come to the **Northstar Hotel,** 618 Second Ave. South, Minneapolis, MN 55402 (tel. 612/338-2288). The reason for this handsome hotel's local popularity is the presence of a five-star restaurant called the Rosewood Room. Live entertainment is offered nightly in the restaurant and in the popular Rosewood Lounge.

The lobby is done in muted shades of beige and peach, and guest rooms feature muted browns and beiges. A drive-up area makes for convenient arrivals; another gracious feature is the presence of uniformed doormen on duty 24 hours a day. Although there are no athletic facilities on the premises, a $2 guest-entrance fee provides you with temporary membership at the International Fitness Center or the YMCA, both of which are located on the downtown skyway system. Rates at the Northstar are $79, single or double.

When you see a big bubble in the sky, you'll know you've arrived at the **Ambassador Resort Motel,** 5225 Wayzata Blvd., Minneapolis, MN 55416 (tel. 612/545-0441). The huge glass dome covers the largest tropical indoor-pool court in the state of Minnesota. The palm trees, ranging from 20 to 60 feet in height, will put you in a frolicsome mood; so will the large whirlpool, which accommodates 20 wet and happy people. Other popular features include two saunas, a shuffleboard court, Ping-Pong tables, a putting green, and pool tables. And there's a video-game room as well as two restaurants, and a lounge featuring live entertainment.

In the unlikely event that you'd ever wish to leave the premises, a courtesy van will take you to shopping centers within a 15- to 20-mile radius, including two of the area's best: Ridgedale and Bonaventure. And there's Byerly's as well, a must-see supermarket with the accent on "super." (See Chapter X for more information on this phenomenon.)

The Ambassador lobby is a bright, cheerful place with natural light streaming in through glass walls. Guest rooms are cheery, done in beiges and natural woods. TV includes complimentary HBO. Room rates are $48 single, $59 double, plus 6% hotel tax.

For nearly 20 years visitors to the Twin Cities have enjoyed staying at the **Sheraton Airport Inn,** 2525 E. 78th St., Bloomington, MN 55420 (tel. 612/854-1771). Now a second beautifully landscaped brown-brick four-story structure has been built adjacent to the original two-story building. Still present and popular in the huge lobby are the cozy nooks and crannies that businesspeople find useful for private conferences.

Another feature of the lobby is the abundance of couches and coffee tables, set amid fresh green plants and palm trees. There's an indoor pool and whirlpool here, as well as free cable TV that includes Showtime and CNN channels. A full-service dining room, the Timbers, is a popular place to dine; also a favorite is the live musical entertainment and the lounge with big-screen live TV coverage of major sporting events. Rates for the individually decorated rooms are $59 single, $65 double. Free transportation is provided to and from the international airport, located just 3½ miles away.

Budget Accommodations (Doubles Under $50)

Remember the privately owned one-of-a-kind hotels and motels of yesteryear? That's what you'll find at the **Center City Inn,** 77 E. 9th St., St. Paul, MN 55101 (tel. 612/227-7331), right on the edge of downtown St. Paul, about three blocks from I-94, and across the street from the start of the skyway system.

This eight-story maroon-awninged gray-brick building stands one block from the Town Square shopping complex and indoor municipal park. You're also within short walking distance here of some of the city's prime attractions: the Civic

Center, Science Museum, Omnitheater, Ordway Music Theatre, Minnesota Museum of Art, and the Park Square Theatre.

The burgundy, pink, and rose tones in the small, comfortable lobby carry through to the 92 spacious guest rooms, all of which have balconies. The rooms are simply furnished: each has either a king-size bed or two doubles; all have dressers, night stands, and large picture windows. Guests on the east side of the building look out on the city; a few rooms offer a spectacular view of the Capitol complex; rooms facing the west side have a less commanding view, but these rooms are particularly quiet, so if you're a light sleeper, one of them might be preferable for you.

The economy rates here are $39 single occupancy, $45 to $47 double. There's a full-service American-fare restaurant on the premises, serving three meals a day, with top breakfast and lunch tabs of $6 and a top dinner tab of $12.

If you're interested in economy-priced accommodations with cooking facilities, you'll be glad to learn about the **Friendly Host Inn,** 1225 E. 78th St., Minneapolis, MN 55420 (tel. 612/854-3322, or toll free 800/453-4511). Single-bedded rooms with a two-burner stove and a small sink rent for $32 single occupancy, $37 double; the much larger two-bedded rooms contain a four-burner cooker, a small refrigerator, and double cupboards. The cost for these rooms is $41 double occupancy, $45 triple. Without cooking facilities, the one-bedded room goes for $28 single occupancy, $32 double; two-bedded rooms are $36 double occupancy, $40 for three. Families pay $36 for standard two-bedded rooms, $41 for rooms with cooking facilities.

Decor varies here, but the rooms are all attractive and comfortable and the motel is well located, just five miles from the airport. An indoor pool and whirlpool are available on the premises.

The **Exel Inn,** 2701 E. 78th St., Bloomington, MN 55420 (tel. 612/854-7200), is located just four miles from the Minneapolis–St. Paul International Airport and provides complimentary airport shuttle service 24 hours a day. This 205-room brick complex of two two-story buildings offers attractive rooms at reasonable rates: $31 to $33 single occupancy, $36 to $38 double occupancy. The rooms, decorated in shades of brown and peach, are kept scrupulously clean. Cable color TV is available in each room, including Showtime at no additional cost.

Day's Inn/University, 2407 University Ave. SE, Minneapolis,

MN 55414 (tel. 612/623-3999), is located at University and Washington Avenues six blocks east of the University of Minnesota's Minneapolis campus. Guest rooms, done in earth tones of rust, brown, and orange with touches of blue, offer two large chairs, a desk, and a credenza; most have a vanity area separate from the bath. There are no restaurants on the premises but there's a branch of the Embers chain right across the street. A free continental breakfast is available each morning. Rates are $36 to $40 for a single, $42 to $46 double. Free local phone calls, free shuttle service to the university and to local hospitals, and two nonsmoking floors are also offered here.

One of the most pleasant neighborhoods in Minneapolis has been the setting for the past 30 years of the **Fair Oaks Motor-Hotel**, 2335 Third Ave. South, Minneapolis, MN 55404 (tel. 612/871-2000). Situated directly across the street from the small, lovely Fair Oaks Park and diagonally across from the famous Minneapolis Institute of Art, this budget motor-hotel shares a city block with the Hennepin County Historical Society. The rooms have recently been remodeled; all contain free HBO and direct-dial phones. Rates here are $35 single occupancy, $45 double. Senior citizen discounts of 10% are available.

You'll also find on the premises here a restaurant that's been popular for the past three decades. The Fair Oaks Restaurant opens at 5 a.m. each weekday morning, at 7 a.m. on weekends, and closes at 10 p.m. each evening.

The very lowest-cost housing in many cities is available on college campuses, but in the Twin Cities area, the dormitories of the University of Minnesota are available only in the summer. Rooms cost about $16 per night, and guests must be associated with the university—prospective students, researchers, and the like.

Low-cost weekly accommodations are available near the university at the **Gopher Campus Motor Lodge**, 925 SE 4th St., Minneapolis, MN 55414 (tel. 612/331-3740), with rates at $231 per week for one person, $269.50 for two.

Less convenient to the campus, but lower still in cost are the rooms at the **YMCA** in downtown Minneapolis, at 30 S. 9th St., Minneapolis, MN 55402 (tel. 612/371-8750). Here, at the only Y in the Twin Cities with sleeping accommodations, you'll pay $16.86 per night for a single room without bath. One floor has been set aside for women. Reservations are not accepted, but rooms are usually available.

At **Macalester College** in St. Paul, two guest rooms are available right on campus at $20 per person per night. Each room has two bunk beds and private bath. Reservations should be made at least two weeks in advance by contacting the Residential Life Office, Macalester College, 1600 Grand Avenue, St. Paul, MN 55105 (tel. 612/696-6215).

Card-carrying members of American Youth Hostels may be able to secure a place to stay in the Twin Cities for a maximum of three nights at $10 per night or less, depending upon availability. Contact **American Youth Hostels,** Minnesota Council, 30 S. 9th St., Room 201, Minneapolis, MN 55402.

And finally there's the alternative offered by **Condo Rentals, Inc.,** 1501 E. 79th St., Bloomington, MN 55420 (tel. 612/854-3089), just seven minutes from the airport. Fully furnished residences are available by the day or week at remarkably low cost, with a minimum stay of three nights. Particularly popular with corporate trainees, Condo offers a home away from home for families as well. (Even family pets are welcome, with a $100 damage deposit.)

For those staying fewer than 30 days, the rate is $39 per night per unit; for 30 days or more, $37 per night. Rates for two-bedroom condos are $49 per night if you're staying fewer than 30 days, $47 per night if you'll be here 30 days or more. Furnishings include complete kitchen facilities with dishes, pots and pans, silverware, mixer, toaster, mixing bowls—everything but the food. Each unit has one and a half baths and two private entrances, one to the outside world and one to the enclosed courtyard where two swimming pools are open from late spring to early fall. Weekly maid service is also part of the package.

Reservations at least two weeks in advance are strongly recommended and can be guaranteed with a major credit card.

Chapter IV

WHERE TO DINE

THE GOOD NEWS about dining out in the Twin Cities is that there's something here to suit every taste and every budget. Far from being the land of lefse and lutefisk, Minneapolis and St. Paul are remarkable for the variety, the quality, and the cosmopolitan nature of their restaurant cuisine. Actually, they're a little short on Scandinavian dining places, but there are plenty of good French and German, Greek and Italian, Chinese, Japanese, Vietnamese, and other ethnic fare to be found here. And in addition, there are fine eating spots that have a special way with basic American steaks and chops and seafood as well as with vegetarian foods.

A number of Twin Cities restaurants have won national and international awards, and they'll be called to your attention, along with those that have become favorites among knowledgeable hometown folks. Many of the places listed here, in fact, are the ones to which local hosts generally bring their own out-of-town guests.

I'll let you in on the not-to-be-missed restaurants in a variety of categories, from the big splurge through the expensive, the moderate, and the budget. One reminder: Even the costliest eating spots tend to be moderately priced at lunchtime. That means you can fulfill two goals simultaneously. You can enjoy the finest in ambience, cuisine, and presentation for a nominal noonday cost, and you can turn these lunches into scouting expeditions for that extra-special evening out, when memories—not money—become the prime consideration.

And now for the cost of dining at local restaurants. I'll divide the prices into four categories—big splurge, expensive, moderate, and budget—but do keep two things in mind.

First, prices in Twin Cities restaurants tend to be lower than in other metropolitan areas, so the "expensive" choice here may be your "moderate." All the better. That's just one more benefit for visitors to these fair cities.

The other thing to remember is that you're only charged for what you order, so a little circumspection can see you through an evening in the priciest restaurant without bending your budget completely out of shape. Here are my per-person price categories for entree + coffee + 15% gratuity + 6% tax: **big splurge,** $30 and up; **expensive,** $20 to $30; **moderate,** $10 to $20; and **budget,** under $10.

Big Splurge ($30 and up)

Where do celebrities head for lunch and dinner while they're in the Twin Cities? Likely as not, you'll find them at an elegant, expensive-and-worth-every-penny-of-it restaurant known simply as **510,** located at 510 Groveland Ave., Minneapolis (tel. 874-6440). Robert Redford has dined here, and so have Carol Channing, Charlton Heston, Pia Zadora, and Richard Dreyfuss. And while they were appearing in *Foxfire* at the nearby Guthrie Theater, Jessica Tandy and Hume Cronyn were here regularly.

This is probably the première special-occasion restaurant in town, the place where lawyers, architects, and business people confer with their peers and where they recruit new members for their firms. It's also a place where tourists come, often because they've read about or heard about 510 and want to try its admirable cuisine for themselves.

While dinnertime is big-splurge time at 510, lunches are surprisingly modest in cost. At either meal, the shimmering crystal chandeliers, the sweeping blue-gray draperies, and the graceful wisteria in its handsome island planter provide a gracious and serene setting in which to enjoy the creativity and commitment to quality that have made Kathleen Craig's fine restaurant as popular as it is.

Unpredictability is one popular characteristic of 510, where your waiter will recite for you the specials of the day including soups, appetizers, entrees, and desserts, as well as the fixed-price tasting menu, a seven- or eight-course dinner for a price which varies between $38 and $42. Reportedly the same tasting menu has never been presented twice; certainly there are no reports of diners dissatisfied with any of the tasting menus that were presented.

It's easy to spend $50 per person for dinner at 510, what with most appetizers going for $7 to $9; entrees, from $15 to $25; and desserts, $3.50 to $5. Add champagne, coffee, a gratuity, and there you are. But again, the cuisine here really is top-drawer.

At the very least, you really should consider coming here for lunch when the top price is $8 for grilled breast of chicken, or warm rabbit terrine with sweet-and-sour cabbage and caraway-thyme sauce. Lunch is served from 11:30 a.m. to 2 p.m. Monday through Friday, and dinner from 6 to 10 p.m. Monday through Saturday.

The transformation of Minneapolis' run-down Warehouse District into a smart Soho section of town with galleries, small restaurants, and popular bars is largely credited to the emergence in 1977 of the **New French Café**, at 128 N. 4th St., Minneapolis (tel. 338-3790).

The bare whitewashed walls, the exposed ducts, and the exposed kitchen, now considered chic, were dictated by the need for economy back when this small storefront restaurant first opened, serving only breakfast and lunch. Today there's a variety of menus for the important breakfast meetings, informal lunches, and big-splurge dinners that are served here. There's also a menu for the late-night set and one for Saturday and Sunday brunchers and economy-minded Sunday-supper regulars who are glad to pick up a tab for about $12 instead of the much costlier one at dinnertime.

Lunchtime prices range from $8 for a fish stew and $8.25 for baked chicken breast to $12 for poached salmon. At night you'll pay about $17 for sautéed rainbow trout or $25 for roast rack of lamb. There's also an à la carte variety of hors d'oeuvres, salads, cheeses, and delectable desserts.

Everything's made right on the premises here—from the crusty French bread, served with every meal, to the croissants to the shells for the house-specialty eclairs. Chocolate mousse is a house specialty too, and so is the array of ice creams and sorbets. (Had espresso ice cream recently? You're likely to find some here. And you're likely to come back for more.)

Breakfast is served from 8 to 11 a.m. Monday through Friday; lunch, from 11:30 a.m. to 2 p.m.; and dinner, from 5:30 to 9:30 p.m. Late-night supper is available on Friday and Saturday from 9:30 p.m. to midnight; Sunday supper, from 5:30 to 9 p.m. Saturday and Sunday brunch is offered from 8 a.m. to 2 p.m. Reservations are recommended.

One of the loveliest Victorian houses in the Twin Cities, **Forepaugh's**, 276 S. Exchange St., St. Paul (tel. 224-5606), is also one of its finest French restaurants. Built in 1870 by Joseph Lybrandt Forepaugh, whose wholesale dry-goods firm was the largest in the Northwest, this three-story mansion faced the home of Alexander Ramsey, first territorial governor of Minnesota. Both houses, now listed on the National Register of Historic Places, still stand on their original sites and are popular with visitors who enjoy seeing fine examples of Victorian architecture and decor; but at Forepaugh's it's possible to enhance the experience further by dining in one of nine lovely 19th-century dining rooms, each with its own unique attraction, and each named for a past governor of Minnesota.

From the Pillsbury Room you can enjoy a panoramic view of downtown St. Paul; in the Olson Room you can admire the richness of fine mahogany paneling; in the Sibley Room you'll be able to view a bit of the past in historic photographs of Victorian tea parties that were held across the street in Irvine Park during the late 19th century.

Since 1982 Forepaugh's has been run by Chef Bernard LaGrande, who brought from his native France a gift for adapting classic French cuisine to American tastes. The state fish of Minnesota takes on a delectably Gallic aspect here as walleye meunière; New York sirloin, prepared to taste with a blend of butter and French mustards, wins local awards as entrecôte au beurre de moutarde. By any name, the menu selections at Forepaugh's are exquisite. Chef LaGarde has a wonderful way with veal, a meat whose proper preparation is widely regarded the hallmark of a chef's excellence. Stuffed with crabmeat Thermidor or sautéed with shallots, mushrooms, cream, and demi-glace, the veal here is superb. So are the seafood, the lamb, the duckling, and the other selections on Forepaugh's distinguished menu.

Entrees, served with bread and butter, salad and potato, average $18 to $20. Dressings, mushrooms, and vegetables are available at additional cost. For these parts, prices at Forepaughs are high, but so is the value. Lunch is served Monday through Friday from 11:30 a.m. to 2 p.m.; dinners, Monday through Saturday from 5:30 to 9:30 p.m., on Sunday from 4 to 8 p.m.; Sunday brunch is offered from 11:30 a.m. to 2 p.m.

You'll feel like a star as you glide down the red-carpeted stairway leading from the lobby of the Saint Paul Hotel to **L'Étoile,** 350 Market St., St. Paul (tel. 292-9292), named for the state motto, "L'Étoile du Nord" (Star of the North).

Booths and banquettes in this fine French restaurant are illuminated by chandeliers of brass and beveled glass; classic oil paintings line the walls. The dignified decor of L'Étoile is complemented by the formality of service in a restaurant that ranks among the costliest and most elegant in either town.

Dinners, served à la carte, include favorite entrees like exquisite chateaubriand for two, carved tableside and served with the bouquetière of vegetables for $42 and fork-tender prime rib of beef at $15. On evenings when the nearby Ordway Music

Theatre is offering programs, you'll find something of a bargain at L'Étoile—sandwiches and cold plates, served with new potato salad or french fries from $5.75 to $8.75. Entrees, which include salad and the vegetable of the day, range from linguine bolognese at $9.25 to gulf scampi at $14.50. Post-performance delicacies lure many audience members back from the Ordway and from the nearby Chimera and Actors Theatres too. Favorites include the chocolate schaume torte, custard brûlée with raspberries, and a really sensational strawberry glacé.

You can enjoy the ambience of L'Étoile for a surprisingly moderate cost at lunchtime. Daily standing specialties, served with green salad and fresh vegetable of the day, range from Wednesday's spinach and pesto tortellini for $6.50 to Friday's West Coast seafood plate for $9.75. Hours at L'Étoile are 11:30 a.m. to 2:30 p.m. and 5:30 to 10 p.m. Monday through Friday, and 5:30 to 10:30 p.m. on Saturday.

Expensive ($20 to $30)

If you like seafood, you'll like what's waiting for you at the **Bristol Bar & Grill,** Riverplace, 1 Main St. SE, Minneapolis (tel. 378-1338), where you'll find one of the most comprehensive seafood menus in the Twin Cities.

This perennially popular restaurant, named for a famous British seaport, has both British and nautical touches in its decor. Along with the dark-green walls and glowing mahogany woodwork in the Dome Room, there's a huge Tiffany-style glass dome and fluted Tiffany-style lamps. And there's an exquisite display of sterling-silver antiques imported from England.

Each of the dining rooms has attractions of its own. Some tables offer a truly spectacular view of the Mississippi River, cobblestoned Main Street, and the Minneapolis skyline beyond. Other rooms contain private dining alcoves for parties of six or so. Another choice and frequently prebooked seating option is on a terrace that offers a breathtaking skyline view, but is only large enough for six tables of fortunate diners.

Mesquite-grilled swordfish is among the most frequently ordered entrees here, with prime rib and shrimp scampi not far behind. Blackened catfish is another favorite. Entrees, all of which can be blackened upon request, are served with the vegetable of the day, a choice of potato or rice, a dinner salad, and as many Bristol biscuits as you can eat.

The price range here is extensive, with dinner entrees ranging from $8.50 for seafood fettuccine to $24 for a New England clambake of Maine lobster, crab cluster, shrimp, clams, and mussels, served with red-skinned potatoes and corn-on-the-cob.

A best-buy is available in the form of "twilight dinners," served between 5:30 and 7 p.m. These include a choice of eight appetizers, entree, and dessert for $11. Another best-buy, especially for families, is the all-you-can-eat Sunday buffet brunch, served from 10 a.m. to 3 p.m. at $11 for adults, no charge for children under 12.

Lunch is served Monday through Saturday from 11:30 a.m. to 2:30 p.m.; dinner, Monday through Thursday from 5:30 to 11 p.m., on Friday and Saturday to midnight, and on Sunday from 5:30 to 10 p.m.

One of the most distinctive restaurants in the Twin Cities is **Camelot**, 5300 W. 78th St., Bloomington (tel. 835-2455). Here, in a medieval castle complete with moat and drawbridge, you'll find superb continental European cuisine, much of it prepared tableside and all of it under the supervision of owner-manager Tor Aasheim, an internationally known chef and restaurateur who was lured to Minneapolis from his native Norway in 1968 by visiting members of the prestigious Minikhada Country Club.

After nine years at Minikhada, Aasheim moved across town to become general assistant manager of L'Hôtel Sofitel, the first French hotel in the United States. And now, as owner-manager of Camelot, he's brought new lustre to a restaurant that's long been noted for fine dining in a delightfully picturesque setting.

Hand-carved oak abounds throughout the restaurant, and spears, swords, and suits of armor add their own authentic touches to the period decor. Only the menu is contemporary—continental European dishes, with a few American favorites.

Fresh Norwegian salmon, broiled or poached, is particularly favored here. Another top choice is the roast rack of lamb. Two beef specialties are the Camelot's version of steak Diane, cooked tableside, and tournedos Camelot, twin filet mignons on wild rice, one with crabmeat and sauce béarnaise, the second with fresh mushroom cap and sauce bordelaise.

Following your entree, you'll be presented with a deliciously difficult choice of pastries and other desserts, but do consider the heavenly soufflé au Grand Marnier with raspberry sauce. It's delectable.

Entrees, served with vegetable and potato or rice, range from $15 to $20, but with additional optional courses and some of

---

A St. Paul Tradition

For 25 years the elegant **Blue Horse**, 1355 University Ave. (tel. 645-8101), has attracted a clientele who care more about quality and consistency than about cost. John Warling is the second-generation owner-manager of this internationally honored restaurant. As you wait for your table in the brick-arched entryway, you'll see citations from Cartier's, *Esquire*, and *Travel and Leisure*. The arrival in 1983 of Chef Peter Grise has led to a notable "lightening" of the menu. Steaks and seafood remain a prime attraction here, but the Blue Horse now offers specialties that have been sautéed and stir-fried, sauces that are more frequently thickened by reduction than by roux. While retaining such Blue Horse standbys as old-fashioned corned beef hash, Grise has introduced new favorites like osso bucco, Florida stone crab, and chicken Antonio.

Along with a reputation for food and service second to none in the Twin Cities, the Blue Horse is known for its extensive wine list. At periodic sold-out Winemakers Dinners, the chef develops menus to complement wines selected by prominent winemakers. The $85-per-couple tab seems more than reasonable to those connoisseurs who vie to attend.

Luncheon specials, served with soup or salad, range from $8 to $11. Dinner entrees, served with Blue Horse Caesar salad and choice of vegetables or rice pilaf, are $15 to $31. Lunch is served from 11:30 a.m. to 4:30 p.m.; dinners, from 5 to 11 p.m. The Blue Horse is closed on Sunday.

---

the fine wine available here, your check can rise into the expensive-and-worth-it sphere.

One good way to enjoy the ambience at a more modest price is to come to Camelot for lunch, when you can have a six-ounce broiled sirloin with French bread and french fries for $8, or a grilled Reuben for $6, or Camelot steak tartare, prepared tableside, for $9.25. And for under $5 you can have soup and a roast beef sandwich in the comfortably furnished Ale House (a.k.a. "bar"). Half a sandwich and soup goes for under $4.

One last note: If someone suggests that you go to the Tower, don't get nervous. That's the place where an engaging group of young singers and dancers entertain on Friday and Saturday nights. The $3 cover charge is waived for dinner guests.

Camelot is open seven days a week. Lunch is served Monday

through Friday from 11:15 a.m. to 2 p.m.; dinner, Monday through Thursday from 5:30 to 10 p.m., on Friday and Saturday to 10:30 p.m., and on Sunday from 5 to 9 p.m. Sunday brunch begins at 10:30 a.m. and concludes at 2 p.m.

If you enjoy dining with music in the foreground as well as the background, don't miss **Gustino's** (tel. 349-4075), the delightful Italian restaurant on the sixth floor of the downtown Marriott Hotel, 30 S. 7th St. A dozen singing servers are on hand here seven nights a week with a varied selection of musical and culinary fare.

The setting is as upbeat as the songs. You're led to your table through a glass-alcove entryway past a white grand piano and a floor-to-ceiling glass triangle containing more than 200 bottles of imported Italian wine.

Northern Italian cuisine is featured here, with veal roast a constant on the menu; the sauce and the stuffing change daily. Another specialty is the awesome Torre di Pisa, a three-level antipasti tower that varies from day to day. The fettuccine Alfredo is rich and delicious, the cioppino a sensational blend of lobster, shrimp, scallops, mussels, clams, and fresh fish in a fish-and-tomato broth. There's a spectacular seafood pizza as well, pizza con aragosta e gamberi, which loses nothing in translation: pizza with lobster and shrimp, pepper, and mozzarella cheese.

You really can't go wrong with any of Gustino's soups, salads, pizza, and pasta on the menu here, but do save room for a slice of the tasty pepperoni bread and for one of the exclusive "painted desserts" concocted daily by the chef.

Entrees average about $20 and antipasti about $7, except for the Torre di Pisa at $15. Wine-lovers will enjoy the wine-of-the-month opportunity to order by the glass two different premium wines which are ordinarily available by the bottle only. Hours at Gustino's are Sunday through Thursday from 6 to 10 p.m., on Friday and Saturday to 11 p.m.

With the opening in March 1987 of the **Whitney Grill**, 150 Portland Ave., Minneapolis (tel. 339-9300), the Mill District, midway between the Metrodome and the Mississippi River, got its first luxury restaurant. (Actually, this is both the newest and oldest part of town—newest because it's in the process of redevelopment, oldest because the historic buildings here date back to the 19th century when this was the birthplace of the milling industry in the United States.)

There's an old-world atmosphere at the Whitney Grill, with its mix of fabric-covered walls, African mahogany woodwork, and extensive use of marble. The handsome traditional European chairs have been upholstered with tapestry and outfitted with European goose-neck arms. An especially nice touch at dinnertime is the piano music that's offered from 6 to 11 p.m. Monday through Friday; from 6:30 p.m. to midnight on Saturday, and from 6 to 10 p.m. on Sunday.

The distinguished cuisine here seems a natural extension of the setting. Executive-chef Richard Groshers and Executive Sous-chef Adam Atwood have won enthusiastic reviews for regional American items including West Coast halibut bisque, East Coast shellfish terrine, Colorado rack of lamb, and Wisconsin veal T-bone. Desserts are fabulous. A particularly popular summertime item is the exquisite raspberry roulade, a concoction of fresh raspberries and chantilly cream wrapped in sponge cake that's been soaked in Triple Sec. Need I say more?

Cuisine and decor are, of course, major reasons for the laurels won so quickly by the Whitney Grill, but don't underestimate the value of vibes. They're a major concern of Michael Kutscheid, a maître d' with a difference. Kutscheid started out to be a lawyer, working part-time as a waiter while he earned his degree at the William Mitchell College of Law in St. Paul. It wasn't until after graduation that he realized he didn't want to give up restaurant work. He says that his years in law school were not wasted because they taught him to think and to organize, both of which abilities serve him well in his capacity as food and beverage manager. One of his greatest assets, though, is the ability to maintain an atmosphere of warmth and hospitality. "We want people who come here to feel that they're special," he declares.

Breakfast is served in the Whitney Grill from 7 a.m. to 10:30 a.m., with prices ranging from $4.50 for pancakes with sliced fruit, maple syrup, and bacon, sausage, or ham, to $8.50 for two eggs served with sirloin steak, scrapple, and toast.

Luncheon entrees, served from 11 a.m. to 4:30 p.m., range from $8.50 for sautéed boneless breast of chicken to $13.50 for broiled prime sirloin. A selection of appetizers, soups, salads, sandwiches, and desserts is available.

Dinner entrees, served from 5 p.m. to 10:30 p.m., include Minnesota walleye at $14, veal T-bone at $21, and chateaubriand for two, carved tableside, for $41.

Moderately Priced ($10 to $20)

AMERICAN / CONTINENTAL: Here in the heartland of America, it's not surprising to find a number of distinguished restaurants that specialize in both traditional and "nouveau" American fare. What follows is a sampling of local dining places that are particularly popular with Twin Citians and their guests.

The accent is all-American at the **Dakota Bar and Grill,** 1021 E. Bandana Blvd., St. Paul (tel. 642-1442), a gathering place that's won many local awards. Menus feature a full complement of seafood, beef, chicken, lamb, and pork, along with tasty vegetarian dishes that have converted many a hard-core carnivore. Although most dishes are made with local ingredients, fresh seafood is flown in from the East Coast each day, and cheeses come from as far away as California. (Try the warm Sonoma goat cheese with toasted almonds—a delightful combination served with grilled eggplant and sweet peppers.)

Executive Chef Ken Hoff's imaginative use of spices and garnishes excels in popular items like Minnesota brie-and-apple soup or fresh saffron spaghetti with marinated shark, scallions, ginger, and cilantro. Popular dinner entrees include sautéed veal with apricot-bourbon sauce, grilled red grouper with sherry-vinegar sauce, and apple, pear, and fennel lasagne.

The selections of wondrous desserts include Dakota's crème caramel with a splash of amaretto, Frangelico, or Grand Marnier and—if calories are absolutely no object—chocolate mousse with strawberry cream.

At the daily all-you-can-eat luncheon buffet, you can fill freshly baked buns with assorted meats and cheeses, and add a green salad and hot selection of the day, for under $5. Sunday brunches feature assorted breads and muffins, granola and yogurt, fresh fruit and fruit salads, and a hot entree that varies from week to week. Outdoor dining is popular here during spring, summer, and early fall, when flowering shrubs served as your setting.

Prices for lunchtime sandwiches are under $5; grilled meats and fish cost less than $9 at lunch and less than $13.50 at dinnertime. Lunch is served 11:30 a.m. to 2:30 p.m. Monday through Saturday; dinner from 5:30 to 10:30 p.m. Monday through Thursday, 5:30 to 11:30 p.m. Friday and Saturday, 5 to 9 p.m. on Sunday. Brunch is served 10:30 a.m. to 2:30 p.m.

Good food and good wine in a comfortable, congenial setting continue to attract diners to **Faegre's Bar and Restaurant,** 430 First Ave. North (tel. 332-3515). Located on one of the busiest corners of downtown Minneapolis, Faegre's has received local awards for its creative continental cuisine and its extensive list of fine California and European wines.

You'll see everything from black tie to blue jeans on diners here in a 120-seat dining room that's minimally decorated—

white walls displaying works for sale by local artists, indirect lighting created by a series of reflective ceiling beams, postmodern windowboxes, and large windows looking out on a diversity of Warehouse District passersby.

Specials change here every day, but there's always a vegetarian entree and there's always the delectable Chinese chicken salad on a bed of Napa cabbage with a savory ginger-garlic-tahini dressing. The roast breast of duckling with sweet-and-sour sauce is another standby here. The Caesar salad has won an enthusiastic following, and so have the French onion soup and crusty French bread. And speaking of French, how about one of the most surprising items at Faegre's—french fries served with béarnaise sauce! It's reportedly a favorite of French

A Minneapolis Tradition

For more than four decades Twin Citians have headed to **Murrays**, 26 S. 6th St., (tel. 339-0909). Silver butter-knife steak is the specialty of this handsome family-owned and -operated restaurant, but you needn't live by beef alone at Murray's. The menu features broiled filet of walleye pike and veal T-bone steak among other favorites.

Situated in the heart of downtown Minneapolis, Murray's has somehow managed to retain its intimacy after being enlarged a few years ago. Mirrored walls, dusty-rose draperies and valances, and wrought-iron chandeliers and balustrades provide the same warm and gracious setting that Art and Marie Murray decided on back in the '40s. Their son, Pat, who now runs the restaurant with some help from a third generation of Murrays, also kept the grand piano with cello and violin accompaniment that provide a lovely melodic background for the evening's experience.

Dinners here are in the expensive-but-worth-it category. Top items, silver butter-knife sirloin steak for two or chateaubriand for two, served with half a bottle of French wine, will cost about $50. But less costly items are notable too—broiled sirloin tips or herb-broiled chicken at $12.50, for example. Dinner includes potato or vegetable along with salad and another specialty, the famous bread basket of baked-on-the-premises garlic toast, soft pretzels, and assorted rolls and crackers. Murray's is open seven days a week.

Lunch is served from 11 a.m. to 2 p.m., tea from 2 to 4:30 p.m., and dinner from 6 to 11 p.m. A special "downtowner" menu, in effect from 4:40 to 6 p.m., offers special rates.

chefs in the privacy of their kitchens, and it's a favorite here at
Faegre's as well.

Everything's made from scratch by a kitchen staff that's as
committed to good, nourishing, flavorful food as co-owners
Lowell Pickett and Sis Longfellow are. Prices are moderate.
Lunches average $7; dinners, $15. Lunch is served from 11:30
a.m. to 2:30 p.m., and a light menu is available from 2:30 p.m.
to 5:30 p.m. Dinner is on from 5:30 to 10 p.m. Monday through
Friday, to 11 p.m. on weekends, with a late-night menu served
until midnight. A popular jazz trio entertains on Sunday
nights.

The jaunty carousel horses that hang suspended from the
ceiling of **Filbert's**, 1021 Bandana Blvd. East (tel. 644-1442),
are probably the first thing you'll notice about this popular restaurant and nightspot. You might also notice that faces are
peering down at you through the upstairs windows of this lively
Bandana Square gathering place. People-watchers from without and within have given Filbert's the "place to be seen" award
in local newspaper polls. But what you'll see here varies widely
according to the time of day or night.

By day this is an attractive suburban dining place with a
beautifully landscaped outdoor plaza that's much in demand
during outdoor dining weather. Cajun cooking is a specialty
here, and if you're a fan, you'll probably enjoy the blackened
catfish or blackened tenderloin or breast of chicken Cajun style.
A variety of popular salads, sandwiches, and burgers is available at $6.50 or less. Luncheon entrees range from $7 to $10.
Dinners are in the $5 to $13 price range.

But it's what happens after dinner that has given Filbert's its
late-night reputation for strobe-lighted dancing, drinking, and
high-energy fun that brings the 20- to 40-year-old crowd back
again and again. Dining hours are 11:30 a.m. to 9 p.m. Monday
through Saturday.

Sunday brunch, served from 10 a.m. to 4 p.m., includes a variety of omelets, waffles, quiches, and filled croissants for $3 to
$6. Mimosas, Bloody Marys and screwdrivers are brunch-
priced at $1.

One of the most popular of downtown St. Paul landmarks is
Gallivan's, 354 Wabasha Ave., St. Paul (tel. 227-6688). This St.
Paul favorite underwent a major expansion in 1982 after it was
bought from the Gallivan family by Jerry and Jean Ann
Landreville. What had been a dining room/bar has now become three separate dining rooms with an adjoining bar/
lounge. The spacious main dining room features dark woods
and subdued lighting; the intimate library boasts a functioning

fireplace along with bookshelves stocked with histories, biographies, lawbooks, and encyclopedias.

The loyal clientele here is composed largely of folks who work in the neighborhood—lawyers, judges, and civil servants from the nearby courthouse and City Hall, as well as journalists from the *St. Paul Pioneer Press,* the local Knight-Ridder newspaper located just one block away.

There are few surprises on the Gallivan's menu, and that's just the way longtime enthusiasts like it. But the prices may prove a pleasant surprise to first-timers. Entrees, which include a choice of soup or salad and a choice of french-fried, au gratin, or baked potatos, range from $8 for a crisp chicken half to $16.50 for porterhouse steak. If you're a liver lover like me, you'll cheer for the broiled baby beef liver with bacon and onions; the broiled walleye pike is a favorite too. There's a long wine and liquor list here for patrons of the dining rooms and of the bar.

You'll think you've come to a small rustic restaurant as you approach **Gregory's,** at 7956 Lyndale Ave. South, in Bloomington (tel. 881-8611), but wait until you get inside! There are three floors of dining rooms and bars here, making Gregory's one of the largest, as well as one of the most popular, restaurants in this burgeoning suburb.

The Old West lives again in the main dining room with its split-log walls and wagon-wheel chandeliers. Other rooms provide a diversity of decor and ambience: the elegance of the Ritz, with its mahogany furnishings; the turn-of-the-century Parlor, warm and inviting with its frosted gas-light globes and hand-carved fireplace; the trendiness of the Rafters' black leather upholstery and stained-glass windows.

But it's the food, not the furnishings, that account for the enduring popularity of Gregory's. You'll find a touch of Cajun here, a bit of nouvelle cuisine there—Gregory's doesn't aim to be left behind—but primarily this is a prime ribs, walleye pike, chicken and shrimp and duck kind of place, with soups made from scratch and three luncheon specials everyday. In fact the next-day specials are noted in each luncheon menu, so regulars can make their plans accordingly.

Lunches range from burgers and fries for $5 to broiled sirloin steak sandwich with fries and salad for $9. Dinnertime entrees, served with salad, potato or rice, toast, rolls, and butter, range from $8.50 for baby beef liver to $16 for Cajun shrimp.

Feel free to come as you are to Gregory's. You'll see everything here from formal attire to sweaters and slacks. Lunches are served from 11 a.m. to 3 p.m. Monday through Friday; dinners, from 4 to 10:30 p.m. Monday through Saturday. The bar remains open until 1 a.m. Gregory's is closed on Sunday.

Phone early for a reservation at **Kincaid's,** 8400 Normandale Lake Blvd., Bloomington (tel. 921-2255). At this writing, there's no more popular restaurant in the Twin Cities than this beautifully appointed steak-and-seafood house, an elegant mix of marble walls, brass chandeliers, and cherrywood furnishings in an indoor park-like setting which describes itself as "behind the times and proud of it."

For all its vaunted traditionalism, though, Kincaid's employed very contemporary marketing research before its October 1986 opening by Restaurants International. Data showed Twin Citians to be "value oriented"—willing to spend money, but only when they feel they're getting their money's worth. What they get at Kincaid's is a choice of top-notch steaks, chops, and fish, mesquite grilled at high temperatures to sear in the flavorful juices. And there's a variety of fine pastas, sauces, soups, and desserts as well.

Luncheon entrees, served with vegetable and herb-pan bread, range from $6 for fish and chips to $9 for boneless New York steak. Dinners, served with a choice of chowder or salad, range from $9 to $17. The chatty dinner menu, which includes a lengthy wine list along with recipes for some of Kincaid's most notable entrees, also carries a money-back guarantee that your steaks, chops, and roasts will be moist, flavorful, and tender.

An elegant back bar has a dining area of its own, and a separate oyster bar features four different varieties daily, flown in from all over—the East Coast, West Coast, Canada, New Zealand, you name it. Desserts come in many forms: for example, brandy ice, the adult milkshake combining ice cream, brandy, Kahlúa, and dark crème de cacão. It'll make you glad you grew up! Lunch is served from 11 a.m. to 2 p.m. Monday through Saturday; dinner, to 9:30 p.m. Monday through Thursday, to 10:30 p.m. on Friday and Saturday, and 5 to 9:30 p.m. on Sunday. Blueberry Brunch is served on Sunday from 10 a.m. to 2 p.m.

The Lexington, 1096 Grand Ave., St. Paul (tel. 222-5878), is an institution in the Twin Cities, an elegant yet gracious, sprawling yet intimate restaurant with a long-standing reputation for fine food served in beautiful surroundings at reasonable prices.

It started out decades ago as a one-room tavern serving steak sandwiches and hamburgers, and has since evolved into a 360-seat restaurant with a 42-item menu. You'll find traditional American fare at the Lexington: New York sirloin and spring lamb chops, Dover sole and lobster tails, chicken Kiev and barbecued ribs. And then there are the specialties of the house—medallions of boeuf bourguignon glazed with a sauce of red wine, veal scallopine sautéed in butter and simmered with sherry wine and mushrooms, Minnesota ringnecked pheasant braised in a sauce of cream and brandy and served over wild rice. Entrees, served with a choice of potato and a choice of salad, range in price from $9 for braised short ribs to $22 for steer tender.

The setting here is as carefully designed as the menu: dark polished woods, gleaming crystal chandeliers, fine oil paintings, and a variety of rare artifacts—from the bronze relief in the main dining room of an elderly couple sharing a bit of snuff to the jovial gargoyle now putting in his time as a wine tureen in the Williamsburg Room. There's really no lovelier setting, no friendlier service, no finer food than you'll find at the Lexington, where families, business associates, and newcomers in search of the flavor of Minnesota are attentively and graciously served.

After you've enjoyed your entree, try one of the splendid desserts that have garnered a following of their own through the years. The incredibly creamy cheesecake amaretto is always in demand, but you won't go wrong with the carrot cake, pecan pie, or anything else on the menu at the Lexington.

This restaurant accepts no credit cards except the ones they themselves issue, but you can pay by check. Food is served from 11 a.m. until midnight Monday through Saturday. The Lexington is closed on Sunday and Christmas Day.

If your silverware's standing in a glass tumbler, and your napkin turns out to be a white terrycloth towel, and the stacked-up saucers await the mixing and matching that diners seem to enjoy, you're at **Monte Carlo Bar & Grill,** 219 Third Ave. North, Minneapolis (tel. 333-5900). There's some question as to whether this popular art deco hangout is a restaurant with a bar or a bar with a restaurant. When the tin ceilings first went in some 70 years ago, the Monte Carlo was exclusively a drinking spot, and that's what it remained until the surrounding Warehouse District turned chic back in the '70s. Now it has broadened its clientele, serving lunchtime and dinnertime chicken soup, plazaburgers, steaks, chops, and more to office workers, antique dealers, salesclerks, and shoppers. The price range is moderate, from $4.25 for a full Caesar salad to $11 for filet mignon. But the best buy of all is what you'll find here during the extended brunch hours from 10 a.m. to 4 p.m. on Sunday: all-you-can-eat scrambled eggs, Canadian bacon, sausage, toast, and hash browns for $4.

The copper bar is still a Monte Carlo focal point, with shelves of more than 500 bottles reaching up to the ceiling. Drinks are served club style—the mix in a large tumbler, liquor in shot glasses, garnishes at the side.

There's free parking in an adjoining lot. Hours are 11 a.m. to 1 a.m. Monday through Saturday, 10 a.m. to midnight on Sunday.

By the way, there's a relatively quiet front room off to the right as you enter Monte Carlo. It's the preference of those who find the rest of this lively restaurant too rambunctious for their taste.

Pearson's, 3803 W. 50th St., Edina (tel. 927-4464), features the kind of down-home cooking that many Minnesotans grew up with. Paul Pearson, the second-generation owner-manager of this family restaurant, got started in the business as a toddler, back in the '50s when a picture of him, dressed in diaper and Indian headdress, was used on Twin Cities billboards to promote an earlier family venture, the first electronic drive-in in the Upper Midwest. Now Paul and his brother, Marston, share responsibility for Pearson's, which their parents opened in 1973 as a coffeeshop near one of the most valuable street corners in the state of Minnesota—50th Street and France Avenue, in the affluent suburb of Edina. That original small diner has since been joined by the Oak Room and the Oak Room West, two elegant, handsomely paneled dining rooms with large stone fireplaces highlighted by large brass chandeliers.

Local families enjoy Pearson's because the menu is varied enough so that the entire clan can choose from among a diversity of entrees. Breakfasts are well under $5; lunches and dinners, under $10. Swedish meatballs, baked chicken, and roast prime rib rank high among the favorites here; so do pastries, soups, salad dressings, and dinner rolls, all of which are made on the premises. Some 90% of the diners here are steady customers, Paul Pearson reports, a measure of the steadfastness of this clientele. Hours are 7:30 a.m. to 9 p.m. Monday to Saturday, 9 a.m. to 7 p.m. on Sunday. Pearson's is closed on major holidays.

Polly Sidney really started something in 1979 when she opened **Polly's Slow Food Restaurant** (tel. 645-2990). Now situated at 1021 Bandana Blvd. in Bandana Square, St. Paul, this homespun restaurant features the recipes of her mother and grandmother. The cabinetmaking skill of her father has provided for Twin Citians a casual, comfortable, picturesque environment in which to enjoy the kind of home-cooking that's fast becoming a lost art.

You'll enjoy the old-world ambience of these attractive restaurants, with their hand-finished tables, benches, and chairs and their intriguing tabletop displays of antique postcards and snapshots. (There's reportedly at least one photo of Polly displayed on each tabletop.)

Breakfast items with an enthusiastic following here include German sour-cream twists and Danish fruit soup. Another favorite is cheese savaren, a bread-pudding look-alike with a cheese-and-onion richness all its own.

At lunchtime you'll be able to try the popular wine-cheese soup, served with lahvosh, a crisp Armenian cracker-bread. Another daily specialty is Polly's just-about-perfect lemon meringue pie. There's a wide and wonderful variety of pastries, sundaes, and malts on hand too, for those untroubled by calories.

Dinner specials, served with soup or salad, range from $6 for spinach lasagne to $11 for ten-ounce char-broiled steak served with fries, hash browns, or baked potatoes.

Polly's is open Monday through Thursday from 6:30 a.m. to 9 p.m., on Friday to 9:30 p.m., on Saturday from 8:30 a.m. to 9:30 p.m., and on Sunday from 8:30 a.m. to 6 p.m.

You probably won't be invited to dinner there, but do try lunch at **Primavera** or at the **Atrium Café International,** both of which are located at the elegant International Market Square, 275 Market St., Minneapolis (tel. 339-8000). Although they share a single phone number, address, and setting, the price ranges in these adjacent luncheon spots are distinctly different. At the "open-air" Atrium, located in what seems to be a New Orleans courtyard, you'll find one of the towns' best buys: an all-you-can-eat hot-and-cold buffet for $7, with the cold buffet alone going for $5. You'll take your selections to an umbrella-topped table and dine to the strains of live piano music. Meanwhile, a few feet away at Primavera you can be tasting some of the showcase items that keep this remarkable dining spot occupied seven nights a week with functions that have included the Symphony Ball, the British Festival, and other fêtes involving five- to six-course sit-down dinners for up to 2,000 invited guests.

Favorite items at Primavera include a salad of grilled chicken stuffed with dried fruits and black-walnut dressing for $7 and salmon filet with piperade of sweet pepper and onion and lemon grass butter sauce for $10. Appetizers are a specialty too; try the warm shrimp flan with sauterne-butter sauce for $4, and for dessert either the chocolate meringue torte or the hazelnut-and-fig bread pudding with Tuaca cream sauce, both of which are under $4.

Reservations are heartily recommended at both restaurants, which share what used to be the Munsingwear factory loading dock. The reception area was the boiler room, but the ambience now is sheer elegance and tastefulness. The rest of the complex houses wholesale showrooms for architects and designers, hence the identification button you'll be given when you enter. You can do a bit of window-shopping and can actually spend some money at an accommodating showroom here and there, but just looking can be fun too. And the dining at Primavera is among the best to be found in the Twin Cities.

You'd have a good time even if you didn't have a single thing to eat at one of the three **Rudolph's Bar-b-que** Twin Cities locations: at Franklin and Lyndale Avenues, Minneapolis (tel. 871-8969); 815 E. Hennepin Ave., Minneapolis (tel. 623-3671); and 366 Jackson St., Galtier Plaza, St. Paul (tel. 222-2226). The decor and the food listings are among the wittiest anywhere, based as they are on the good old steamily romantic days when screen idol Rudolph Valentino reigned supreme. In fact, on the purple-hued oversize menu, a photo of the turbaned Valentino and a blonde beauty bears the legend "Your eyes, your lips, your ribs!"

Wit, whimsy, and wonderful ribs are what you'll get at Rudolph's, along with a secret barbecue recipe that has won innumerable national awards. Owner Jimmy Theros has also won national devotees among rib-fanciers at his Coral Gables, Florida, and Akron, Ohio, branch restaurants. How to describe Rudolph's ribs? I've got a book to write; you go and taste them for yourself. If you're not a devotee of barbecued ribs, there are plenty of other moderately priced items ranging from the unadorned Hollywood-and-Vine hamburger at $4 to the shrimp Fantasia at $14. And save room for the "Happy Ending" desserts. The peach Melba, at $3, is a real treat in every sense, and so is the "Last Tango at Rudolph's," a blending of warm fudge brownie, vanilla ice cream, hot fudge, whipped cream, and crushed nuts.

There are "early bird" and "late-night" special menus here, and a lavish Sunday brunch at $11 for adults, $5 for children under 12. On your way in and out, take a look at some of the wonderful vintage Hollywood photos that line the walls. They're irresistible too.

Hours at the various locations vary. The Rudolph's at Lyndale Avenue is open from 11 a.m. to 3 a.m. Monday through Saturday and 10 a.m. to 2 a.m. on Sunday; Sunday brunch is served from 10 a.m. to 2 p.m. At Hennepin Avenue, Rudolph's is open from 11 a.m. to 1 a.m. Monday through Friday, 8 a.m. to 1 a.m. on Saturday, and 8 a.m. to midnight on Sunday. And in St. Paul the hours are 11 a.m. to 1 a.m. Monday through Saturday, to midnight on Sunday; Sunday brunch is served from 11 a.m. to 2 p.m.

There's something for everybody at **T.G.I.Friday's,** with three locations, at 7730 Normandale Blvd., Bloomington (tel. 831-6553); 5875 Wayzata Blvd., St. Louis Park (tel. 544-0675); and 2480 Fairview Ave. North, Roseville (tel. 631-1101).

As the name implies, this is a place for unwinding after work is done. It's also a place for lunch and dinner on weekdays and weekends alike. The extensive menu, in effect throughout the day and evening, features nearly ten pages of suggestions for dining and drinking, either at the large square center bar or in one of the elegantly cluttered dining rooms which abound with Tiffany-style lamps, stained-glass windows, mounted animal heads, and assorted antiques. The red-and-white striped tablecloths here are a signature item at T.G.I.Friday's throughout the country and, most recently, across the waters in England as well.

Best described as an American bistro, this congenial, convivial gathering place is remarkable because of its tilt toward non-alcoholic drinks. Friday's Flings are a delightful alternative to the liquor that used to be considered a social necessity. Flings are particularly popular at lunchtime with office workers and at any time with those who enjoy the atmosphere at the bar but don't care to drink alcohol. Drinks are not discounted for the popular daily Happy Hour, but a wide assortment of hors d'oeuvres is.

Prices here are easy to take. Burgers with all sorts of extras go for $5.50. Beef, chicken, and seafood entrees range from $8 to $12. A delightful children's coloring menu, reportedly designed by children for their peers, features everything kids love best, from hot dogs to grilled cheese to pigs-in-a-blanket to you-name-it. Prices are in the $2 range, give or take a dime or two. Friday's is open seven days a week: Monday through Friday from 11 a.m. to 1 a.m., on Saturday from 10 a.m. to 1 a.m., and on Sunday from 11 a.m. to midnight.

A hundred years ago everybody in the elegant Ramsey Hill neighborhood of St. Paul knew that an establishment named for pharmacist W.A. Frost stood on the corners of Selby and

Western Avenues. That's true today too, but now it's a restaurant, **W. A. Frost and Company,** 374 Selby Ave. (tel. 224-5715), located in the restored Dakota Building, not far from the Minnesota State Capitol and on the edge of one of this country's best-preserved Victorian residential districts.

The ambience of bygone days dominates the dining rooms here with their tin Victorian ceilings, marble tables, Oriental rugs, and illuminated oil landscapes that date back to the turn of the century. There are two functioning fireplaces here as well, a popular feature during the winter months; as the seasons change, though, diners look forward to some of the Twin Cities' most picturesque outdoor dining amid flowering bushes and trailing vines under a living canopy of trees.

The menu offers an eclectic cuisine with a variety of European, Oriental, and American selections. Favorite appetizers include the savory smoked salmon and cream cheese torte at $4.25 and crispy Chinese chicken wings at $3.75. A wide range of seafood is served here, everything from walleye to monk fish. And there's a large selection of beef, chicken, and pasta dishes as well.

This is one fine restaurant where people customarily come just as they are; don't be surprised to see a casually clad neighborhood couple fresh from working in their garden, while at a nearby table the governor or a bevy of businessmen or legislators sit in somewhat more formal attire.

Prices at W. A. Frost are moderate, ranging from $6 to $9 for an entree which includes potato and fresh vegetable. You'll also find one of the largest selections of imported beers and fine liquors in the area. Hours are 11 a.m. to 1 a.m. Monday through Saturday, with lunch served from 11 a.m. to 5 p.m.; dinner, from 5:30 p.m. on. Sunday hours are 11 a.m. to midnight.

CHINESE: Many local Asian restaurants fall into the budget category, but here are a couple of more elegant Chinese dining places.

There hadn't been a Chinese buffet in the Twin Cities until Leeann Chin opened one back in 1979. Now there are three branches of **Leeann Chin Chinese Cuisine:** 1571 Plymouth Rd., Minnetonka (tel. 545-3600); 214 E. 4th St., Union Depot Place, St. Paul (tel. 224-8814); and 900 Second Ave. South, International Center, Minneapolis (tel. 338-8488).

There are also five take-out delis located throughout the Twin Cities and suburbs, and of course there's that cookbook, *Betty Crocker's Chinese Cookbook, Recipes by Leeann Chin.*

Leeann Chin, who had joined forces with another Twin

Cities-based food manufacturer, General Mills, now heads an investor group and that's good news for you because the intent is to make her food services available beyond the Twin Cities. One Leeann Chin restaurant has already opened in Chicago, and others are on the way.

This unassuming woman's achievements are the more remarkable because Leeann Chin spoke no English when she first arrived with her five children in 1955. She could sew, though, and ultimately established a small dressmaking and alterations business. In 1982 she hosted a luncheon for the women she'd sewn for, and their requests for lessons in Chinese cooking led ultimately to an invitation to teach classes at the Bonaventure Center in suburban Minnetonka. The rest, as they say, is culinary history.

Certain signature items have evolved in Leanne Chin's restaurants during the years. Shrimp toast and crab puffs, lemon chicken, and Szechuan beef rank high among general favorites. Buffet selections change from day to day, but you'll always find three appetizers, two entrees, and fried rice on the long, fully laden tables. In addition, you'll be served your choice of Chinese soup or salad, and of course, tea. And, happily, there's no limit on the number of trips you may take to either the appetizer or entree tables.

Prices are $8 for the luncheon buffet, $12 at dinnertime. By the way, be sure to look closely at the exquisitely carved ivory and jade artifacts in each of the restaurants—they're exceptional!

One of the best buffets in the Twin Cities is the one you'll find at **Ping's,** 1401 Nicollet Ave. South (tel. 874-9404). From 11:30 a.m. to 2 p.m. Monday through Friday, $6 entitles you to unlimited visits to tables piled high with appetizers, fried rice, and assorted entrees. Even more lavish Sunday buffets, served from noon to 3 p.m. and 5 to 9 p.m., cost $8.

Amid gray walls and pillars, pink Chinese kites hang suspended in this attractive informal dining room where a pink tile bar serves as focal point on the lower of two dining levels. Chef Mingh Tran's selections consistently attract downtown business people, local high-rise residents, and more far-flung Twin Citians who savor the spicy Szechuan entrees featured here. There's complimentary valet parking at Ping's own nearby lot on the edge of downtown Minneapolis.

One of the most famous specialties of this house is the crispy, flavorful Peking duck, an appropriate specialty in a restaurant named for one of the more famous ducks of our time, the protagonist of Marjorie Flack and Kurt Wiese's children's tale *The*

Story About Ping. In Minneapolis, Ping's Peking duck can be brought to you as an entree for two persons for $25 or as appetizers for four or more persons for $20. Other entrees range from $6.25 for the vegetable stir-fry to $13 for sesame beef or chicken.

Ping's is open Monday through Thursday from 11 a.m. to 10 p.m., on Friday to midnight, on Saturday from 4:30 p.m. to midnight, and on Sunday from noon to 9 p.m.

FRENCH: Country French cuisine in a casual, comfortable setting is the specialty of the house at **Edward's Restaurant and Bakery,** 9920 Wayzata Blvd., St. Louis Park (tel. 546-6871). Chef Eric Schlenker, who apprenticed at London's Savoy Hotel where the prevailing language in the kitchen is French, brought his recipes and savoir faire to New York City's Brasserie before coming to the Twin Cities. It's his philosophy, and that of owner-maître d' Ed Christie, that authentic French fare doesn't have to be expensive, exotic, or laden with heavy sauces.

The kind of items French families order at their local brasseries—or the kind of meal you'd be offered if a French family invited you to their home for dinner—is what you'll find at Edward's in a setting that couldn't be warmer or more congenial. But before you reach the handsome dining rooms, with their pale stucco walls, dark woodwork, dark-green upholstery, and profusion of live greenery, some of it trailing down from massive ceiling supports, you'll feel your mouth watering uncontrollably as you step inside the front door. First there's the tantalizing aroma and then, straight ahead, the dazzling display of pastries and desserts in the bakery showcase that adjoins the open kitchen. Behind the case you'll glimpse, among oversize steel appliances, the long preparation table, the tall proofer in which croissants rise to their proper proportions, and the overhead pot rack where a profusion of pots, pans, and miscellaneous utensils hang suspended. The distinctly different dining rooms are a contrast in decor—the large bay windows in the main dining room, the oversize skylight in the family room, the casual elegance of the piano area combine to impart a remarkable sense of both expansiveness and intimacy.

Lunchtime choices include veal cutlets, smoked trout, quiche Lorraine, a choice of omelets, and for those who must take continental cuisine one step at a time, hamburger provençal. Prices range from $2 to $4 for hors d'oeuvres, $5 to $7 for entrees, and $6 to $8 for salads.

In the evening you'll be able to choose among chicken, pork, veal, beef, lamb, and shrimp entrees, all of them served with salad and potato along with French bread for prices between $9 and $13. Hors d'oeuvres, soups, salads, and cheese-and-fruit plates are available as well, and so are those—sigh!—pastries that are brought to your table as the end of the meal draws near.

And then there's the Sunday brunch at Edward's—surely one of the best bargains in the twin towns. You can order a brunch entree—Parisian French toast or the quiche du jour or a sirloin steak and eggs, or any of the other items listed in the menu, or for $10.50 you can have any of these items plus juice and a glass of champagne plus croissants and fresh fruit and soup and a pasta dish and an assortment of pastries and coffee or tea.

And there's one more thing you should know about Edward's. The bakery opens at 7 a.m. to sell breakfast take-out croissants, muffins, and assorted rolls to office workers in the area. Enterprising tourists line up there as well.

Lunch is served at Edward's Monday through Friday from 11:30 a.m. to 2 p.m., and dinner is on from 5:30 to 9:30 p.m. On Saturday you can dine at Edward's from 5:30 to 10 p.m. Sunday champagne brunch is served from 10:30 a.m. to 2 p.m.

Music drifts from twin pianos situated in the center of a dimly lit dining room that's been tastefully decorated in warm shades of mauve and gray. Sound romantic? It is, and it's part of what brings diners back again and again to **Yvette,** in Riverplace, 1 Main St. SE, Minneapolis (tel. 379-1111). But there's more to recommend this lovely French-American restaurant which overlooks the Mississippi and historic St. Anthony Falls. The food's as outstanding as the decor.

The dry-aged beef steak here is among the best that you'll find in the Twin Cities, and the daily seafood specials feature a mouthwatering selection flown in from Boston each day. (Days when tile fish is on the menu are the happiest ones for many local enthusiasts.) Sauces are light and seasonings are too, especially on the bestselling Cajun chicken. Desserts are another specialty, with the top draw being the chocolate velvet cake, baked on the premises with tasty touches of crème de cocoa.

Wines are very much a specialty of this house; they range in price from a Canteval house wine for $10 to Château Mouton Rothschild Pauillac 1897 for $2,000.

A dinner entree, served with potato, vegetable, and salad, is priced from $10 to $15. In the adjoining café, an informal alternative to the elegant dining room, you'll find a menu whose top entree price is $11. This restaurant is open from 11 a.m. to midnight every day, with lunch served from 11 a.m. to 5 p.m. and dinner from 5 p.m. to midnight. There's outdoor dining on a flower-bordered terrace, weather permitting.

GERMAN: The handsome German castle you'll see pictured on an outdoor wall of the **Black Forest Inn**, 1 E. 26th St. (tel. 872-0812), says a lot about this popular restaurant and its clientele. It was local artist and theater set designer Jack Barkla who painted the distinctive mural, and it's artists and theater folk like Barkla that you're likely to encounter at the Black Forest when evening performances are over. Late-night audience members also find their way there for the informal atmosphere and for the extensive selection of domestic and imported beers and wines served amid the dark woods and stained glass of a German "gasthaus." Families and couples find this a comfortable setting for lunch or dinner with authentic German specialties or more familiar American fare, depending on your inclination.

Luncheon entrees include wienerschnitzel and sauerbraten as well as chicken wings and corned beef on rye. The much more comprehensive dinner menu includes German favorites like schweinbraten (roast pork, apple dressing, and red cabbage) and gefuellte krautrolle (stuffed cabbage roll with rice); entrees are served with a vegetable and, more often than not, a potato pancake or spaetzel.

The Black Forest features a long list of German, French, and California wines as well as a variety of liqueurs, brandies, and cognacs. Luncheon prices range from $3 to $7.50; dinner entrees, from $4.50 to $13.50. In warm weather, an enclosed courtyard turns into a convivial outdoor beer garden. Lunches are served from 11 a.m. to 5 p.m. Monday through Saturday, and dinners are on from 5 to 11 p.m., with a late-night menu from 11 p.m. until midnight. Sunday dinner is served from noon to 10 p.m., with a late-night menu available from 10 until 11 p.m. The bar is open until closing time. Reservations are available for parties of five or more.

GREEK: For more than a decade, one of the most popular ethnic restaurants in the Twin Cities has been the **Acropol Inn**, 748 Grand Ave., St. Paul (tel. 298-0151). Now this fine Greek-American restaurant is one of the handsomest too. Etched glass plays a prominent part in the current decor: Juno greets you at the front door while large figures of Zeus and Dionysius dominate the first of two spacious dining rooms. Greek landscapes are illuminated by ceiling spotlights and taped Greek music adds the penultimate touch. The ultimate touch comes when you taste the homemade fare prepared for you by Aris and Cassandra Apostolou and served, likely as not, by their son, George, or teenage daughter, Vicki.

Early each morning, Monday through Saturday, Cassandra Apostolou begins baking the day's supply of bread, baklava, and assorted pastries while Aris readies the soups, roasts, salads, and other specialties. Lamb, roasted on a spit, is a favorite here; so are the seafood, beef, and chicken entrees prepared American style. But mostly it's the authentic Greek dishes that keep people coming back again and again for everything from moussaka (ground meat, fried eggplant, and a special topping) to dolmades (ground meat and rice wrapped in grape leaves and topped with lemon sauce) to steefatho (beef in wine sauce with potatoes and onions). The Greek salads are delectable too, enhanced with imported feta cheese and olive oil. Dinner prices range from $9 to $13 including soup, salad, and homemade bread. Luncheon entrees range from $5 to $9.

And maybe the best news of all is that for less than $6 you can lunch on a gyro sandwich with soup; many local diners consider that the perfect combination. Hours are 11 a.m. to 9 p.m. Monday through Thursday, to 10 p.m. on Friday and Saturday. The Acropol is closed on Sunday.

ITALIAN: The next best thing to a flight to Italy is a drive to **Cocolezzone,** 5410 Wayzata Blvd., Golden Valley (tel. 544-4014). Inspired by and named for a popular trattoria in Florence, this large, lively, and very beautiful spot became an instantaneous success when it first opened its doors in June 1985. With marble floors, beeswax-finished walls, and a plenitude of imported artifacts, Cocolezzone is a casual, sometimes clamorous, but altogether delightful place where pizzas fly through the air on their way to oak-fired ovens in the large display kitchen.

Because northern Italian fare is featured here, prepare to see, along with the usual tomato-laden toppings, such relatively unfamiliar sights as seafood pizza and pizza with spinach leaves, cheese, and a cooked egg in the center. Tomatoes, of course, make many appearances here, most notably perhaps in tortellini rosa, a delectable meat-filled pasta in tomato-and-cream sauce.

Dining here can be a very expensive or a remarkably inexpensive experience, depending on how you approach the lengthy northern Italian à la carte menu. Sharing is encouraged by the waiters, who delight in guiding you through the traditional succession of courses. The lunchtime menu lists a variety of antipasti, or you may prefer to select your own assortment from the tempting display case. Next comes the pizza, followed by soups, primi (a selection of pastas), meat, fish, and finally salad—for reasons of digestion, you'll be told.

For dinner, when the prices and portions are somewhat greater, the succession includes antipasti, pizze, primi, secondi, contorni, and dolci. The average dinnertime tab here comes to about $20, exclusive of wine. For lunch, $12 is the average amount. An extra treat that comes with dining at Cocolezzone is the free ticket you get to Rupert's, a popular nightclub right next door.

Lunch is served at Cocolezzone from 11 a.m. to 5 p.m. Monday through Friday, from 11:45 a.m. to 5 p.m. on Saturday. Dinners are served from 5 to 11 p.m. Sunday through Thursday, to midnight on Friday and Saturday.

Figlio's, 3001 Hennepin Ave., Minneapolis (tel. 822-1688), is a bustling beauty of an Italian restaurant-cum-bar with a marked California accent. One of Figlio's dining rooms overlooks busy Lake Street with some of the best people-watching hereabouts. The other, larger room has a view of its own—the busy demonstration kitchen with an oversize built-in wood-burning oven flanked by brick walls on which pizza paddles hang suspended.

The northern Italian cuisine is overseen by Executive Chef Vittorio Renda, famed locally for his version of carpaccio, paper-thin slices of raw beef tenderloin marinated in olive oil, shallots, capers, and herbs, topped with thinly sliced imported parmesan cheese, and assembled into open-faced sandwiches on Italian bread with three kinds of mustard at the ready.

Another Renda specialty is something called Morto nel Cioccolato, "Death by Chocolate," of which happy locals contentedly declare, "What a way to go!" Do consider a portion of this extravagantly rich and utterly delicious concoction composed of alternating layers of sublime chocolate cake and heavenly chocolate-amaretto gelato, served with thick chocolate sauce.

The rest of the menu contains a wide assortment of Italian and American favorites—from fettuccine Alfredo and stuffed tortellini to blackened red fish and ten-ounce burgers.

There are a lot of nice touches to the service here, foremost among them perhaps the heated plates that keep your selection piping hot as well as flavorful. Outdoor dining on Lake Street, take-out items, and Sunday brunches (from 10:30 a.m. to 2:00 p.m.) are some of the perennially popular attractions at Figlio's.

Hours are 11:30 a.m. to 1 a.m. Monday through Thursday, 11:30 a.m. to 2 a.m. on Friday and Saturday, and 10 a.m. to midnight on Sunday.

You've got a lot of choices to make at **Spazzo,** a unique Italian-American restaurant located in the Union Depot, 214 E. 4th St., St. Paul (tel. 221-1983). First there's the long list of Italian and American menu selections listed under such headings as "Appetizers," "Entrees," and "I Just Want a Sandwich." And then there's the matter of plate size. Diners here are encouraged to sample a variety of different dishes, so rather than order a large entree and a small side plate, you might choose several small ones. Or if you're not feeling particularly hungry, you might settle for just one small plate—that's fine too.

Most diners at Spazzo enjoy sampling a number of selections, and that requires another choice. Do you have your plates brought to the table all at once, or do you take them in succession? The mixing and matching opportunities are many, varied, delectable, and sometimes surprising.

An appetizer that has caught on quickly here is buffalo mozzarella with roasted sweet peppers, olive oil, and fresh basil. Spaghettini with artichoke hearts, goat cheese, and sun-dried tomatoes tossed in cream, parmesan, and egg is an unexpectedly popular entree too. But old favorites are available as well—everything from hamburgers small and large, to calves' liver to grilled New York sirloin.

Prices are moderate to high, depending on your selections. Pasta ranges from $4 for a small plate of fettuccine Alfredo with four kinds of cheese to $7 for fresh linguine with bay scallops, clams, and bay shrimp tossed in cream, parmesan, and egg. Entrees, which come in one size only, range from $10 for the boneless breast of chicken to $14 for tenderloin medallions.

Hours are 11 a.m. to 10 p.m. Monday through Thursday, to 11 p.m. on Friday, and 5 to 11 p.m. on Saturday. The large bar is open from 11 a.m. to 1 a.m. Monday through Saturday. There's free valet service for your car and, weather permitting, outdoor dining for you.

JAPANESE: Japanese cuisine, both traditional and contemporary, is featured at **Kikugawa,** Riverplace, 45 Main St. SE, Minneapolis (tel. 378-3006). Owner-operator John Omori recalls the reaction of Twin Citians to sushi when it first appeared on the menu during the early '80s, while his restaurant was still located across the river in downtown Minneapolis. "They'd look at the sushi and say, 'Wow!' or 'Yuck!' " he declares with a smile, then adds that this raw-fish delicacy has by now gone from less than 10% of food orders to about one-third.

This handsome restaurant, with its pale-wood pillars and beams, offers nabemono table cookery throughout the different dining rooms. Particularly popular are the tatami rooms, where Occidental diners leave their shoes at the door and simulate the experience of old-fashioned Oriental dining. In the tatami rooms or the main dining room or the riverfront room, choices these days are likely to include beef shabu, paper-thin slices of filet mignon cooked in two or three seconds in hot shabu broth. A current favorite in Japan, beef shabu is particularly popular with the growing number of local residents who first tried it during visits to Japan. Another current favorite that John and Miyoko Omori have introduced at Kikugawa is the yakitori bar, a broiling station for skewered chicken, beef, seafood, and vegetables. And then there's the selection of delicious desserts here, including two notable intercontinental triumphs— tempura ice cream and green-tea ice cream. They'll surprise and delight you.

Kikugawa is open for lunch from 11:30 a.m. to 2 p.m. daily and for dinner Monday through Thursday from 5 to 10 p.m., on Friday and Saturday to 11 p.m., and on Sunday from 4 to 9 p.m. Popular items here include sukiyaki at $7.50 and nabemono table-prepared items including shabu shabu (Japanese fondue) at $16. For haute cuisine Japanese style, try the combination tempura—seafood, chicken, and beef, with seasonal vegetables —at $16. It's justifiably famous in these parts. There are other specialties too, in a variety of price ranges. If you like Japanese food, you'll like Kikugawa.

Budget Dining (Under $10)

AFGHANI: Faculty members and students from nearby Macalester College and St. Thomas University make up more than half the regular diners at the **Khyber Pass Café**, 1399 St. Clair Ave., St. Paul (tel. 698-5403). But diners come from throughout the Twin Cities to check out for themselves the high praise they've read and heard since this unique neighborhood eating place first opened in June 1986.

Afghani artifacts decorate the white walls of this small family-run café, and the strains of Afghani music provide a somewhat exotic background in the spare, comfortable dining room. Owner Habib Amini, who does all the cooking at the Khyber Pass, explains that unlike other Middle Eastern cuisine,

Afghani cooking uses relatively few spices to enhance rather than overpower the food's natural perfume.

Chicken, lamb, and vegetarian dishes are among the top favorites here. One popular selection is the kebab-e murgh—chunks of boneless chicken cooked on a skewer and served with tomatoes, onions, and chutney. Korma-e sabzee is a delicious spinach dish served with chunks of lamb; korma e dahl, another popular entree, features chunks of lamb with yellow lentils cooked in onions and garlic.

Luncheon entrees range from $3.80 to $4.80. Dinners are served à la carte with flat bread for $4.50 to $5.25. A full dinner, served with basmati rice, salad, chutney, and flat bread, runs about $5.75 to $6.85. There's a flat $1.50 charge for desserts, afternoon or evening. If you like puddings, you're bound to enjoy the firni, rich and creamy and flavored with a blend of cardamom, rosewater, and pistachios. If you're a yogurt lover —and even if, like me, you're not—try a glass of doh, plain yogurt diluted with water, mixed with cucumber, and garnished with mint. Delightfully refreshing! Lunches are served from 11 a.m. to 2 p.m., and dinners are from 5 to 9 p.m. The Khyber Pass is closed on Monday.

AMERICAN: There's a lot of coming and going at the **Loon Café**, 500 First Ave. North (tel. 332-8342). Downtown office workers and shoppers find this a good place for a quick lunch. The oblong burger served on a sourdough bun is popular, and so are the "championship chilis," listed on the menu with asterisks to indicate how hot a choice is being made. There's also a selection of soups, salads, and cold sandwiches. Prices range from $3 to $6.

Primarily, though, this is a bar that sells food, not a restaurant that sells drinks, and the Loon really comes into its own in the evening when it becomes one of the busiest, noisiest spots in the chic Warehouse District. Many young professionals find their way here before heading home. Ticket-holders on their way to or from a performance or a game find this a good place to stop for a while. And celebrities, local and national, wander in from time to time: Bob Dylan, Morgan Fairchild, and other personalities have been sighted at the Loon.

Named for the official bird of Minnesota, this café displays and sells a variety of wildlife prints as well as sweatshirts and T-shirts bearing a loon's likeness.

Taped music, overpowering when you walk in, soon subsides into a background of general din which somehow doesn't seem to inhibit conversation. Hours here are 11 a.m. to 1 a.m. Monday through Saturday, and 5 p.m. to midnight on Sunday.

You'll find a lot more than the name implies at the **Malt Shop,** 809 W. 50th St., Minneapolis (tel. 824-1352), 208 Main St., Minneapolis (tel. 378-7251), and 1021 Bandana Blvd. East, St. Paul (tel. 645-4643). Famous for their hamburgers and ice-cream desserts, the Malt Shops offer in addition an international array of specialties—everything from bird's-nest soup to feta salad. All soups, salad dressings, and sauces are made on the premises, and so is the special cheesecake—a combination of cream cheese and ricotta. Salads come in two sizes and so do the "gourmet hamburgers," which include variations like the Beach Burger with Canadian bacon, Colby cheese, and barbecue sauce, and the Greenhouse, with sautéed mushrooms and melted Monterrey Jack cheese.

Daily specials at $6, served with soup or salad and grilled onion roll, range from Monday's lasagne to Sunday's chicken Monterrey. Popular box lunches include a sandwich, potato chips, fruit or feta salad, chocolate-chunk pecan cookie, pickle, condiments, and utensils for under $4. Hours are 11 a.m. to 10:30 p.m. Sunday through Thursday, to 11 p.m. on Friday and Saturday.

At which beautifully appointed Minneapolis restaurant can you enjoy three pieces of fried chicken, french fries, soup or salad, toast, vegetable, and a small ice-cream sundae for $4? Or shrimp in garlic butter baked in wine sauce, with potato, soup or salad, vegetable, toast, and a sundae for $6? Or an eight-ounce tenderloin filet with the same sort of accompaniments for under $8?

During the past 30 years there's been one place in town where you could find prices like this for selections like this in a setting like this—**Nora's,** 2107 E. Lake St. (tel. 729-9353.) Now there's a second such restaurant at 3118 W. Lake St. (tel. 927-5781), and that's particularly good news for visitors to the Twin Cities because the new Nora's is just a block from Lake Calhoun, about a mile from the heart of Uptown, and thus squarely within one of the most popular and interesting parts of Minneapolis.

The breads, soups, and sauces are made on the premises, and so are the popular onion rings, which come fully into their own when they're dipped into the drippings of a broiled-to-order steak (just a personal observation that I'd like to pass along). Another popular item is the Uncle Nels broiled sandwich, a combination of turkey breast, light wine sauce, mushrooms, and cheddar cheese on toast. According to owner Nora Truelson, it came into being as a bribe to one of her five sons: "We'll name the sandwich for you if you'll work tonight." He did and they did.

Nora's is open from 11 a.m. to 10 p.m. Sunday to Thursday, to 11 p.m. on Friday and Saturday.

Three years after the first **Old Country Buffet** opened in March 1984 at 9 E. 66th St., Richfield (tel. 869-1911), there were five more doing SRO business at suburban locations surrounding Minneapolis and St. Paul: 2480 Fairview Ave., Roseville (tel. 639-0088); 6540 University Ave., Fridley (tel. 572-8627); 4801 Hwy. 101, Minnetonka (tel. 474-1684); 14150 Nicollet Ave. South, Burnsville (tel. 435-6711); and 5526 W. Broadway, Crystal (tel. 536-8497). You'll understand the reason for this overwhelming success during your first visit to one of these clean and pretty family restaurants where the country-style decor features small patterned wallpaper in designs of blue, rust, and white, and where there's an abundance of booths and tables to accommodate parties of any size—and parties of absolutely all sizes do dine regularly at Old Country Buffet.

Certain items always appear, afternoon or evening, on the succession of buffet tables. You'll always find fluffy mashed potatoes and golden fried chicken along with gravy, rolls, vegetables, salads, beverages, desserts, sundaes, and hot cinnamon rolls. But those are only the starters. In addition, there's a long list of daily specials—meatloaf on Monday, fried cod on Tuesday, lasagne on Thursday, Swedish meatballs on Friday—and that's only lunch I'm talking about. For dinner, seven nights a week, you can have roast beef or ham carved to your specifications, along with other items du jour.

If you try Old Country Buffet once during your visit to the Twin Cities, you'll probably come back. It couldn't be more pleasant or more budget-pleasing. Complete lunches cost $4; dinner, $5.40. Sunday breakfast, served from 8 to 10:30 a.m., costs $4. Lunches are served Monday through Saturday from 11 a.m. to 3:30 p.m., and dinner, Monday through Thursday from 4 to 8 p.m., on Friday and Saturday to 9 p.m., and on Sunday and holidays from 11 a.m. to 8:30 p.m.

DUTCH: You'll have a sense of déjà vu when you get your first look at a **Pannekoeken Huis Restaurant:** 1505 S. Robert St., West St. Paul (tel. 455-1653); 2217 Hudson Rd., St. Paul (tel. 735-8860); 3020 W. 66th St., Richfield (tel. 866-7731); and 9830 Aldrich Ave. South, Minneapolis (tel. 881-5635). Then you'll remember where you saw this trim, pretty blue-and-white building before. It was on the last piece of Dutch Delft porcelain that you admired.

The most popular item on the menus in these family restaurants, as popular as they are picturesque, is, of course, the pannekoeken, a soufflé-style pancake, baked in the oven, flipped, and then rushed to the table before its puffiness disappears. The average deflation time has been clocked at 20 seconds, and that's why, from time to time, you'll see a waitress dashing from the kitchen with a plate held aloft as others clear out of her way. You can choose from 11 (a Dutch dozen?) different toppings for your pancake or choose to eat it plain with powdered sugar and lemon wedges—you'll love it either way.

There are other delights here as well: hearty Dutch stews and soups and omelets, for example. But much of the menu here is Dutch-American—metworst sausage and eggs, pannekoeken burgers, Netherlander sandwiches. And finally there are wholly domestic items, like grilled Reubens, barbecued ribs, batter-fried chicken strips. So maybe you won't find a truly authentic Dutch experience here after all. What you will find is tasty, healthful fare in delightful surroundings at modest prices: a $6 top tab for entrees, with soups, accompanied by Sytje's house salad and a thick slice of fresh-baked nine-grain bread well under $4.

And save room for some of the imported candies and take-home pastries you'll pass on your way to the door. You'll be glad you did! Hours are 6 a.m. to 11 p.m. Sunday through Thursday, to 1 a.m. on Friday and Saturday.

INDIAN: Anyone for murgh makhni, shahi korma, saag gosht, or shrimp scampi? You'll find them all at **Kebabi Bar & Restaurant,** a northern Indian dining place at 1 Main St. at Riverplace, Minneapolis (tel. 623-0501). You'll also find that underneath the exotic names for some of the entrees here, there's top-notch dining on tasty, nourishing Indian and American selections. And if you get here at lunchtime, you'll find one of the most popular, and popularly priced, luncheon buffets in the Twin Cities—an all-you-can-eat choice of the chef's special of the day plus roasted chicken, curries, lentils, rice pilaf and potatoes, salad bar, and fruit-salad bar for $5.50.

You'll know you've arrived at Kebabi when you spot a large bell-shaped clay tandoor oven in the window. Once inside the restaurant, you'll find a small, comfortable room dominated by brilliantly colored deerskin shadow puppets, illuminated by concealed tube lights which show up the subtlety of the artwork. The culinary artwork here features tandoor cooking of meats marinated in yogurt or lime juice, specially seasoned, and then roasted on skewers in traditional bell-shaped ovens. You can watch flat breads baked in three to five minutes on these same oven walls. This naan bread, a specialty at Kebabi, is a bestselling take-out item. Curries are popular here too, and so is the extensive vegetarian selection.

The bar is a busy place where nearly 40% of the orders are for nonalcoholic specialties like the rich and delicious mango shake. Dinner entrees range from $7 to $12.

Kebabi is open Monday through Thursday from 8 a.m. to 10 p.m., on Friday and Saturday from 10 a.m. to 10 p.m. Sunday brunch is served from 10 a.m. to 4 p.m.

ITALIAN-AMERICAN: It's been nearly 25 years since the first **Shakey's Pizza Restaurant** arrived in the Twin Cities at 1494 Portland Ave. in Richfield (tel. 866-2591). Now there are six other suburban locations here as well: I-35W at Burnsville Parkway, Burnsville (tel. 894-1010); 47th Street and Central Avenue NE, Columbia Heights (tel. 571-9139); Snelling and West Larpenteur, Falcon Heights (tel. 646-6316); Hwy. 7 west of I-494, Minnetonka (tel. 933-2288); Hwy. 12 west of Hwy. 100 in St. Louis Park (tel. 544-3162); and on South Robert Street in West St. Paul (tel. 451-1769).

The menu and the ambience have changed a lot through the years. What was originally a pizzas-only parlor with banjo-playing waiters has since become a chain of more decorous family restaurants featuring luncheon and dinner buffets which are notable for the profusion of their offerings: fried and barbecued chicken, mojo potatoes, a lineup of pasta dishes, and a very good salad bar. Thin-crust pizza remains king here, though, in a wide variety of forms including dessert pizzas, birthday pizzas, and Shakey's Special, a pizza with six toppings. (You'll find anchovy pizzas here too, a delicacy that's sometimes hard to find in these parts—don't ask me why.)

What's in the name of this hugely successful chain of budget restaurants is a bittersweet story that dates back to the Korean War when Californian Sherwood Johnson came away from his military service with spells of uncontrollable shaking. He dubbed himself "Shakey" and gave this name to his first pizza parlor and to the successful franchise that grew out of it. (Some people make lemonade when life hands them a lemon. Sherwood Johnson made pizza!)

You'll find the value unbeatable here: all-you-can-eat luncheon buffets for less than $5, dinner buffets for less than $6. Daily dinner specials go for $4, and senior citizens will find their own special perks here—complimentary coffee and 10% discounts on all food orders.

The decor differs a bit from place to place, but you'll probably find Tiffany-style lamps, hanging plants, wooden beams, and an aquarium at whichever Twin Cities location you visit. Hours differ too, so phone ahead for specific information.

VIETNAMESE: Budget dining doesn't get any better than what you'll find at the **Lotus,** 3037 Hennepin Ave., Minneapolis (tel. 825-2263); 313 Oak St., Minneapolis (tel. 331-1781); 3907 W. 50th St., Edina (tel. 922-4254); and Cliff Road at Hwy. 13 in Burnsville (tel. 890-5573).

Don't be put off by the decor—or lack of it—at these casual, congenial Vietnamese restaurants where large white Oriental lampshades are about as far as Le and Hieu Tran went in 1983 when they decorated the first of what has since become four busy neighborhood eating places.

Because sharing is encouraged, you can try a number of savory, nutritious entrees from beginners' fare like chicken or beef with vegetables to less familiar selections such as curried mock duck, sautéed with onion, garlic, and lemon grass in spicy coconut gravy. The chow mein here is delectable—a hearty mixture of chicken, beef, and shrimp, along with crunchy slabs of cabbage, carrots, celery, onion, and broccoli, that in no way resembles the gelatinous mound you'll find in some other Oriental eating places.

The menu indicates which items are hotter than others, but a lot of flexibility goes with the territory. Because most dishes are stir-fried to order, the chef will adjust particular dishes to suit individual tastes and tolerances.

Although Le and Hieu Tran and their four teen-age children have made many friends in the Twin Cities, few people are aware of the symbolism in the name and the logo of the Lotus restaurants. The blue curves of neon in the windows symbolize the ocean from which the Trans and other desperate boat people were rescued before being flown to the United States. And the blossoming lotuses, like the refugees' lives since their escape, become robust despite the murky waters in which they lived for so long.

You may have to wait for a table at the Lotus Restaurants, but the food and the value are well worth waiting for. Entrees range from $4 to $8. Hours vary from restaurant to restaurant, so call ahead.

Vietnamese restaurants were a rarity in the Twin Cities before the opening in 1970 of **Matin,** 416 First Ave. North, Minneapolis (tel. 340-0150). Today there are reportedly more Vietnamese restaurants here than in any other major city in the country, thanks in large part to the prominent role of local churches in sponsoring families seeking to leave that war-ravaged country.

None of these restaurants, though, has remained more authentic than Matin. The authenticity of seasoning and preparation accounts for the popularity not only of the savory entrees but of the assortment of frozen Matin eggrolls which are now on limited sale at several local supermarkets. Actually the demand for these delicacies is practically unlimited, but since they're prepared and packed right on the premises of this small restaurant, the limitation is built in.

You'll want to try the eggrolls imperial, crammed with black mushrooms, cellophane noodles, carrots, onions, pork, and chicken; there's a version for vegetarians as well as carnivores. Other favorites on the menu include the hot-and-heavenly imperial chicken, and the curried beef sautéed with onions, garlic, and lemon grass in coconut gravy, topped with peanuts. Sound good? The neighborhood office workers come back for it again and again, and so do the artists and gallery-goers who frequent this part of the Warehouse District. Most entrees here are in the $5 to $6 range, except for Vietnamese beef fondue at $10.50.

Matin is open for lunch Monday through Friday from 11 a.m. to 2:30 p.m., and for dinner Monday through Thursday from 5 to 10 p.m., on Friday and Saturday to 11 p.m. The restaurant is closed on Sunday.

Chapter V

THE SIGHTS OF MINNEAPOLIS AND ST. PAUL

A BEAUTIFUL BLEND of the old and the new is what you'll find here in the Twin Cities. Many of their proudest buildings, like the splendid mansions on St. Paul's Summit Avenue, have been listed on the National Register of Historic Places; many other buildings, newer than tomorrow, will dazzle you with their soaring expanses of reflective glass. Don't miss City Center and Phillip Johnson's award-winning IDS Tower in downtown Minneapolis. Be sure to see, too, the brand-new Conservatory on the Nicollet Mall, designed as downtown Minneapolis' answer to the shopping centers of suburbia. And note that the internationally famed arts of the Twin Cities are often housed in buildings that are themselves works of art.

But not all the Twin Cities' sights are man-made. The lakes of Minneapolis and St. Paul are legendary, not only for their beauty but for the many popular activities that take place there throughout the year.

Let's start our mini-tour in St. Paul because that's where the Twin Cities started.

Historic St. Paul

THE STATE CAPITOL: The grandest of all Twin Cities sights is the Minnesota State Capitol, built in 1905 on a hill at 700 Wabasha St. overlooking downtown St. Paul. Approached by a succession of broad gray granite terraces and crowned by the world's largest unsupported marble dome, this magnificent structure was the design of Cass Gilbert, a young St. Paul architect whose later work included the Woolworth Building in New York City. At the base of the dome, modeled after the one Michelangelo created for St. Peter's in Rome, a dramatic group of gilded figures represents *The Progress of the State.* Four prancing horses, symbolizing the power of nature, are held in check by two women, representing Civilization. A charioteer, Prosperity, holds aloft a horn of plenty in one hand, and in the other he grasps a banner bearing the inscription "Minnesota."

The interior of the capitol building is equally impressive, with its marble stairways, chambers, and halls, and its diversity of fine oil paintings depicting important events in Minnesota history. Free guided tours through the Senate, House of Representatives, and Supreme Court chambers are offered Monday through Friday from 9 a.m. to 4 p.m., on Saturday from 10 a.m. to 3 p.m., and on Sunday from 1 to 3 p.m. Phone 296-2881 for details.

THE CATHEDRAL OF ST. PAUL: On a nearby site, at the corner of Summit and Selby Avenues, stands another of St. Paul's proud architectural achievements, the 3,000-seat Renaissance-design Cathedral of St. Paul, constructed of Minnesota granite. John Ireland Boulevard, the street which extends just half a mile from the Capitol to the cathedral, is named for the dynamic archbishop of St. Paul who served as a fighting chaplain during the Civil War and later diverted his energies and determination toward raising the funds for the creation of this magnificent structure, which he dedicated to the people of St. Paul.

SUMMIT AVENUE: Beyond the cathedral, Summit Avenue, long the most prestigious of St. Paul's addresses, extends 4½ miles to the Mississippi River. On this distinguished street stands the country's longest span of intact **Victorian mansions** and here, at 240 Summit Ave., you'll find one of the city's perennially popular tourist attractions, the mansion of "Empire Builder" James J. Hill, founder of the Great Northern Railroad, a network which made possible the development of the American Northwest. (For information about tours, phone 297-2555.) Among the more modest homes on this avenue is the one at 599 Summit, where F. Scott Fitzgerald lived in 1918 while finishing his first literary success, *This Side of Paradise.* And farther down toward the Mississippi, at 1006 Summit, you'll find the governor's stately residence.

Elsewhere on Summit Avenue, you'll find several famous colleges and universities—**Macalester College,** at Summit and Snelling Avenues South; the **College of St. Thomas,** at 2215 Summit Ave.; and at 875 Summit Ave., arguably the most influential small college anywhere in the country, the **William Mitchell College of Law,** whose graduates include two former colleagues on the United States Supreme Court, Chief Justice Warren Burger and Justice Harry Blackmun.

Distinguished houses of worship stand on this avenue as well, including **Mount Zion Temple,** 1300 Summit Ave., home of the oldest Jewish congregation in the state of Minnesota. Members of this congregation, which dates back to 1856, selected the famous architect Frederick Mendelsohn to design their new temple for them in the early 1950s. Mendelsohn had gained earlier international fame for his work in pre-Nazi Germany. Tours of this beautiful building are popular with Gentiles and Jews alike. Call 698-3881 for more information.

DOWNTOWN RESTORATIONS: In the downtown area, two twin-towered churches are particularly interesting and photogenic. **Assumption Church,** 51 9th St. West, was constructed in 1873 for the city's German-speaking Catholics, and it looks like a bit of Bavaria transplanted in a midwestern American city. That may be due to the fact that this picturesque church was designed by Joseph Reidl, architect to the king of Bavaria. Relatively austere on the outside, it contains within a wealth of beautiful statuary, magnificent murals, and an exquisite gilded back altar. The twin-towered **Saint Louis Catholic Church,** 506 Cedar St., is a quietly elegant structure of red brick and limestone. It was built in 1909 for French-speaking parishioners.

The **St. Paul Union Depot,** at the corner of East 4th and Sibley Streets, is a massive sandstone building with an imposing columned entrance which once welcomed train travelers to the Twin Cities. The Union Depot was opened to the public in 1920, then reopened in 1983 after it had been restored and refurbished. Now it houses restaurants and in the Union Depot concourse, exhibits such as the multi-million-dollar art collection of Milanese collector Count Giuseppe Panza di Biumo, expected to arrive by 1989.

Elsewhere in Lowertown, at Mears Park, Sibley and 6th Streets, stands **Park Square Court,** the 19th-century warehouse credited with having inspired the redevelopment of St. Paul's historic Lowertown. Now primarily an office complex, Park Square is accessible by skyway.

Nearby **Galtier Plaza,** on Sibley Street between 5th and 6th

Streets, is now an entertainment, retail, restaurant, and residential complex.

But perhaps the most dramatic of all St. Paul's restored structures is the **Landmark Center,** facing Rice Park at 106 W. 6th St. This massive early French Renaissance structure with Gothic towers and pillars, turrets and gables, 20-foot ceilings and hand-carved mahogany and marble decoration, served for decades as the Old Federal Courts Building and Post Office. Eventually it fell into disrepair and was slated for demolition when a determined coalition of private citizens and public officials intervened and prevailed. In 1972 the Landmark was taken over by the city, and today, returned to its former grandeur, it houses a diversity of arts and civic offices and is open to the public for free guided tours.

The Landmark Center is just one of several significant structures that encircle **Rice Park,** the oldest of St. Paul's urban parks and a treasure in itself, with its lovely central fountain and meticulously manicured lawns.

On another side of the park you'll find the exquisite **St. Paul Public Library,** donated to the city in 1916 by James J. Hill, whose own private reference collection is also contained here. (Hill's donations also played a major role elsewhere in the city, most notably perhaps in the establishment of the College of Saint Thomas and of the Cathedral of St. Paul.)

Forming the fourth "wall" around Rice Park is the restored and refurbished **Saint Paul Hotel,** which has made a graceful transition from its turn-of-the-century origins to its present-day role as host to visitors to this city. Elegant accommodations are offered to out-of-town guests and superb dining is enjoyed here by visitors and hometown folks alike. (See Chapter III, "Where to Stay," and Chapter IV, "Where to Dine," for further details.)

THE WORLD THEATRE: It was St. Paul's favorite son, Garrison Keillor, who spearheaded a national crusade to save the World Theatre, one of the city's most beautiful and beloved restorations. The World, built in 1910 by Sam S. Schubert, and originally named for him, was for decades an Upper Midwest showplace for stage and later for movie productions. Ultimately it became the home of Keillor's "Prairie Home Companion," the radio show that provided weekly reports on Lake Wobegon, the mythical town "where all the women are strong, all the men are good-looking, and all the children are above average." By 1977, when plaster started falling from the ceiling, safety officials demanded that the theater be closed, so a massive fund drive got under way which ultimately led to the

World's rehabilitation and then to its gala reopening on April 26, 1986. Today, restored to its original splendor, the World is one of the country's few remaining two-balcony "dramatic house" proscenium theaters, with none of its 925 seats more than 87 feet from the stage.

The New St. Paul

THE ORDWAY MUSIC THEATRE: The Ordway received national attention when it first opened on January 1, 1985. Its grace and grandeur led to comparisons with the grand old concert halls of Europe, but the expanses of its glass walls provide a distinctly contemporary touch to the exterior of the structure. These glass walls also provide a superb view of the city for those within. (See Chapter VII, "Music, Dance, Museums, and Galleries" for details.)

The Skyway System

St. Paul's skyway system has become so integral a part of city life that we tend to forget how remarkable it is. Extending for nearly three miles from one end of St. Paul to the other, this is the largest publically owned skyway system in the world. Built and maintained by the city, St. Paul's skyways, like any other public thoroughfares, are uniform in design and patrolled regularly by the police department. Although hours in different parts of the system vary, depending on the kinds of buildings they're connecting, those that tourists are likely to use are generally open from 6 a.m. to 2 a.m.

The city has made good use of its skyways for festive as well as functional purposes. During one St. Paul Winter Carnival, lines of marchers, musicians, clowns, and tap-dancers started out at the north, south, east, and west corners of the skyway, ultimately convening at the center of the skyways, Town Square. In the process they made their way into the *Guinness Book of World Records* for having participated in the world's longest indoor parade.

The skyways have made this a second-story city, where a vast majority of retail business is conducted above street level. Visitors needn't worry about the weather as they walk from hotels to shops, restaurants, and theaters. This is, after all, wonderful, weatherproof downtown St. Paul.

TOWN SQUARE: At the heart of St. Paul's extensive skyway system is the remarkable 27-story Town Square, with its shopping, office, dining, and entertainment facilities. There are hotel accommodations here too, at the unique Holiday Inn Town Square, the first hotel in America with built-in solar heating and hot-water systems. Easily the most beautiful part of Park Square, though, is still unexplored territory to many Twin Citians. Tucked away above the retail area is the world's largest indoor public park, lush greenery on the fourth level, dancing waterfalls, cozy seating alcoves, and even a playground where children can have fun while their elders enjoy the beauty and serenity of it all.

THE WORLD TRADE CENTER: Also new on the St. Paul landscape is the nearby World Trade Center, a sleek, imposing 40-story tower, opened in the fall of 1987 for the purpose of encouraging and expediting international trade. Town Court, the adjoining retail complex, includes an indoor fountain, shops and restaurants.

LANDMARK CENTER: This beautiful castle-like structure was formerly the Old Federal Court Building where famous gangster trials were held back in the 1930s. The courtroom has been elegantly restored and so has the magnificent sixth story courtyard. Landmark now serves as the art center for St. Paul, with one of the main galleries of the Minnesota Museum of Art located here.

THE SCIENCE MUSEUM OF MINNESOTA: Exhibits at the Science Museum, 30 E. 10th St., ranging from the anthropological to the technological, have enthralled visitors of all ages and all backgrounds since 1980. Its distinctive concave entranceway encloses a portion of the circular second-story Omnitheater, where exciting and educational 70-mm movies are projected onto a massive tilted screen for a sometimes scary sense of involvement.

THE MINNESOTA MUSEUM OF ART: Overlooking Kellogg Boulevard and the Mississippi River, the handsome art deco Minnesota Museum of Art, 305 St. Peter, is the repository of a distinguished collection of contemporary paintings, sculpture, photography, and drawings from throughout the world. A large portion of the street level has recently been turned over to the Park Square Theatre, a highly regarded company whose popular productions add yet another dimension to the interesting offerings here.

TWO SPECIAL ST. PAUL STATUES: There are two St. Paul statues that rank high on any list of sightseeing attractions.

In the St. Paul City Hall / Ramsey County Courthouse, at Fourth and Wabasha Avenues, Carl Milles's majestic 36-foot tall onyx figure, the *Indian God of Peace*, stands in regal splendor. This 60-ton statue, which rotates very very slowly, has been seen and admired by most Twin Cities children and by the grownups who bring them here during viewing hours: Tuesday through Friday from 8 a.m. to 5 p.m., on Sunday from 1 to 5 p.m. Many Twin Cities parents saw this statue for the first time when they themselves were children.

And on the slope between the Capitol and the cathedral there's an often-overlooked symbolic tribute to a history-making Minnesotan. Charles Lindbergh, who grew up in Little Falls, Minnesota, went on in 1927 to become the first pilot ever to make a nonstop solo flight across the Atlantic Ocean. Sculptor Paul Granlund has honored him by creating two bronze figures, Lindbergh as the young man who observes you as you drive or walk by, and Lindbergh as the small boy who looks the other way, toward downtown St. Paul and the Mississippi River just beyond.

Natural Attractions

More than a million visitors a year make St. Paul's **Como Park** one of the most popular of all Twin Cities attractions. The glorious **Como Park Conservatory**, site of innumerable weddings and other festive events, would in itself be a prime attraction, but there's a great deal more to be enjoyed in this vicinity. Adjacent to the conservatory are two smaller but equally exquisite showplaces: the **McKnight Formal Gardens** with their famous Paul Manship sculpture of an Indian boy and his dog, and the **Japanese Gardens**, designed by Masami Matsuda of Nagasaki, St. Paul's Japanese sister city. (Masada's attention to detail extended even to the angle of the rocks.)

Another favorite destination at Como Park is the long-popular **Como Zoo**, not far from a small, privately operated amusement park which has pony rides among its many attractions.

Golfers will be glad to know about the elegant new octagonal clubhouse that overlooks one of the city's best 18-hole **golf courses** here at Como Park. A vast pavilion, restored to its early–20th-century grandeur, enables Twin Citians to again enjoy seeing and being seen as they promenade and listen to lakeside concerts.

Lake Como provides delightful swimming and sunning, and paddleboats are a popular diversion here as well, making their way among the ducks, gulls, and other birds at home on the lake.

If you've a question, comment, or concern during your visit, look for one of the attractive park rangers, in their beige-and-brown uniforms, who patrol regularly and are unfailingly courteous and helpful. Como Park is located about 2½ miles north of the juncture of I-94 and Lexington Avenue in St. Paul. See Chapter IX, "Sports and Recreation," for details on park activities, and phone 292-7400 for information on the many beautiful lakes and parks in St. Paul.

Historic Fort Snelling

One of the most popular sightseeing attractions in the Twin Cities isn't properly in either Minneapolis or St. Paul, but in between them at the confluence of the Mississippi and Minnesota Rivers (now Hwy. 5 at Hwy. 55, one mile east of the Minneapolis–St. Paul International Airport). This is the place where in 1819 Col. Josiah Snelling and his troops began construction of a fort to establish an official U.S. Government presence in the wilderness that had recently been won from Great Britain. President Thomas Jefferson had hoped this outpost would become a "center of civilization," and that's what occurred as families arrived and built homes on the perimeter of land that had been ceded to the army by the Sioux. In 1837, after a treaty opened additional land for settlement, these families moved across the river to establish a community of their own, one that would later be known as St. Paul.

Fort Snelling continued as a military installation which played an important role in the lives of those who lived and worked there. In 1837 Dred Scott, the slave of an army surgeon, was married in a Fort Snelling lookout built of limestone from nearby bluffs. After the doctor's death in 1846, Scott sued for his freedom on the basis of having lived for a time in the free state of Minnesota—and lost the case. The now-famous Dred Scott Decision is often cited as a contributing factor to the American Civil War.

And in 1864 a young German military attaché named Count Zeppelin ascended 300 feet above the Old Round Tower in a large gas-powered canvas bag. Later such vehicles, bearing the count's name, served as a common means of aerial transportation.

Since 1937 the Minnesota State Historical Society has maintained a **living museum** at Fort Snelling, where costumed guides re-create the activities and ceremonies of everyday army life during the 1820s. Phone 726-9430 for information about hours and admission; you can get specifics on tours and special events by calling 726-1171.

Historic Minneapolis

THE ARD GODFREY HOUSE: In the mid-1800s, on the east bank of the Mississippi River, the village of St. Anthony took its name from the nearby waterfalls which had earlier provided the power to build Fort Snelling. St. Anthony lost its name and its separate identity in 1872 when it merged with Minneapolis, but its cobblestoned main street remains, and so does the small yellow wooden house that was built by Ard Godfrey, a mid-19th-century millwright from Maine. Prior to this time, most houses in the area were made of log; a few were adobe huts.

The Ard Godfrey House, now located at the corner of University and Central Avenues SE, reflects the New England heritage of its builder in the cornices, the moldings, and the divided window sashes that he designed in 1848 for the 1½-story dwelling made of lumber from the village's first sawmill—the sawmill was powered, of course, by St. Anthony Falls. Godfrey's house, which originally stood on the corner of Main and 2nd Streets, was turned into a museum and moved to its present site in 1909. Somehow in the process its kitchen wing was lost, but much of interest still remains, including original furnishings as well as flags, snowshoes, and the city's first directory, dated 1859. Tour information is available by calling 330-0181 or 870-8001.

OUR LADY OF LOURDES: Just a short walk away, at 21 Prince St. SE, you'll find the church that's been in continuous use longer than any other in Minneapolis. Our Lady of Lourdes Church, serving parishioners since 1877, is a small, Gothic-style limestone structure that retains its original statuary, tapestries, and stained glass. French readings are presented at Easter, Christmas, and New Year's (about 25% of the church's congregation is of French descent). Tours are available by appointment (tel. 781-2337), with a $1 donation requested. Visitors wishing to attend services here are welcome at 5:30 p.m. on Saturday and at 9 and 11 a.m. on Sunday.

The neighborhood in which this dignified historic building now stands would no doubt astound the mid-19th-century French Catholics who originally attended services here. Among the parishioners was Zepherin Demoules, a French-Canadian who founded *L'Echo de l'Ouest,* the state's only French newspaper. Today Our Lady of Lourdes is surrounded by two bustling shopping-and-entertainment centers, St. Anthony Main and Riverplace.

THE WAREHOUSE DISTRICT: Although 19th-century Minneapolitans firmly believed that Main Street, the center of the Warehouse District, would remain the city's major thoroughfare, when railroads superseded ships as the primary means of transporting goods, the business and industrial interests moved across the Mississippi River. In what's now known as the Minneapolis Warehouse District, chic restaurants, bars, artists' galleries, and antique shops have moved into the restored sprawling structures that once housed local products awaiting shipment to other parts of the nation.

HENNEPIN AVENUE: Between the Warehouse District and the beautiful Nicollet pedestrian mall a few blocks away lies a short section of Hennepin Avenue that's been accurately described as "this clean city's gritty side." Pornographic bookstores and strip-tease shows have become entrenched in a small concentrated area, so if they're your cup of tea, you know where to head. But you'd better hurry because a determined move is now under way to upgrade this part of downtown, and when public and private interests in Minneapolis band together, the impossible takes hardly any time at all. Much of what's newest and most exciting about Minneapolis—the pedestrian mall, the skyway system, the sleek, futuristic structures that house offices and shops and more—came about because of coalitions bent on giving a new face to the downtown skyline. Here and there, though, you'll find something old that somehow eluded the massive reconstruction of recent decades.

THE FOSHAY TOWER: The venerable Foshay Tower, at 821 Marquette Ave., is a proud survivor of the past. Built in 1929, the 447-foot-high obelisk was known for decades as the tallest structure in the entire Upper Midwest. Today it has been dwarfed by its sleek new neighbors, but for one brief shining interlude in 1981 the tower received national attention in newspapers and on TV when an immense, much-photographed yellow ribbon was wrapped around its upper portion as a welcome-home greeting to America's liberated Iranian hostages.

A DIVERSITY OF DOWNTOWN CHURCHES: Among the distinguished old buildings in downtown Minneapolis, many on the perimeter are, not surprisingly, churches of various denominations and descriptions—the Romanesque Revival **Methodist Church** at 101 East Grant St., the imposing **Westminster Presbyterian Church** at 1201 Nicollet Ave., the modified Gothic **St. Mark's Episcopal Church** at 15th Street and Hennepin Avenue, the magnificently spired **Hennepin Avenue Methodist Church** at Groveland and Hennepin Avenues, and the neobaroque **Basilica of Saint Mary** at 16th Street and Hennepin Avenue.

THE LUMBER EXCHANGE BUILDING: There's an interesting bit of architectural history to be seen at 425 Hennepin Ave., site of the Lumber Exchange Building, built in 1885 and refurbished in 1980. It was in this elegant 12-story structure, fashioned of granite and Lake Superior brownstone, that much of the city's extensive lumber trade was conducted. It currently houses offices, shops, and a night club.

POWERS DEPARTMENT STORE: At 5th Street on the Nicollet Mall stands an old structure which has recently been pressed into new and distinctly unusual service. Powers Department Store, which closed its doors to shoppers in 1985, had long occupied a significant role in local retailing. It was in this friendly, family-owned department store, for example that the Twin Cities' first "moving stairway" was introduced to a properly impressed public in 1929. What you'll find at Powers now is an institution dedicated not to shoppers but to scholars. St. Paul's **College of St. Thomas** has come across the river to establish in this old department store off-campus classes for the benefit and convenience of downtown Minneapolis workers and residents. A storefront private college of this kind is a first for the area and represents a superb addition to the mall that has played so central a role in the continuing revitalization of downtown Minneapolis.

The New Minneapolis

THE NICOLLET MALL: Here's an important word of warning to tourists taking their first look at the picturesque Nicollet pedestrian mall. Those cabs, buses, and emergency vehicles you see on the mall are the only exceptions to the firmly enforced ban on vehicular traffic. The beautifully landscaped mile-long thoroughfare is primarily for use by pedestrians, and you'll be glad that's so as you enjoy your walk amid the mall's trees, flowers, and graceful statuary.

The Skyways

As in St. Paul, the first thing you'll notice in downtown Minneapolis is its extensive skyway system, which was a nationwide first in the 1960s. In fact this is the longest privately owned skyway system in the world. In general, Minneapolis skyways remain open during the business hours of the buildings they connect.

Because the design, maintenance, and security of Minneapolis' skyways are primarily the responsibility of the owners of these linked buildings (there are some public buildings here too), the respective designs and hours of the Minneapolis skyways tend to differ from one another. While you're walking through downtown Minneapolis, you'll see the eclectic skyway designs of the individual architects engaged by various building owners. One particularly interesting skyway, which links Crossings Condominiums and the Norwest Operations Center, at South Second Avenue near Washington Avenue, looks like the car of a sleek, streamlined train. In fact the skyways have given a sleek, streamlined look to all of well-connected downtown Minneapolis.

NEW FACES DOWNTOWN: If downtown Minneapolis looks like a brand-new city, that's because so much of it is. Let's take a walk down the Nicollet Mall, starting at the northern end, not far from the Mississippi River. We'll see along the way some of the award-winning buildings that have changed the face of the city.

Shortly after being completed in 1963, the **Northwestern National Life Insurance Company**, at 20 Washington Ave. South, was pictured on the cover of *Time* magazine. Modeled after the Parthenon, this magnificent marble structure with its graceful Doric columns has become one of the loveliest and earliest landmarks in the new Minneapolis.

The remarkable 11-story **Federal Reserve Bank Building**, at 250 Marquette Ave., is reportedly the first American building designed on the cantilevered suspension system usually reserved for bridges. It's said that the building could easily support a structure of identical size, turned upside down and placed on top.

City Center, a six-acre expanse occupying the square block from 6th to 7th Streets and Nicollet to Hennepin Avenues, houses the Marriott Marquis Hotel, the International Foods

Building, and a three-level, atrium-illuminated shopping area that contains dozens of fine shops in addition to one of the city's best department stores, Donaldsons.

The 51-story **Investors Diversified Services Center,** across the street at 777 Nicollet Mall, contains the **Crystal Court,** which serves as the focal point of the skyway system. Today shops, restaurants, and offices keep this a busy area, but a great number of visitors to the IDS Crystal Court are here to see for themselves this beautiful IDS Building, which rises out of the Crystal Court and is considered by many the finest work of famed architect Phillip Johnson.

The **Conservatory,** a spectacular glass-and-marble fashion center at 8th Street on the Nicollet Mall opened late in 1987 and certain to add to the fun and excitement of shopping in downtown Minneapolis, contains an elegant collection of shops and boutiques.

Peavy Plaza is a picturesque addition to the Nicollet Mall at 11th Street, where it adjoins Orchestra Hall and serves each year as site for the joyous Sommerfest (see Chapter VII). With its ice skaters in the wintertime and fountains in the summer, the plaza has been called a small version of New York's Rockefeller Center.

Now, walking a few blocks east, we'll find at 222 S. 9th St. the 42-story **Piper Jaffray Tower,** featuring innumerable panes of aqua-blue window glass and providing a particularly dramatic addition to the Minneapolis skyline.

Marble and copper-colored glass distinguish the beautiful 17-story curved-glass **Lutheran Brotherhood Building** at 4th Avenue between 6th and 7th Streets.

The **Hennepin County Government Center** links two square blocks of downtown Minneapolis at 5th Street between Third and Fourth Avenues. You'll find here beautiful landscaping and lots of benches from which to admire it.

The two-towered marble **Pillsbury Center,** at Second Avenue South between 5th and 6th Streets, is a contemporary example of a famous family's historic commitment to the Twin Cities.

The massive **Northstar Center,** at 110 7th St., where a ten-story hotel sits atop six stories of offices and parking ramps, was a harbinger of exciting things to come when it opened in 1963. This was the first new complex of office, retail, and dining areas in downtown Minneapolis, and its early promise has been more than fulfilled.

The end of this mini-tour finds you near 5th Street and Chicago Avenue, where the **Hubert H. Humphrey Metrodome** sprawls on the eastern edge of downtown. Tourists and teams seem to like it a lot more than home folks do.

THE ARTS IN MINNEAPOLIS: The Twin Cities is widely known for its wealth of cultural presentations—borrowings from other times and places to be shared today. I'll be telling you more in Chapters VI and VII about some of the specific features and facilities that you'll enjoy in the Twin Cities, but here's a quick look at some of the internationally known theaters, museums, and concert halls that await you here.

Located on Vineland Place on the southwestern rim of downtown Minneapolis, the glass-walled **Guthrie Theater** looks bright and welcoming with its cheerful view of the lobbies and levels within, and its colorful banners proclaiming the titles of plays presently in production.

Although the **Walker Art Center** and the Guthrie Theater share the same Vineland Place site and the same outer lobby, they don't share architectural styles. With its brick-and-concrete exterior, the Walker, despite the color and excitement within, looks relatively austere and even severe to passersby. A more inviting feature will be the sculpture gardens due to open in June 1988.

At **Orchestra Hall,** 1111 Nicollet Mall, what you see on the outside is a far cry from what's within, where painstaking and imaginative attention to design have been responsible for superlative acoustics. The exterior, though, brightened only by huge blue ducts, serves simply as an unadorned shell for the massive lobby and 2,200-seat concert hall within.

The classic **Minneapolis Institute of Art,** at 2400 Third Ave. South, is one of the greatest and grandest museums in the country. It shares an outer lobby with the famous Minneapolis Children's Theatre company.

THE UNIVERSITY OF MINNESOTA: Established in 1851 and now the largest university on one campus in the United States, the University of Minnesota has gained recent fame for the organ transplants and other surgical miracles accomplished at its on-campus University Hospital. You probably won't get to watch an operation during your stay, but there are many on-campus activities that visitors can enjoy.

Whether or not you're able to attend a performance, do drive down to the riverfront for a look at the **Centennial Showboat,** docked on the east bank of the Mississippi. This authentic 19th-century sternwheel river packet was secured by the University Theatre Department for the state's 100th anniversary celebration in 1958. It's been here ever since, staging summer-time melodramas and musical olios for booing, hissing, and cheering audiences. There are concerts, recitals, lectures, and exhibits on campus as well, many of them free of charge.

If you'd like to tag along on the campus tours provided for incoming and prospective students, they're conducted daily at 11:15 a.m. and 2:15 p.m. on the Minneapolis campus and at noon on the St. Paul campus. Phone 624-6868 for further information.

A Chain of Minneapolis Lakes

Three of the most popular lakes in Minneapolis form a chain that's believed to be part of the course followed by the Mississippi River some 25,000 years ago. For information about all the Minneapolis lakes and parks, phone 348-2243.

LAKE OF THE ISLES: Although property close to Lake of the Isles is very expensive these days, you couldn't have given it away 100 years ago. What stood here then was a mess of swamps and marshes that were feared as breeding places for the dreaded malaria. But after years as a dumping ground, the property was dredged during the late 1880s and by the turn of the century had become valuable real estate. Now a man-made lake, popular with fisherfolk because it's stocked with tasty sunfish and croppies, and small wooded islands are a picturesque part of the city. Lake of the Isles is popular with canoeists too, because of its irregular shoreline and varied landscape. (At 20 to 25 feet deep, this is the shallowest of the chain of lakes.) During the wintertime a regulation hockey rink is set up, along with areas for general skating—and of course a warming house is set up too.

If you decide to walk around Lake of the Isles, remember that the path closest to the shore is for you; the other path is for bicyclists.

LAKE CALHOUN: A channel connects Lake of the Isles to Lake Calhoun, so boaters can paddle from one to the other. (No power-boats are permitted on city lakes, partly because of the noise and partly because the rapid churning of the water erodes the shoreline.) Lake Calhoun is the largest of the chain of lakes, and at 90 to 100 feet, it's the deepest as well. Whatever the season, you're likely to see boats here, lots of one-man skimmers and sailboats in the summertime, iceboats (sailboats on blades) in the winter. This is perhaps the most popular lake with young adults, who do a lot of sunning on its shores, swimming in its depths, cross-country skiing and socializing in the nearby Hennepin and Lake-Uptown area.

LAKE HARRIET: The third link in the chain of lakes may have the greatest appeal to families because of its delightful gardens, bird sanctuary, and summertime band concerts at the pavilion, which was remodeled in 1985. The All-American Rose Selection Test bed in the **Lake Harriet Rose Gardens** provides an annual display of glorious colors and scents for visitors. The **Lake Harriet Rock Garden** has been a popular display since it was first built in 1929 and refurbished in 1984. And the adjacent **bird sanctuary** features a woodchips path for visitors who enjoy the solitude and serenity of an unspoiled woodland setting, the more remarkable because it's located in the heart of a busy metropolitan city.

If you're visiting the Twin Cities during the summer months, from late May until early September, join the many men, women, and children who arrive by boat, by bike, or by automobile, with or without picnic supper, to enjoy the nightly Lake Harriet **bandstand concerts.** And if there are children in your party, remember the restored-streetcar ride that may be the only opportunity today's youngsters may ever have to enjoy that form of transportation (see Chapter XIII, "Family Fun," for further details).

Sailing is another popular mode of transportation at Lake Harriet, one of the city's three sailing lakes. Along with Lake Calhoun and Lake Nokomis, Lake Harriet features weekend sailboat races which draw throngs of participants and observers throughout the summer months.

Selected Twin Cities Tours

Of course there's more to be seen in the Twin Cities, and one of the best ways of getting your bearings is to make your first order of business the kind of narrated tour that I always seek out in an unfamiliar city. Here are four good ways to go in Minneapolis and St. Paul, depending on your preference and your pocketbook.

GRAY LINES TOURS: As in so many cities across the country, city tours are offered by Gray Lines, which in the Twin Cities is run by the Metropolitan Transit Commission. Tours last about 3½ hours and take passengers through both Minneapolis and St. Paul, with time out at Minnehaha Falls and the State Capitol. Prices are $13 per adult, $6.50 for children from 5 to 14 (children under 5 can ride free as long as they don't take a seat that could go to a fare-paying passenger). Tours run Tuesday through Saturday, departing from a number of Twin Cities locations including the popular souvenir shop, Hello Minnesota, at 7 S. 7th St., and the Radisson University Hotel, at 615 Washington Ave. SE in Minneapolis. In St. Paul, buses depart from the Radisson St. Paul Hotel, at 11 E. Kellogg Blvd., and the Holiday Inn Town Square, at 411 Minnesota St.

Ben Shanks was the personable, knowledgeable, and accommodating young driver of the Gray Line tour I took, and it's impossible to recommend him too highly. He's also a seminary student with an interest in playwriting, so he'll be going on to other kinds of work in the future, but he assures me that all Gray Line guides are carefully and thoroughly trained.

For further information on Gray Line tours, call 827-7733.

SUBURBAN LIMOUSINE TOURS: If you prefer seeing the cities as part of a smaller group in a smaller vehicle, consider **Twin Cities Sightseeing Tours,** operated by Minneapolis and Suburban Airport Limousine Service (tel. 827-7777). This tour lasts 2½ hours, costs $13 per person, and will take you to many landmarks in both cities, with a stop en route at Minnehaha Falls. Individuals can board at the main office, 3920 Nicollet Ave. South, leaving their cars in the parking lot free of charge. The sights you'll see on a Minneapolis and Suburban Limousine tour are pretty well determined in advance, but you'll find that different drivers bring their individual perspectives to the matters at hand. If your interest is primarily historical or literary, or directed toward some other specific area, you might mention that when you call.

TOUR DU JOUR: Everyone connected with the guided tours of Minneapolis and St. Paul speaks highly of Millie Resch's Tour du Jour, Inc. After earning a degree in cultural anthropology at the University of Minnesota, she treated herself to a course in Twin Cities geography just for the fun of it and discovered that she was more interested in the way people live today than in ancient times. Tour du Jour uses a ten-passenger van for an entertaining and educational Twin Cities tour that takes about 3½ hours, with one 20-minute stop. The cost is $15 per person. Millie picks up passengers at designated times and places. Call 823-0291 for details.

A VIEW OF TWO: And then there's the Rolls-Royce of local tours, View of Two, an enterprise of two canny suburban women.

They had studied the local scene exhaustively in order to show the Twin Cities off to visiting friends and relatives, and then decided to share their knowledge and enthusiasm with others as well. Mary McGovern and Patty Bailey can take individuals and small parties to places inaccessible to larger groups. Want to see the world's largest embroidered tapestry, now on display in a local guild hall? They'll take you there. Want to view the local home that was built of materials "left over" from construction of the Minneapolis City Hall? No problem. Or maybe you're interested in the tiny homes, now considered chic, where Swedish immigrant laborers were housed by the Milwaukee Railroad in the late 1800s. They're well worth seeing, but only View of Two is prepared to take you there and tell you all about them. These custom-designed tours vary in price according to the size of the group. You're invited to phone 476-0130 for further details.

STERNWHEELER BOAT TOURS: For a change of pace, consider a tape-narrated, round-trip boat trip from Harriet Island to Fort Snelling. You'll get to experience a bit of local history as you travel the Mississippi on one of the old sternwheelers belonging to the **Padelford Packet Boat Company** (tel. 227-1100). Prices are $6.50 for adults, $4.50 for senior citizens, $4 for children under 12. Tours last about 1¾ hours.

Chapter VI

THEATER IN THE TWIN CITIES

THE QUALITY AND VARIETY of the Twin Cities theater scene will surprise you in its many year-round productions. During any month you can attend dozens of first-rate stagings of plays from the classical to the contemporary, the traditional to the avant garde—and all at prices that are remarkably low.

Although Twin Cities theater didn't gain international prominence until the establishment here in 1963 of the Tyrone Guthrie Theater, first-rate productions had been steadily attracting theater-goers for a long time before that. The Old Log, now one of the country's oldest stock companies, began staging professional productions in 1941. Theater in the Round, now one of the country's longest-lived community theaters, staged its first performance in 1952. The Brave New Workshop, the country's oldest satirical revue, was founded in 1958, five years before Chicago's Second City got under way. And the University of Minnesota Theatre consistently drew audiences from throughout the Twin Cities for a wide variety of productions that were popular not only at home but also on the road.

The famous Irish-English director Sir Tyrone Guthrie selected the Twin Cities as the home for his repertory company in part because a committed theater-going public already existed here. But there was another consideration as well—one that had to do with dollars and cents. "We will put our various skills and experiences at your service," he had declared. "We will create for you a professional theater, which you will own. . . . You, however, must undertake the formidable task of raising the dough."

In Minneapolis, that was no problem: corporate support for the arts is greater here than anywhere else in the country.

The "dough" was raised handily and the Guthrie Theater is by now an integral part of cultural life in these parts.

What's best about Twin Cities theater is that it's a year-round activity for audiences of widely varied tastes. There's mainstream theater and avant-garde theater, dinner theater and coffeehouse theater, theater in the park and theater in the round, children's theater, history theater, showboat theater, and a lot more.

In the Twin Cities theater is not primarily a business but an art. As such, it's supported in large part by contributions from individual and corporate benefactors. You'll see the names of these patrons listed in the programs of many local not-for-profit resident theaters, including the Guthrie, where actors work for wages far lower than those associated with Broadway's "star system." These factors, plus lower production costs, combine to keep ticket prices relatively low in Minneapolis and St. Paul. A good seat will seldom cost more than $15, and student, senior citizen, and standby rates are lower still. In addition, **Tickets-to-Go** counters at the Crystal Court in Minneapolis and Town Square in St. Paul can cut the cost of tickets in half, if they're purchased on the day of the performance. The Minneapolis office is open Tuesday through Saturday, noon to 6 p.m., and the St. Paul office from 11 a.m. to 6 p.m. on those same days.

Transportation poses few problems here: even outlying theaters are easy to reach by highway and freeway, and parking is either free or nominal in cost.

And because the investment of time and money is not as staggering here as elsewhere, theater-goers can afford to be a bit more adventurous and tolerant than they might otherwise be. That makes experimentation, and therefore variety, more feasible.

Then there's the crucial corporate connection. Business interests in the Twin Cities have a distinguished record of support for the arts, and this has played a major role in their continuing growth and development.

All these factors have helped to keep theater alive and well and living a full, rich life in the Twin Cities, and this, in turn, has led to a self-perpetuating situation. Theater has begotten more theater. The opportunities here have drawn talented artists in great numbers, and this abundance of talent has in turn attracted film and TV production companies to these parts. Casting directors and agents pass through regularly to check performances at the Guthrie and other local theaters—with consequences that have by now become legendary.

The progress of Peter MacNicol is one example. This aspiring young actor came from Texas to study theater at the University of Minnesota because he'd heard of its close ties with the Guthrie. After his talents had been showcased in a variety of amateur productions hereabouts, he was offered a contract by the Guthrie. There he was seen by a visiting New York casting director and, not long afterward, was appearing in a featured role on Broadway in the Pulitzer Prize–winning *Crimes of the Heart.* From there he went west for a leading movie role with Meryl Streep in *Sophie's Choice.* He has since starred in a number of plays, movies, and TV films, appearing with such luminaries as Colleen Dewhurst, Jason Robards, and Burt Reynolds. And in addition to his other activities, he's taken time to return to the Twin Cities for a leading role in the Guthrie's *Execution of Justice,* a controversial play which garnered favorable notices nationwide.

Maybe what's most important about MacNicol's story is that like Loni Anderson, Linda Kelsey, Prince, and others who've gone on from the Twin Cities to make national names for themselves, MacNicol was able to develop his talents at local theaters employing "amateurs," a term that identifies artists not only as unpaid performers, but also as lovers of their craft. Members of the original Moscow Art Theater were amateurs; so were members of the Provincetown Players. And so are members of many troupes in Minneapolis and St. Paul.

While certain Twin Cities actors, writers, directors, and technicians have gone on to spend their professional lives on one coast or the other, many others remain to enjoy fulfilling careers in Twin Cities productions.

It's been said that you can make a fortune in the theater, but not a living. Not so in the Twin Cities, where a great many talented theater people are making a comfortable living. This, in turn, enhances the quality of life for the rest of us.

Major Twin Cities Theater Companies

Here's an alphabetical listing of some of the theatrical companies that await you in Minneapolis and St. Paul.

ACTORS THEATRE: At 28 W. Seventh Pl., St. Paul (tel. 227-0050), this ensemble company of Equity actors is committed to working together, year after year, and to developing their talents in a wide variety of roles. Since the company was first founded in 1977, Actors Theatre has presented plays by Shakespeare and Pinter, Chekhov and Athol Fugard. They've also performed works by the Czech playwright Vaclav Havel, the West Indian playwright Derek Walcott, and the Hungarian playwright Gyula Hernadi.

From the early years when they offered four plays each season, they've grown to an annual subscription series of six productions. And in their 330-seat proscenium theater, located on a small pedestrian mall in downtown St. Paul, they stage works-in-progress and present guest appearances by companies from other parts of the city and other parts of the world.

In August 1986 the touring South African production of *Asinamali!* broke attendance records at the Actors Theatre in St. Paul, months before its successful run in New York. And in January 1987 Actors Theatre was written up in *USA Today* and *American Theater* magazine for its presentation of the largest one-act play festival outside New York.

Audiences have responded enthusiastically to the adventurous Actors Theatre. Subscriptions increased from 100 in 1977 to more than 2,300 ten years later. And what's best of all, perhaps, is that Twin Citians turn out for the unfamiliar works as well as for the familiar ones—and they've gotten adventurous too.

Ticket prices range from $7 to $16, with students, children, and senior citizens paying $7.

BRASS TACKS THEATER: Patty Lynch, who founded this enterprising company in 1979, remains artistic director to this day. She's also the author of the recently produced *Pretty Girls Aren't That Smart,* a contemporary suspense thriller with a feminist twist. Other hit première productions include actor/director/playwright Jim Stowell's highly praised series of monologues, *Travelling Light,* and a companion piece, *Rio Grande.*

It's the preeminence of language and the commitment to developing dynamic new works that keeps this avant-garde company on the cutting edge of the Twin Cities theater scene. Brass Tacks productions (tel. 341-8207) are staged in a number of spaces around town, but primarily at the Hennepin Center for the Arts in the restored downtown Masonic Building in Minneapolos, or at the Southern Theater, which started life as a vaudeville house near the west bank of the University of Minnesota's Minneapolis campus. The Brass Tacks' address changes regularly, but their phone number remains the same, so call for word on their presentations during your Twin Cities stay. You can count on an interesting and dynamic evening in the theater.

Tickets are $9 on Thursday and Sunday evening, $10 on Friday and Saturday evening.

BRAVE NEW WORKSHOP: For nearly 30 years, Dudley Riggs's Brave New Workshop, 2605 Hennepin Ave., Minneapolis (tel. 332-6620), has been fulfilling its self-proclaimed role as loyal opposition to all parties. By now the oldest satirical company in the United States, Brave New Workshop company members write their own material. After each evening's series of sketches, the company does improvisations based on audience suggestions, and many of these impromptu skits are in turn developed into titled sketches. Past productions, which have also toured successfully in New York, Boston, Miami, and San Francisco, include *I'm OK, You're a Jerk, National Velveeta or What a Friend We Have in Cheeses,* and *The Vice Man Cometh.*

You can't miss the storefront theater in which this company performs: the bright lights and red, white, and blue stripes serve loud notice that you've arrived. Performances are at 8 p.m. Tuesday through Thursday, at 8 and 10:30 p.m. on Friday and Saturday. Ticket prices are $8.50 Tuesday through Thursday, $10 on Friday and Saturday. For $6.50 on Sunday, *On the Wall, Off the Wall* offers a combined program of improvisations and award-winning short films.

CHANHASSEN DINNER THEATRE: In 1988 this unique theater complex at 521 W. 78th St., Chanhassen (tel. 934-1521), celebrates an important anniversary: 20 years ago general amazement, if not amusement, greeted the announcement that Herb Bloomberg, a prominent local builder, was venturing into entirely unfamiliar territory. After completing construction of the beautiful Old Log Theater in Minnetonka, Bloomberg decided to open and run a 600-seat dinner theater of his own in the tiny suburban town of Chanhassen, some 20 miles from downtown Minneapolis.

Another unlikely announcement followed the first: productions staged here would not be limited to the usual forced feedings of Broadway musicals; the Chanhassen would be offering polished productions of highly regarded theater works in a handsome and congenial dinner-theater setting. One of their earliest hits turned out to be the 19th-century French farce *A Flea in Her Ear.* One member of that cast, incidentally, was TV-star-to-be Linda Kelsey.

Today the Chanhassen has grown into the only theater complex in the world with four playhouses under one roof, offering performances throughout the year. And the seating capacity has nearly doubled, from 600 to 1,150. The Chanhassen has consistently earned high marks for the quality and diversity of its productions: *Equus, Loot, On Golden Pond, The Dining*

Room, and *The Foreigner,* among others. There have been superb productions of musicals as well—hits like *A Little Night Music, Camelot, Company, Gypsy, West Side Story,* and *Fiddler on the Roof.* In the last, a dark-haired Loni Anderson acted and sang the role of Tevye's daughter, Tsietel.

The first thing visitors notice as they enter the enormous, but somehow intimate, theater complex is the oversize fireplace in the long lobby that leads to the various theaters, bars, alcoves, lounges, and other gathering places. There's a selection of entertainment here seven days and nights each week, with dinner-and-theater package prices ranging from $17.50 to $21.50 for matinees, $19.50 to $31.50 evenings, and $18.50 for Sunday brunch.

Chanhassen is easily reached at the juncture of Hwy. 5 and Hwy. 11, about 30 minutes from either downtown St. Paul or downtown Minneapolis.

CHILDREN'S THEATRE: Located at 2400 Third Ave. South, Minneapolis (tel. 874-0400), in the huge white-brick building that houses the Minneapolis Institute of Art, the Children's Theatre presents productions geared toward multigenerational audiences—kids of absolutely all ages. The rows in the 746-seat auditorium have been raked with youngsters in mind, so small people can look over the heads of tall ones with no difficulty at all. Plays, based primarily on tales familiar to children and teenagers, are lavishly produced and skillfully acted by a company of child and adult players. Since 1984, when the Children's Theatre School, from which many of the acting company were previously drawn, was discontinued, open auditions have provided young cast members for the productions.

Authors are often invited to participate in the staging of their plays at Children's Theatre; Dr. Seuss (Theodore Geiss) worked with the company on the CTC production of *The 500 Hats of Bartholomew Cubbins,* Astrid Lindgren came to the Twin Cities to advise on the production of *Pippi Longstocking,* and illustrator-author Tomi de Paoli served as consultant for the staging of *Strega Nona.*

Ticket prices range from $6.75 to $11.75 for children under 18 and for students or senior citizens. The price for those above 18 years of age is $8.75 to $15.75.

CRICKET THEATRE: At 9 W. 14th St., Minneapolis (tel. 871-2244), the Cricket Theatre concentrates on staging contemporary plays by living playwrights, some of whom have already made a name for themselves, some of whom are still emerging. Along with contemporary classics like *American Buffalo, The Gin Game, Streamers, Fool for Love,* and *Who's Afraid of Virginia Woolf?* this company has produced lesser-known works by finalists in the New Plays Program, sponsored by the Dramatists Guild and the Columbia Broadcasting System, thus giving fledgling dramatists the chance to watch their plays being brought to life on the stage and to work closely with professional theater artists. There have been 13 world premières and 47 area premières among Cricket's offerings since the theater was founded by Bill Semans in 1968.

In 1987 the Cricket made two important changes: it moved to a new home in a beautifully renovated old theater on the southern edge of downtown Minneapolis, and it expanded its mission to include one guest production each season by a foreign theater company.

Performances are at 8 p.m. Wednesday through Saturday evenings; Sunday times vary, so phone for information. Tickets sell for $11 on Wednesday and Thursday, $13 on Friday and Saturday; students and seniors get a 20% discount.

E.T.C.: Located at Seven Corners, 1430 Washington Ave. South, Minneapolis (tel. 332-6620), near the west-bank campus of the University of Minnesota, Dudley Riggs's Experimental Theatre Company shares a building with Café Expresso, reportedly the Midwest's oldest coffeehouse. There's a full bar in the café and one in the theater, and dinner can be brought to your table any night of the week. Stand-up comedy and musical satire are on the bill of fare here. *What's So Funny About Being Female?,* an all-women production, was brought back for its third anniversary during the 1987 January-through-May run. The other side of the story followed in June with an all-male company's musical satire, *Fixing Men, or A Woman's Guide to Home Repair.*

Like its older sibling, Dudley Riggs's Brave New Workshop, E.T.C. is considered a fine training ground for young performers, with alumni who have included the Flying Karamazov Brothers and former "Saturday Night Live" performers Franken and Davis.

Performances are at 8 p.m. on Wednesday and Thursday, and at 8 and 10:30 p.m. on Friday and Saturday. Prices for dinner theater are $20 on Wednesday and Thursday, $22 on Friday and Saturday. Performance-only prices are $8.50 on Wednesday and Thursday, $10 on Friday and Saturday. On Sunday at 8 p.m. local amateurs and professionals do stand-up comedy, and tickets cost $6.50.

GUTHRIE THEATER: In 1964 the Tyrone Guthrie Theater, 725 Vineland Pl., Minneapolis (tel. 377-2224), gained worldwide fame as the home of a new classical repertory company, selected by the distinguished director for whom it was named. The fact that Tyrone Guthrie intended to produce classics during his three-year stay at the theater did not imply that these productions would be conventional; in fact, the *Hamlet* he directed during that first season was done in modern dress. The spirit of the production, though, was true to the original; indeed, the topical touches seemed to enhance its universality.

After Guthrie's departure, the theater went through good times and bad under a succession of artistic directors. The original commitment to classics eroded somewhat along the way, but in early 1987 things took a turn for the better, at least in the view of those who had been bemoaning a perceptible shift toward lighter, more "commercial" fare. The newly named and widely admired artistic director, Garland Wright, announced for his first official season an array of classics that qualified in all ways as the kinds of works originally identified with the Guthrie. Theater-goers understood that Wright's production of Molière's *The Misanthrope,* and Livieu Culei's guest production of Euripides' *The Bacchae,* would have contemporary resonances, but these works and others on the program were consistent with the original Guthrie commitment.

The move back toward a true repertory company after years of short runs by guest stars was another cause for celebration in some theater-going circles.

Whatever your taste in theater entertainment, you'll surely want to include a Guthrie performance in your Twin Cities agenda. This is one of the most famous theaters in the world—I've been questioned about it in Great Britain, on the continent, and in the Caribbean—and your afternoon or evening is bound to prove memorable.

There are several reasons to arrive early for a Guthrie performance: you'll want to see one of the country's largest public sculpture gardens, just installed across the street, and to explore the theater itself. Even before you enter the auditorium with its hundreds of multicolored upholstered seats, you'll be surrounded by a tempting array of dining and sipping and shopping choices. At certain times of year you can carry a drink and a snack to the outdoor terrace overlooking Vineland Place. And year round you can try to find a table in the Aisle 10 section of the lobby, where glass walls provide a view to the outdoors of those who arrive later than you do.

The Guthrie shares an entry lobby with the adjacent Walker

Art Center and is just steps away from the Walker's extensive, and often expensive, selection of gifts and souvenirs. The Guthrie's own smaller gift shop carries a variety of theater-related items, and you'll want to check those as well. And once in your seat you'll enjoy looking at the large, handsome complimentary program, which provides interesting and informative background about the production you're about to see. Shortly before the lights dim, you'll hear the trumpeters signaling that the auditorium doors will soon be closed just before the performance gets under way. Performances begin at 7:30 p.m. Tuesday through Thursday, 8 p.m. Friday and Saturday, and 7 p.m. on Sunday (the theater is dark on Monday). Matinees are usually presented on Wednesday and either Saturday or Sunday, but do call to confirm the day and time. Ticket prices range from $7 to $25.

ILLUSION THEATRE: Headquartered at the Hennepin Center for the Arts, 528 Hennepin Ave., Minneapolis (tel. 339-4944), this eight-member company, which started in 1974 as a mime troupe, has made a name for itself in two distinctly different arenas. In 1977 Illusion Theatre became the first company in the country to use drama as a means of preventing sexual abuse and interpersonal violence. *Touch,* an original play for children, has been performed throughout the country in schools, churches, and at conferences for community education. So have two other works, *No Easy Answers,* written for adolescents, and *For Adults Only,* designed for grownup audiences. In addition to the touring productions of these plays, the Illusion Theatre maintains a February-through-July Twin Cities season, during which it creates new works collaboratively and presents productions of lesser-known European scripts.

Illusion productions are staged at the eight-story sandstone Masonic Temple at 6th Street and Hennepin Avenue. Ticket prices are $11 on Thursday and Sunday, $15 on Friday and Saturday. All performances are at 8 p.m., except on Sunday when they begin at 7 p.m.

MIXED BLOOD THEATER: This professional theater at 1501 S. 4th St., Minneapolis (tel. 338-6131), was founded in 1976 to produce new works in a color-blind fashion. Mixed Blood has by now received numerous local awards for productions like *Glengarry Glen Ross, A My Name Is Alice,* and *For Colored Girls Who Have Considered Suicide When a Rainbow is Enuf.* Founder Jack Reuler has also received national awards, none more prestigious perhaps than his selection by *Esquire* in December 1984 as one of those under 40 who were changing the face of America. Reuler was cited not only for Mixed Blood's color-blind casting of all productions, but for his theater's being the largest employer of minority professional actors in the entire country.

Mixed Blood productions are presented in a 100-year-old firehouse with a large, flexible space where plays can be presented in a proscenium setting, on a thrust stage, or as "theater in the rectangle." It's said that you never know when you walk into Mixed Blood which way you'll be facing. What you do know, though, is that you'll be seeing a top-quality production that's very likely making its area or world première here in the Twin Cities. Alumni of this theater include Carl Lumbley, a one-time regular on TV's "Cagney and Lacey."

Showtime is 8 p.m. on Thursday, Friday, and Sunday; on Saturday there are two performances, at 7 and 9:30 p.m. You'll pay $7 on Thursday and Sunday, $9 on Friday and Saturday.

OLD LOG THEATER: This popular playhouse, located at 5175 Meadville St., Excelsior (tel. 474-5951), is very much a family affair out in suburban Lake Minnetonka, where since 1941 Don Stolz has been staging Equity productions at one Old Log Theater or another. The small original theater, now used as a scenery shop, was replaced in 1960 by the present Old Log, closer to the water's edge and, with 655 seats, one of the largest theaters in the Twin Cities area.

Comedies are the specialty of this house, and eldest son Tom Stolz has developed through the years into an adept comic actor, notable for his droll dead-pan delivery in productions as diverse as *Brighton Beach Memoirs* and *Bedfull of Foreigners*. Other family members make their own contributions behind the scenes and at the front of the house. Jon Stolz is the scenery and lighting designer, Tim Stolz the stage manager. And it's Donny Stolz who will greet you at the box office, of which he's the manager. By the way, if one of the characters onstage during your visit is portrayed by a pretty teenage actress, check the program to see whether you're watching one of Don's talented granddaughters, Theresa or Alison Stolz, who made their joint debut during the 1986 season as sisters in Neil Simon's *Brighton Beach Memoirs*.

Broadway and London comedy and farce are the prevailing fare that's offered here, but from time to time more serious work has been presented, including admirable productions of *Look Homeward, Angel* and *84 Charing Cross*.

If you're in the Twin Cities during the Easter season, you might want to phone the theater for word on Tom Stolz's annual tour-de-force performance in *The Gospel According to Saint Mark.* But at any time of year a visit to the Old Log will introduce you to the work of the Twin Cities' oldest professional theater company. Shows are at 8:30 p.m. Wednesday through Saturday and at 7:30 p.m. on Sunday. Tickets are $9.25 for the Saturday performance, $8.50 on other days.

RED EYE COLLABORATION: The only resident experimental theater company in the Twin Cities, Red Eye Collaboration performs in a 70-seat studio theater in the downtown Minneapolis Warehouse District at 126 N. Washington Ave. (tel. 339-1191). You'll know you've arrived at Red Eye when you see a historic warehouse with a large red neon sign featuring a blue neon fish swimming above it. One of this troupe's greatest successes to date was, conventionally speaking, not a play at all but an "animation"—essentially a prose poem divided among members of a group, each one representing a different aspect of the central animal character.

Four mixed-media productions are staged each year by the Red Eye Collaboration, along with one work-in-progress series. Tickets for these productions are $8 on Thursday and Sunday, $9 on Friday and Saturday; two-for-one on Thursday evening. All performances are at 8 p.m.

THÉÂTRE DE LA JEUNE LUNE: This unique international ensemble was founded in 1978 by four students, two Twin Citians and two Parisians, who met while studying at the École Jacques-Lecoq in Paris. Their name is taken from lines in a Berthold Brecht poem: "The young moon holds in its arms for one night the old moon." This symbolic blending of past traditions into modern, dynamic forms has been at once the mission and the method of the company that now calls Minneapolis home. Productions by this constantly interesting group tend to be highly physical and visually exciting, reflecting elements of clowning, farce, mime, and vaudeville. Recent hits include the wild comedy *Yang Zen Froggs in Moon over a Hong Kong Sweatshop* and a production of *Romeo and Juliet* in which the title roles were portrayed as two middle-aged characters.

Although this company has no home of its own, it performs regularly at Hennepin Center for the Arts in downtown Minneapolis and at the Southern Theater in the heart of the west-bank theater district. Tickets for Théâtre de la Jeune Lune productions range from $7 to $12. Call 333-6600 for more information.

THEATER IN THE ROUND: Since 1952 talented Twin Citians have contributed their time and their talents, onstage and behind the scenes, to community-theater productions by Theater in the Round, 245 Cedar Ave., Minneapolis (tel. 333-3010), or TRP as it's known locally. More than half a million theater-goers have attended productions in an old one-story brick building at Seven Corners in the west-bank theater district. Some of the Twin Cities' top directors have worked here with aspiring actors and technicians who later went on to professional careers in theater, TV, and the movies.

Play selection here is eclectic: the biggest hits to date have been *Equus, Of Thee I Sing, The Mouse Trap, Mrs. Warren's Profession,* and *Cyrano de Bergerac.* Plays by aspiring authors are produced as well. Although arena staging poses special problems for directors, actors, and designers, audiences enjoy the intimacy of the well-staged in-the-round productions for which TRP is known. You'll also enjoy the chance during intermission to browse in the back gallery where works by local artists are displayed.

TRP ticket prices are $8 on Friday and Saturday, $7 on Sunday, with a $1 discount for students and senior citizens.

Other Area Theaters

Several additional Twin Cities theaters offer different delights.

The **History Theater,** located in the Weyerhauser Auditorium at St. Paul's magnificent Landmark Center, 75 W. 5th St. (tel. 292-4323), stages original plays dealing with representative people and important events in Minnesota's past.

The **Park Square Theatre,** 253 E. 4th St., St. Paul (tel. 291-7005), offers two distinctly different seasons, the main Classic Season and the summertime Festival Season, when new American plays are staged, usually in conjunction with their authors.

At the Foot of the Mountain, 2000 S. 5th St., Minneapolis (tel. 375-9487), is one of the country's most important feminist theaters. Its resident troupe is comprised of four women—Asian, black, white, American Indian.

The **University of Minnesota Theatre Department's** four separate stages at the handsome Rarig Center theater complex (tel. 625-4001) consistently present a wide variety of enjoyable entertainment. You'll also enjoy the perennially popular productions aboard the university's Centennial Showboat, when audiences are welcomed aboard for hissing-and-booing summer-time productions of 19th-century melodramas.

Local newspapers carry comprehensive listings of current and upcoming presentations by these and other theater companies. A call to **Tickets-to-Go** (tel. 333-0159) at the IDS Crystal Court, 7th Street on the Nicollet Mall in Minneapolis, will provide you with information about specific offerings and about the availability of same-day half-price tickets for the rich array of Twin Cities theater fare.

Chapter VII

MUSIC, DANCE, MUSEUMS, AND GALLERIES

THE TWIN CITIES ARE RICH not only in theater, but in music, art, and dance as well. With two world-class music halls and two famous art museums, it's noteworthy that facilities in Minneapolis and St. Paul complement rather than compete with each other.

Orchestra Hall is an assertively modernistic building; the Ordway Music Theatre has an old-world beauty. The Walker Art Center is famous for its collection of modern art; the Minneapolis Institute of Art is associated primarily with more traditional works.

Music

MUSIC HALLS: There are two major ones in the Twin Cities, Orchestra Hall and the Ordway.

Orchestra Hall

As its name implies, Orchestra Hall, 1111 Nicollet Mall, Minneapolis (tel. 371-5656), was built as a home for the internationally acclaimed Minnesota Orchestra. In addition, since it first opened in 1974, this acoustically acclaimed hall, which seats more than 2,300, has offered a wide diversity of programs from symphonic to jazz to pop and featuring a range of artists from Isaac Stern and Itzhak Perlman to Andy Williams and Pearl Bailey. The highly praised purity of sound transmission here results in large part from the remarkable cube-like shapes you'll see set into the ceiling of the auditorium. These hundreds of surfaces disperse sound to every corner of the vast hall. Other steps have been taken as well. Lockers, available without charge in the lobby, serve still another acoustical purpose: heavy woolens and furs brought into the auditorium tend to absorb a great deal of the sound produced onstage.

Since 1980 Orchestra Hall has also become identified with one of the Twin Cities' most popular annual events. Sommerfest brings guest conductors and performers and very large audiences to Orchestra Hall for programs of waltzes, polkas, and light Viennese classics. There's also a Marktplatz, set up on adjacent Peavey Plaza, where colorful booths display delectable Viennese food and beverages. Dance groups and musical ensembles provide free entertainment, and from time to time, al fresco mid-morning fashion shows and late-night vintage movies are presented too. By the way, the benefits of all this fun extend well into the regular season when Kinder Konzerts are made possible in part by proceeds from the Sommerfest pastry booths.

The Ordway Music Theatre

The exquisite structure of the **Ordway Music Theatre,** 345 Washington St., St. Paul (tel. 224-4222), says a lot about the Twin Cities, where private and corporate generosity have played a prominent part in the quality of life the residents enjoy. After St. Paul's only major downtown performing arts building was closed in 1980 because of structural deterioration, the family of Lucius Ordway offered to pay for plans to be drawn for a new theater. They offered to donate $10 million toward a new music hall if public and private interests in the Twin Cities would match that commitment and that contribution.

Since its triumphant opening on January 1, 1985, the Ordway Music Theatre has been praised not only for the programs it presents, but for the beauty it imparts to the historic Rice Park area of St. Paul. Hailed as "the most contemporary classic theater in the United States," the Ordway's design combines the new and the old—faceted glass walls set into a façade of bricks and copper, and state-of-the-art acoustics in a traditional horseshoe-shaped Main Hall.

Liveried doormen await theater-goers at the entrance to the handsome lobby; a magnificent spiral stairway leads to the Grand Foyer and upper Promenade, both of which offer spectacular views of the city. The spacious lobby provides upholstered couches and window-wall mahogany benches just right for conversation, refreshments, and people-watching.

The 1,800-seat Main Hall and the 315-seat studio theater

have played host to a wide diversity of programs by distinguished musicians from the Minnesota Orchestra, the Schubert Club, the St. Paul Chamber Orchestra, and the Minnesota Opera Company. And there have been a succession of notable visiting artists as diverse as Leontyne Price, Mel Torme, and the Ballet Folklórico Nacional de México.

MUSICAL AND CONCERT ORGANIZATIONS: In addition to the many local bands and musical groups, there are two major orchestras and an organization sponsoring musical recitals and concerts in the Twin Cities.

The Minnesota Orchestra

The Minnesota Orchestra was born in 1903, the eighth major orchestra to be established in the United States. In 1923 it was heard on crystal radio sets; one year later it became the second major American orchestra to make recordings of its performances. Under the leadership of Eugene Ormandy from 1931 to 1936, the orchestra gained international recognition through its records and its international touring.

Dmitri Mitropoulos led his musicians geographically as well as musically from 1937 to 1949, during which time the orchestra accomplished a 34,000-mile State Department–sponsored tour of the Middle East.

During the 19-year tenure of Stanislaw Skrowaczewski, the Minnesota Orchestra increased in size to 95 musicians and took up residence in its new home at Orchestra Hall. The Minnesota Orchestra performs regularly at St. Paul's Ordway Music Theatre as well, and makes guest appearances throughout the state, the nation, and the world.

Since September 1986 the Minnesota Orchestra has been led by the distinguished conductor Edo de Waart.

St. Paul Chamber Orchestra

The St. Paul Chamber Orchestra, 75 W. 5th St., St. Paul (tel. 291-1144), the nation's first full-time professional chamber orchestra, may be performing at the Ordway Music Theatre while you're here, or you may find them in one of the shopping centers, churches, or school auditoriums that used to welcome them during the homeless years when they were identified with the concept "Music on the Move." The group was originated in 1959 by a group of St. Paulites who decided to find a conductor to head a group of freelance professional musicians who performed educational programs. They eventually established a ten-concert season, went on tour, and gained enough backing to incorporate under the name St. Paul Chamber Orchestra.

By the late '70s the group had undertaken a number of important tours to 140 American cities, as well as to Western and Eastern Europe and to the Soviet Union. During this time they also gained a reputation for regularly combining classical works and world premières on the same program.

Under the leadership of Pinchas Zukerman, the chamber orchestra has hosted a musical *Who's Who,* including Isaac Stern and Misha Dichter. And under Zukerman's leadership the local season expanded to 80 concerts and the St. Paul Chamber Orchestra gained fame as one of the country's best musical groups, with frequent guest appearances at Carnegie Hall, Avery Fisher Hall, and the Kennedy Center.

The Schubert Club

The Schubert Club, 75 W. 5th St., St. Paul (tel. 292-3267). Vladimir Horowitz, Isaac Stern, Robert Casadesus, and Beverly Sills are among the artists who've been brought—and brought back again—to St. Paul by the Schubert Club, founded in 1882 and by now one of the oldest musical organizations in the United States. If you're a music lover, you might want to inquire about whether one of the 50 or so recitals they offer each year will be at the Ordway Music Theatre during your stay.

In addition to bringing celebrated artists from throughout the world to perform in the Twin Cities, the Schubert Club, in a spirit of "venturesome conservatism," regularly commissions work from selected composers of recital music. One of these commissions, "From the Diary of Virginia Woolf," by Dominick Argento, won the Pulitzer Prize for Music in 1975. This work was sung by Dame Janet Baker both here in St. Paul and at Carnegie Hall in New York City.

Among the club's other projects has been the establishment and maintenance of a musical museum containing over 75 keyboard instruments dating back to the mid–16th century.

Dance

No cities except New York and Washington, D.C., offer a more active professional dance scene than the one you'll find in Minneapolis and St. Paul. Whatever the season, there's likely to be at least one major performance during your stay. Calendars of local and touring dance programs are published weekly in both local daily newspapers, and a call to the **Minnesota Dance**

Alliance (tel. 340-1900) will provide specific information about current and upcoming presentations.

Since 1929 music and dance have been the mainstay of the classic **Northrop Auditorium,** University of Minnesota main campus, 84 Church St., SE, Minneapolis (tel. 624-2345), but the major focus didn't turn to dance until after the Minnesota Orchestra moved in 1974 from Northrop to its own home across town in Orchestra Hall. Companies like the American Ballet Theatre, the Joffrey, the Moiseyev, the National Ballet of China, and the Sakailuku, a brilliant Paris-based Japanese company, have all appeared at the 4,800-seat Northrop Auditorium. International stars including Margot Fonteyn, Mikhail Barishnikov, Twyla Tharp, and Merce Cunningham have performed here too.

The **O'Shaugnessey Dance Series,** a six-week program offered during the spring of each year, is the only one of its kind in the country. Committed to spotlighting local professional dance companies, it undertakes a major selection process, then presents the annual series in the beautiful and flexible O'Shaugnessey Auditorium at 2004 Randolph Ave., St. Paul (tel. 690-6700), on the campus of the College of St. Catherine, where a "magic ceiling" can turn an imposing 1,800-seat hall into an intimate 600-seat chamber.

Among the local troupes that have appeared in the O'Shaugnessey series have been the Zorongo Flamenco Company, one of only five professional Spanish Gypsy dance troupes in the country. Their dynamic versions of narrative drama have earned them high marks at home and in the many cities to which they've toured.

Summerdance, a two-week series sponsored by the Minnesota Dance Alliance in June, also showcases the work of selected local companies and choreographers. In 1987 this festival took place in the intimate McKnight Playhouse at the Ordway Music Theatre (see above). The Minneapolis Children's Theatre (see Chapter VI) and the Hennepin Center for the Arts, 528 Hennepin Ave. (tel. 332-4478), also play host to these programs from time to time.

The **New Dance Ensemble** (tel. 341-3050) may be the best known nationally of the Twin Cities' local dance companies, with performances winning plaudits in far-away places like Paris and New York. Performing in the Merce Cunningham modern-dance tradition, their physically demanding pieces and interesting use of space have won them widespread recognition.

The **Ethnic Dance Theatre** (tel. 872-0024) has made a national and an international name for itself. Comprised of nearly 50 dancers and musicians, this company travels to distant destinations at home and abroad, from Appalachia in the United States to Uzbekistan in the USSR, learning traditional dances and then using these as the basis for original choreography. A recent première piece was researched in the Soviet republic of Tadzhikistan and concerns the legendary Tamara Khanum, the first Russian dancer ever to risk execution by casting aside her veil while performing in public.

You'll find the price of tickets to dance performances is remarkably low in the Twin Cities. Prices for touring dance productions range from $8 to $23; for local companies, $5 to $15.

Museums

From the major art and science museums to smaller, more specialized collections, the Twin Cities has a variety for all tastes.

THE AMERICAN SWEDISH INSTITUTE: At 2600 Park Ave. in Minneapolis, the American Swedish Institute (tel. 871-4907) is a museum that doesn't have to be entered to be enjoyed. This is a fairytale castle of pale limestone with arches and turrets, a small balcony, and a tall tower. It's equally grand within: decorative ceilings, intricately designed rugs of Swedish wool, and a glorious stained-glass window copied from a famous and historic Swedish painting.

This magnificent 33-room mansion was donated to the American Swedish Institute by Swan J. Turnblad, who came to this country in 1887 at the age of 8. By the time he was 27 Turnblad had become manager of the *Svenska Amerikanska Posten,* a Swedish-language weekly, and ten years later he was its owner, having increased circulation from 1,500 to 55,000 in the interim, making this the largest Swedish-language newspaper in America. His general purpose, to "foster and preserve Swedish culture in America," has been admirably fulfilled with artifacts in the mansion demonstrating over 150 years of the Swedish experience in the United States. There are examples in this museum of the items Swedish immigrants brought with them from the Old Country and examples of works of art created by Swedish and Swedish-American artists.

Museum hours are Tuesday through Saturday from noon to 4 p.m., on Sunday from 1 to 5 p.m. Admission is $2 for adults, $1 for senior citizens and students under 21. Children under the age of 12 must be accompanied by an adult.

A film program is presented every Sunday at 2 p.m. and musical programs are offered at 3 p.m. on Sunday afternoons during the winter months.

MINNESOTA MUSEUM OF ART: Two historic structures house the Minnesota Museum of Art (tel. 292-4355) in St. Paul: the striking 1931 art deco Jemne Building, St. Peter Street at Kellogg Boulevard, St. Paul, and two blocks away the majestic 1906 Romanesque-style Landmark Center, 5th Street at Market Street, St. Paul.

Holdings at the Jemne include works from the ancient as well as the contemporary world. The most recent additions to the museum's collections of American and non-Western art are exhibited at the Jemne, where the building itself is a treasure, with its original terazzo floors, brass railings, and lighting.

The museum's temporary exhibition galleries at the Landmark Center include the work of new midwestern artists as well as major exhibitions. At times touring exhibitions are on display here too. In the fifth-floor gallery known as "Kidspace," children can enjoy a "hands-on" experience with art.

Hours at both museums are Tuesday through Friday from 10:30 a.m. to 4:30 p.m. (on Thursday to 7:30 p.m.), on Saturday and Sunday from 1 to 4:30 p.m. Admission to the museum and to most exhibitions is free.

By the way, there's food for the palate as well as the soul in both buildings of the Minnesota Museum of Art. At the Jemne, one of the best Sunday buffets in either town can be found on the fourth-floor Deco Restaurant overlooking the Mississippi River. And at the Landmark, budget-pleasing soup-and-sandwich lunches are a popular weekday feature.

JAMES FORD BELL MUSEUM OF NATURAL HISTORY: The James Ford Bell Museum of Natural History, at University Avenue and 17th Avenue SE, Minneapolis (tel. 624-7083), is the oldest museum in the state of Minnesota—and one of the most popular. Located on the Minneapolis campus of the University of Minnesota, this museum is famous for its three-dimensional scenes of Minnesota wildlife, works of art in themselves, which have proved endlessly fascinating to generations of visitors.

Animals and birds in their natural habitats are painstakingly reproduced and displayed here; accompanying legends provide information in a concise and interesting way.

In the popular "Touch and See" room, children can examine for themselves the skins, bones, and skulls of a wide variety of animals, including mammoths and dinosaurs. Among the creatures on hand are stuffed wildlife specimens such as moose, elk, and caribou, as well as Lenny, a live gila monster, which is sometimes kept company by visiting animals from the Como Park Zoo.

Hours are Tuesday through Saturday from 9 a.m. to 5 p.m., on Sunday from 1 to 5 p.m.

THE CHILDREN'S MUSEUM: Children get to do all sorts of grownup things at the Children's Museum, a hands-on "aware house" at 1217 Bandana Blvd. North (tel. 644-3818), in St. Paul's historic Bandana Square complex. Here, in a two-story reconverted blacksmith's shop, children can experience for themselves some of the activities they've only observed before coming here. At a DJ desk they can control cassette decks and dancing colored lights. At the telegraph station they can operate Morse Code devices that signal simultaneously with a clicker and blue lights so deaf children can receive messages of their own. In the health-care department, one of the most used and abused areas of all, a dental chair awaits; so do a skeleton, crutches, splints, and wheelchairs. Another top draw here is the crane-and-train exhibit where children can use an electromagnetic crane to pick up and deposit metal discs. At the Now-and-Then fountain, visitors can compare prices in the 1950s with those of the present. At the bank, after examining foreign and domestic currency on a light table, children can climb onto the back of an armored truck.

Elsewhere in the museum, the past and present coexist: there's a medieval chapel with its own drawbridge and there's Topo, a robot which can be programmed or moved with a joy stick.

Although the museum is always closed on Monday, hours change from season to season; you can receive the latest update from a recorded message at 644-3818. (For more personalized information, call 644-5305.)

GIBBS FARM MUSEUM: This popular living museum at Cleveland and Larpenteur Avenues, Falcon Heights, St. Paul (tel. 646-8629), re-creates life on a seven-acre urban fringe farm at the turn of the century. Costumed guides are on hand to answer questions about the artifacts and activities on this homestead where the Gibbs family's home grew from a one-room cabin in 1850 to a large, comfortable farmhouse complete with parlor, sitting room, kitchen, bathrooms, and more. In a red barn you'll find friendly barnyard animals, and there's a one-room schoolhouse with wooden double-desks, pump organ, slate boards, and school bell. Quilting, baking, and blacksmithing are demonstrated, and a slide presentation explains what farming on the fringe of St. Paul was like in those days.

Information about individual programs, which vary from month to month, can be obtained from the Ramsey County Historical Society, 323 Landmark Center, 75 W. 5th St., St. Paul (tel. 222-0701). The Gibbs Farm is open May 1 through October 31. Hours are Tuesday through Saturday from 10 a.m. to 4 p.m., on Sunday from noon to 4 p.m. Admission is $1.75 for adults, $1.50 for seniors, 75¢ for those under 18.

THE SCIENCE MUSEUM OF MINNESOTA: At the entrance of this immensely popular two-building complex at 30 E. 10th St., St. Paul (tel. 221-9454), you'll be greeted by *Iggy,* a 40-foot steel iguana that, appropriately enough, was sculpted by a 16-year-old St. Paul schoolboy. Boys and girls of all ages have an entertaining and educational time at this massive museum which offers hands-on exhibits dealing with natural history, science, and technology. Members of an acting troupe turn up here and there to bring to life some of the figures who have played a part in the development of this area.

The East Building holds *Our Minnesota,* a permanent exhibit featuring a 12- by 14-foot map of the state that permits visitors to walk or crawl across forests, marked in green; croplands, marked in gold; mines, represented by taconite pellets; and lakes—an expanse of blue plastic representing "sky-blue waters." A woodsman is on hand here to tell tales about the immortal lumberjack, Paul Bunyan. Another living exhibit, the Ice Giant, looms large in the section dealing with the factor that glaciers played in the development of Minnesota's topography.

Exhibits in the West Building take you from the achievements of long-ago Mayans and Egyptians in the Hall of Anthropology to present-day strides in the Hall of Technology, where the model of a Jarvik-7 artificial heart is on display.

And then there's the **Omnitheater,** with its domed screen 76 feet in diameter, which puts viewers right into the center of adventures dealing with every time and every place. A recent double feature, *Water and Man,* was produced for the museum at La Villette in Paris and made its North American première at the Omnitheater. The other part of the bill, *Skyward,* had been produced for the 1985 International Exposition in Tsukuba, Japan.

Hours for the exhibit halls and the Omnitheater differ according to season. Call 221-9454 for information.

Prices for the exhibit halls only are $3.50, $2.50 for those 65 and older and those 12 and under; for the Omnitheater alone, prices are $4.50, $3.50 for seniors and juniors. Combination tickets are $5.50, $4.50 for seniors and juniors.

MINNEAPOLIS SCULPTURE GARDEN: You may have figured out by now that spreading the word about Minneapolis and St. Paul is a real pleasure for me. There is, though, one big problem when you're telling about an area as dynamic as this: it keeps on changing—it's always evolving, so it's hard to keep up. And here more than anywhere else in the country, it's the generosity of family, corporate, and civic groups that continues to enhance our enviable quality of life. A good example is the newly completed Minneapolis Sculpture Garden, on Vineland Place.

Between the time I write these words and the time you read them, work will have been completed on a spectacular new addition to the Twin Cities. A magnificent sculpture garden, one of the largest urban sculpture spaces in the country, is now being created on seven acres of land facing the Walker Museum–Guthrie Theater complex.

All the works of art displayed in this garden will be selected by the Walker Art Center; the Minneapolis Park and Recreation Board will be responsible for maintenance and security of the site, where four tree-lined plazas will display commissioned works of sculpture. Other artworks will be placed in a tall glass gallery whose wings will serve as an enclosed walkway to the Walker–Guthrie complex from a parking lot at the north of the garden.

At this end of the garden, a large-scale sculptural fountain and reflecting pool will stand in honor of William Weisman, the immigrant father of the Minneapolis-born philanthropist, art collector, and donor, Frederick R. Weisman. And the family of the late Irene Whitney has contributed funds for a graceful new pedestrian bridge, to be named after her, that will extend across busy Lyndale and Hennepin Avenues and link the Minneapolis Sculpture Garden with Loring Park and downtown Minneapolis.

Galleries

Night turns into day and staid city streets take on a festive air on the Saturday nights every six weeks or so when openings at more than a dozen galleries in the Warehouse District of Minneapolis attract many hundreds of artists, patrons, and passersby. (Estimates vary, but reliable word has it that more than 2,000 first-nighters typically turn out for these events.) Whatever the season, you'll find gallery-goers strolling from one historic building to another to get their first glimpse of works that range widely in form, style, and price. Some viewers come to buy, some to browse, and some just for the fun of it. After the works have been studied and the plastic wine glasses discarded, it's time to repair to the New French Café or Faegre's Bar and Restaurant or Café Brenda or some other nearby gathering place for discussions and disputes on the paintings and sculpture and other art forms that were introduced that evening.

Actually, the people-watching is an important part of the evening's fun. As one gallery director puts it, "You see every kind of clothing from ripped-out jeans and T-shirts to $70,000 fur coats. It's as mixed as Minneapolis is." And so are the works on display. It's their sheer variety that accounts for the coordination of these openings. Like so many other elements in the Twin Cities, these galleries complement rather than compete with one another. Each has its own niche, its own clientele, and its own unique appeal to the sophisticated gallery-goer and to the neophyte. The concentration of so many galleries within a few city blocks makes this a delightful destination for visiting art fanciers.

Most galleries are open from 11 a.m. to 4 p.m. Tuesday through Saturday, and by appointment. Some remain open Thursday evening until 8 p.m. Do phone to confirm hours.

IN THE WYMAN BUILDING: The Wyman Building at 400 First Ave. North houses nearly a dozen galleries which have combined into a loosely formed co-op. Here are a few of them:

Thomas Barry Fine Arts, Suite 304 (tel. 338-3656), offers contemporary American work including photography, prints, drawings, paintings, and sculpture. Artists include Don Gahr, Lynn Geesaman, Bruce Charlesworth, and Ken Moylan.

Peter M. David Gallery, Suite 236 (tel. 339-1825), shows the drawings, prints, paintings, photography, and sculpture of contemporary American and British artists. Midwestern artists represented here include Cynthia Starkweather, William Weege, and Mark Rediske.

Flanders Contemporary Art, on the first floor of the Wyman Building (tel. 344-1700), features museum-quality contemporary painting, drawing, and sculpture by nationally and internationally known American and European artists, among them Eric Fischl, Nancy Graves, and Tom Holland.

McGallery, Suite 332 (tel. 339-1480), is an avant-garde gallery offering works in a variety of forms—painting, sculpture, and lithography, among others. Paul Benson, Sheldon Hage, Jean Murakami, and Barbra Nei are among the artists represented here.

Jon Oulman, Suite 706 (tel. 333-2386), represents photography by such artists as Melisande Charles, Dennis Farber, Timothy Lamb, and Ruth Thorne-Thomson.

NEARBY MINNEAPOLIS WAREHOUSE DISTRICT GALLERIES: Other galleries in the district, all within easy walking distance of one another, include the following:

Artbanque, Suite 150, 300 First Ave. North, Minneapolis (tel. 333-1821), is one of the largest galleries in the Twin Cities, and one of the most diverse. The work of promising young unknowns can be found here, and so, twice a year, at investment art shows, can the works of giants like Rembrandt, Picasso, and Moore.

Imprimature, 415 First Ave. North, Minneapolis (tel. 333-9174), specializes in photography, much of it impressionist, but you'll also find other forms of art here, including a wide variety of sculptured pieces. Many of the artists represented here are known internationally.

Momentum Fine Arts, 129 N. 4th St., Minneapolis (tel. 341-2546), is worth a visit if only to see the unusual selection of structurist reliefs on display here. This art form, relatively unfamiliar even to many sophisticated art fanciers, is best described as a blend of painting and sculpture; colored rectangles are arranged in three-dimensional designs. David Bart, one of the few contemporary structurists working today, is an artist whose work has been shown here.

Thomson Gallery, 321 Second Ave. North, Minneapolis (tel. 338-7734), offers contemporary drawings, paintings, prints, photography, and sculpture by such artists as Philip Larson, Lance Kiland, Steven Sorman, and Tom Rose. Much of the work shown here is of museum size and quality.

Warm Gallery, 414 First Ave. North, Minneapolis (tel. 332-5672), offers a wide variety of work, much of it related to the concerns of feminists. The Women's Art Registry of Minnesota, more than a decade old, is the country's oldest nonprofit collective of women artists. Members, who share the responsibilities of directing this gallery, include artists Harriet Bart, Carol Lee Chase, and Jean Murakami.

Dillard Voigt Gallery, 212 Third Ave. North, Minneapolis (tel. 332-1661), is one of the newest and most avant-garde galleries in the Warehouse District—or anywhere else. All superior contemporary art is welcome here, from crafts and jewelry to the mixed-media abstract collages of Sam Gilliam to the performance art of visiting jazz groups. Incidentally, this gallery is unusual not only in the art it displays but also in the background against which it's shown. Dark walls, illuminated by a low-voltage lighting system, provide the unexpected and unexpectedly effective setting here.

A considerably more conservative approach to the display and sale of art can be found at the southern end of downtown in **Groveland Gallery**, 25 Groveland Terrace, Minneapolis (tel. 377-7800). Here in a beautiful old mansion you'll find mostly representational art. Minnesota artists and Minnesota settings are featured. Artists represented here include Greg Kelsey, Carol Lee Chase, Mike Lynch, and Larry Hofmann.

ST. PAUL GALLERIES: Meanwhile, over in St. Paul there's the **Suzanne Kohn Gallery**, 1690 Grand Ave. (tel. 699-0477). Regional painters are featured here, and if you don't see what you want on the walls of this small gallery, you're welcome to go downstairs for a look through the works stored there. After nearly a quarter of a century as a gallery owner, Suzanne Kohn still favors beauty of subject and of expression in art. Deborah Brown and Jerry Rudquist are two of the contemporary midwestern artists that she represents.

The work of late–19th-century and early–20th-century regional artists is featured at **Kramer Gallery**, 229 E. 6th St. (tel. 228-1301). Other American and European painters of that period are shown here as well, along with turn-of-the-century Indian art and artifacts. Among the famous painters represented here are Alexis Fournier, who left St. Paul to study with Barbizon masters in France, and Nichola Brewer, another notable turn-of-the-century painter of the Barbizon School. You're also likely to find work by regional impressionists George Ames Aldrich and Alfred Janssen, as well as western works by John Fery, Edgar Payne, and Frank Hoffman.

If you're interested in bringing top-quality crafts back from your visit to Minnesota, you might try the **Raymond Street Gallery**, 761 Raymond Ave. (tel. 644-9200). You'll find baskets, jewelry, blown glass, and more here, where the nationally known pottery of Warren MacKenzie is exclusively available in the Twin Cities.

Chapter VIII

TWIN CITIES NIGHTSPOTS

EXCITING ENTERTAINMENT can be found in late-night clubs all around these towns, although the term "late-night" is used advisedly. By early morning—1 a.m. Monday through Saturday and midnight on Sunday, to be exact—our chariots turn back into pumpkins as nightclub doors close and lights go out. The 1987 legislature was the latest group of local lawmakers who decided to keep Twin Cities closing hours unchanged, but the effort to extend them will undoubtedly continue and may someday actually prevail. For the present, though, you'll find lots to see and do and still get a good night's sleep before rising to another full day of activities here in Minneapolis and St. Paul.

Rock-and-roll, jazz, and comedy clubs are great favorites hereabouts, with some of the country's foremost performers appearing on stages in nightclubs that are themselves often worth writing home about.

A cavernous converted bus depot serves as the site of one of Minneapolis' largest, busiest, and most famous nightspots. The 1,200-seat **First Avenue Club,** 701 First Ave. North (tel. 338-8388), is familiar to movie-goers around the world as the setting for Prince's 1984 movie *Purple Rain.* Actually this multitalented young star, a resident of the Twin Cities, got his start at First Avenue and still makes appearances here to try out new material before a live audience. These performances are never advertised, but word gets around quickly when Prince is to appear. A purple Cadillac parked near the club or a large U-haul at the curb is taken by fans to be proof positive that Prince and his band will be onstage that evening. Crowds follow as the night the day.

There's recorded music for dancing four times each week at

First Avenue, where hi-tech sound and lights provide a noisy and exciting atmosphere. Live national soloists and groups perform on Sunday, Monday, and Wednesday.

While some promising unknowns play the First Avenue from time to time, the usual launching pad for new talent is the adjoining **7th Street Entry,** 701 First Ave. North (tel. 338-8388). Formerly a storage area, this room has become the club in which publicists try to book their young clients, hoping to catch the eye of scouts who've made this a regular stop in their search for new talent. All First Avenue customers have access as well to 7th Street Entry. There's a separate cover charge for each place on Thursday, Friday, and Saturday, and it varies according to the current entertainment. You'll find drinks of all kinds here, but no drink specials because First Avenue is here primarily to sell entertainment, not refreshments. Its small kitchen serves only snacks like nachos and pizzas. It's food for the ears—and strong ears at that—which you'll find featured at First Avenue and at 7th Street Entry. Phone 332-1775 for daily recorded information about performances.

A few blocks away at **Juke Box Saturday Night,** 14 N. 5th St., Minneapolis (tel. 339-5890), you'll find a huge entertainment complex predicated on nostalgia for the '50s and '60s. Entered a hula-hoop, twist, or jitterbug contest lately? They're frequently featured here. So is music of the era from 1955 to 1967, played by a disc jockey who's seated behind the front end of a '57 Chevy. Two large TV screens project old "Howdy Doody" and "Leave It to Beaver" episodes, and portraits of Annette Funicello and Frankie Avalon decorate the walls. Other decorations range from a ceiling display of legs and feet in sneakers, ski boots, socks, and other assorted gear to blinking traffic lights and Tootsie-Roll wallpaper. Jocks can display their skills at popular indoor basketball hoops. Summer 1987 saw a delightful innovation at Juke Box Saturday Night—outdoor dining in an adjoining area that serves as a parking lot during other seasons. You'll have to see it all to believe even part of what goes on at this designated "playpen for yuppies." Hours are 4 p.m. to 1 a.m. Monday through Friday, noon to 1 a.m. on Saturday, and noon to midnight on Sunday. The cover charge is $2 during the week, $3 on weekends. And should you decide to put on a big affair while you're in town, be aware that complete banquet facilities are available here for weddings, bar mitzvahs, birthdays, and other celebrations (the second-floor banquet hall is booked heavily for private parties of these and other kinds.

The other member of Minneapolis' Big Three downtown

nightspots dates back, in decor at least, to the 1890s with its red plush interiors and Victorian bric-a-brac. But the current claim to fame of the **Gay 90's,** 408 Hennepin Ave. South (tel. 333-7755), is that it's not only the largest gay bar in the area but reportedly the largest gay entertainment complex in the country. Hours at the restaurant, with its two floors of bars, discos, and lounges are 8 p.m. to 1 a.m. Monday through Saturday, 10 a.m. to midnight on Sunday.

Right next door you'll find another gay nightspot, the smaller, more restrained **Brass Rail,** 422 Hennepin Ave. South (tel. 333-3016). A pianist plays modern classics here from 9 p.m. until closing, Tuesday through Sunday. Hours are 10 a.m. to 1 a.m. Monday through Friday, noon to 1 a.m. on Saturday, and noon to midnight on Sunday.

Comedy clubs are an important part of the after-hours scene here in the Twin Cities, where one of the most popular of all is David Wood's **Rib Tickler,** on the lower level of the beautiful historic Itasca Building, 716 1st St. North (tel. 339-9031). There's always a nationally known magician and comedian on the bill, along with an emcee, and the caliber of entertainment here is second to none. Acoustics are excellent in this beautifully appointed club, but if you're not tall and stately, you might do well to find a chair on the elevated portion of the room or at one of the high bar stools and tables set here and there. The magicians are phenomenal, and you wouldn't want to miss a trick. The cover charge on Wednesday, Thursday, and Sunday night is $6, $8 on Friday, $9 on Saturday; a current student identification card will get you in for $3. There are exceptions to the above schedule, though. On Wednesday night, Ladies Night, women are admitted for $3; men get in for $3 on their night, Sunday.

Jazz enthusiasts claim that our local clubs rank among the best in the country. The **Dakota Bar and Grill,** at Bandana Square, 1021 E. Bandana Blvd., St. Paul (tel. 642-1442), offers live jazz seven nights a week, with groups ranging from 3-piece combos to 17-piece big bands. Many of the attractions here have impressive credentials. Pianist Baby Doo Caston used to tour with Alberta Hunter and Dizzy Gillespie; saxaphonist Frank Forster worked with Count Basie. Musicians booked to appear at the Ordway or other large halls in town frequently end up here to enjoy the late-night entertainment, which lasts until 12:45 a.m. on Thursday, Friday and Saturday night, until 12:30 a.m. on Monday, and to midnight on Tuesday, Wednesday, and Sunday. No cover, no minimum.

Back in Minneapolis, you'll find the **Artists' Quarter,** 14 E. 26th St. (tel. 872-0405), a club that prides itself on bringing in nationally known jazz musicians 365 days each year. You'll find "straight ahead jazz" here—today's version of the music identified with Dizzy Gillespie and Charlie Parker 20 years ago. The excellence of the acoustics in this 110-seat bar is attributable to the prevalence of wood, which acts as a resonator in the narrow, low-ceilinged area. Hours at the small Artists' Quarter restaurant are 8 a.m. to 1 a.m. Monday through Saturday, 10 a.m. to midnight on Sunday. Entertainment starts at about 9 p.m. Monday through Saturday and about 8 p.m. on Sunday, but you might want to telephone ahead because starting times sometimes vary.

If you want specific information about the jazz entertainment being offered during your stay in the Twin Cities, call **Jazzline** (tel. 633-0329), a service of the Twin Cities Jazz Society. They provide a lengthy run-down on the artists appearing throughout the Twin Cities at clubs, bars, restaurants, hotels, parks, plazas, and even on local radio. During the summer months, much of the jazz hereabouts is performed outdoors, an added attraction.

Interested in other types of music? At the popular suburban **Rupert's Nightclub,** 5410 Wayzata Blvd., St. Louis Park (tel. 544-3550), a 13-piece house band and four singers are on hand to entertain seven nights a week. This huge three-tiered club offers a wide range of entertainment, from Motown to Top-40 to rock and roll to the big bands. The diversity of its offerings probably accounts for the diversity of the crowds. You'll encounter people of all ages gathered here, dressed in styles from the most formal to the most casual. One exception, though: if you want to wear jeans, better check with the management first. Reportedly jeans are the only kind of garb that's unwelcome at Rupert's. Many of the people here look as though they've just arrived from the office, and that may be true because a popular Happy Hour, weekdays from 5 to 7 p.m., features a tasty variety of complimentary appetizers. They seem a perfect prelude to an evening in the club. Hours here are 4:30 p.m. to 1 a.m. on Tuesday, 5 p.m. to 1 a.m. on Wednesday, Thursday, and Friday, 7:30 p.m. to 1 a.m. on Saturday, and 7:30 p.m. to midnight on Sunday.

At the **New Riverside Café,** 329 Cedar Ave. South, in Minneapolis (tel. 333-4814), you'll hear a variety of music by Twin Cities bands and vocalists. In this 15-year-old west-bank collective, where the owners also serve as managers and maintenance staff, the often first-rate musicians are paid by tips from patrons and a meal from the café. You'll find the work of local artists mounted on the wall here as well. "The Riv" is a vegetarian, alcohol-free restaurant with a reputation for tasty food in a wholesome environment. Check it out. Music entertainment begins each night at 9 p.m. and lasts until 11 p.m. on weekdays, to midnight on Saturday.

If it's Irish tunes your ears have been craving, you've come to the right locale. Head for **Patrick McGovern's Pub and Restaurant** at 225 W. 7th St. (tel. 224-5821), just two blocks west of the World Trade Center. Here in a building that dates back to the 1880s, you'll find popular international beers and ales, including Guinness and Harp on draft from Ireland, Bass Ale from England, and Moosehead lager from Canada. A satellite brings in sporting events and the sporting enthusiasts to enjoy them. Irish music is performed by a live band each Saturday evening. Good, reasonably priced food is available at lunch and dinner. Bar hours are 9 a.m. to 1 a.m. Monday through Saturday, 10 a.m. to midnight Sunday.

At **O'Gara's Bar and Grill,** 164 N. Snelling, St. Paul (tel. 644-3333), you'll find a complex that's far outgrown the pub founded in March 1941 by James Freeman O'Gara of County Sligo. Originally serving food and liquor to locals who helped manufacture World War II munitions hereabouts, O'Gara's has expanded since those early days and now boasts a game room (which was formerly a barber shop run by the father of "Peanuts" creator, Charles Schultz). Nowadays you can enjoy music in O'Gara's piano bar, listen to a variety of bands in the Garage, and, of course, sample food and drink in the expanded dining and drinking areas. Students, professors, and white-collar types mix affably with the blue-collar regulars.

In the two adjoining rooms of **Sweeney's Saloon and Champagnerie,** 96 N. Dale St., St. Paul (tel. 221-9157), you'll find two totally different milieus. The saloon is a boisterous place with a large selection of beers, to say nothing of food specials that really are special.

On the much more staid champagne-bar side, you'll find a more serene setting in which to enjoy your choice from over 100 champagnes and wines along with champagne-cooked entrees and champagne-dressed salads. The saloon is open from 11 a.m. to 1 a.m. Monday through Saturday, 11 a.m. to midnight on Sunday; the champagne bar, which features three or four champagnes by the glass each night, is open only six days a week, from about 5 p.m. to 1 a.m. Monday through Saturday. (You might want to phone ahead to check the exact time.)

At **Fitzgerald's** in St. Paul's Galtier Plaza, on Sibley

Street between 5th and 6th Avenues (tel. 297-6787), you'll find a pub with an open contemporary air; window walls offer a lovely view of Mears Park below. Featured here is a wide variety of Scotches and cognacs, after-dinner cordials and premium imported and domestic wines. Popular for lunches with local businesspeople, Fitzgerald's comes to life late at night when it's frequented by out-of-towners staying at nearby hotels with skyway access to Fitzgerald's until closing time. This is also a popular place for after-theater audiences. The bar is open 11 a.m. to 1 a.m. Monday through Saturday, 11 a.m. to midnight Sunday.

Over at 788 Grand Ave., St. Paul (tel. 227-7328), the popular **Grand Central** features live music and dancing seven nights each week. Deejays offer top 40 hits each evening from 9 p.m. until 1 a.m. Things really get lively from 10 or 10:30 p.m. on, with a variety of imported beers to add to the merriment. There's a $2 cover charge on Friday and Saturday nights after 9 p.m.

If you're a jazz enthusiast in town on a Friday or Saturday evening, do consider the **Emporium of Jazz,** 1351 Sibley Memorial Highway, Mendota, MN (tel. 452-1830), located across the Mississippi River from the International Airport. Open from 8 p.m. to 1 a.m. with a $3 cover charge, the Emporium features the much admired New Orleans Dixieland jazz of pianist Stan Hall and his group. (If you opt for dinner at the adjoining Mariner restaurant, your cover charge will be only $1.50.)

Back in downtown Minneapolis, you'll want to check out the **Pacific Club,** 10 S. 5th St (tel. 339-6206 or 339-6100), a new spot whose tropical decor is echoed in the scanty aqua and fuchsia sarongs worn by the waitresses. The Pacific Club gained instant popularity with its absolutely lavish happy hour served from 4 p.m. to 7:30 p.m. Monday through Friday, 6 p.m. to 8:30 p.m. Saturday. The big draw for the hundreds of downtowners who flock here after work each day is the full dinner buffet with more than 20 selections, from appetizers to desserts —all for a single $1 charge. And when the bountiful buffet tables come down, the high-energy music and dancing get underway. There's a $2 cover charge after 7:30 p.m. from Tuesday to Thursday, a $4 cover on Friday after 7:30 p.m. and after 8:30 p.m. on Saturday. A strict dress code here prohibits denim and athletic garb of all kinds, and only those 23 years of age or more are admitted.

On the ground floor of Riverplace, the trendy shopping and entertainment complex on the shores of the Mississippi River, you'll find **J. Cousineau's** at 15 Main St. S.E. (tel. 623-3632), a tiny pub with two patios, one on the mall and one outdoors. It's famous for its enormous half-yard and full-yard ale glasses, reproductions of the glasses used in England during the 17th and 18th centuries. After quaffing your selection, feel free to purchase the one-foot glass at $29.95, half-yard glass at $35.75, or the full-yard at $59.95. (Less hearty or less thirsty souls can imbibe from smaller vessels. Steins and tankards are available for the likes of them.)

And if you feel like an after-hours big splurge, try **Cleo's** on the 50th floor of the Vista Marquette Hotel, 710 Marquette Ave., Minneapolis (tel. 349-6260), where you'll dance among the stars to top-40 music in a setting of hieroglyphics, smoke-breathing cobras, and other Egyptian effects associated with the legendary queen of the Nile. There's a $3 cover charge and drink prices range from $2.50 to $5, but a lovely skyline view of the cities and a complimentary buffet accompany your drinks.

On the strip in Bloomington, you'll find other nightspots including the **Cattle Company,** 4470 W. 78th St. Circle (tel. 835-1225), with deejays on hand from 4 p.m. to 1 a.m. six nights a week (Sunday until 12 midnight). A wide mix of dance music from the 50's and 60's to the current top 40 is featured here.

And across Hwy. 494 at **Stonewings Night Club** and **Lounge,** 8301 Normandale Blvd. (tel. 831-4811), you'll find four-piece house band to play contemporary music for your dancing pleasure from 8:15 p.m. to 1 a.m. seven nights each week.

Finally, in a class by itself, is **Champps Sports Bar and Gourmet Hamburger Grill,** 2431 W. 7th St. at Sibley Plaza in St. Paul (tel. 698-5050), where people of all ages, sizes, backgrounds, and temperaments mix merrily amidst six large TV screens and two bars arched by pennant-decorated ceilings. When visiting the Twin Cities, sports celebrities from out of town head for Champps, and local sports figures congregate here as well. Kirby Puckett, star extraordinaire of the World Champion Minnesota Twins has served as guest bartender here, as have other sports luminaries. The atmosphere is jovial, food and drink prices are moderate. Known as "one of the top six sports bars in the nation," Champps is always busy, bustling and, to a degree, blasé. A note on the menu says it all: "If your order doesn't arrive in 5 minutes, you'll be served in 9 minutes, . . . or maybe 12 . . . Relax . . ." Patrons seem to do just that.

Chapter IX

SPORTS AND RECREATION

WHATEVER THE SEASON, Twin Citians turn out in large, enthusiastic numbers to watch and participate in a wide variety of sporting events. With four major-league teams to support, fans find excitement and fun in superb sports facilities like the Metrodome in Minneapolis and the Civic Center in St. Paul. During the past few years they've enjoyed thoroughbred horseracing at suburban Canterbury Downs as well.

But Twin Citians don't spend all their time watching sporting events. They're participants too. What else would you expect in cities that pride themselves on their remarkable abundance of parks and lakes, athletic activities and events. Delightful walking and jogging, boating and swimming, golf and tennis, and a variety of wintertime activities enhance the quality of life hereabouts for residents who call St. Paul and Minneapolis home and for visitors who call the Twin Cities a great place to enjoy top-notch sports and recreation.

Spectator Sports

BIG-LEAGUE TEAMS: Minneapolis and St. Paul are big-league towns. With four professional sports teams to their credit, and a fifth on the way, the Twin Cities are unique in the diversity of sports competition that they offer and the state-of-the-art facilities that are provided for them.

Home clubs include the Minnesota Vikings football team, Minnesota Twins baseball team (winner of the 1987 World Series), Minnesota North Stars hockey team, and Minnesota Strikers soccer team. And during the 1988–1989 professional basketball season, look for the brand-new big-league professional basketball team, the Minnesota Timberwolves. Tickets to Viking games are $18 for any seat, and can be obtained by writing to 500 11th Ave. South, Minneapolis (333-8828). Twins games range in price from $3 to $9. Write to 501 Chicago Ave. South, Minneapolis (375-1366).

As to sports facilities, consider that in downtown St. Paul each March, at the **Civic Center,** Kellogg and 7th Streets (tel. 224-7403), nearly a quarter of a million spectators come from everywhere to attend the Minnesota State High School League wrestling, basketball, and hockey tournaments. And that in suburban Bloomington, the **Metropolitan Sports Center,** 7901 Cedar Ave. (tel. 853-9310), plays host to the growing number of fans who turn out for Striker soccer and North Star hockey.

But the **Hubert H. Humphrey Metrodome,** 5th Street and Chicago Avenue, Minneapolis (tel. 375-1116), is the area's most famous sports installation. Opened in 1982, this massive facility—it accommodates 55,000 baseball fans or 62,000 football fans—was really built with you in mind. Visitors enjoy knowing for certain that the baseball game they've come to see won't be rained out and that wintry blasts won't make their football viewing uncomfortable. Only the locals look back longingly on the pre-Metrodome days when tailgate parties, held in the vast suburban parking lot, were part of the fun to be found at outdoor Metropolitan Stadium on the Bloomington strip. In its downtown location on the eastern edge of Minneapolis, the Metrodome has no facilities for the convivial get-togethers that were virtually a ritual in these parts.

For better or worse, though—and you'll get lots of eloquent arguments on both sides—then was then and now is now, and there's a lot to be said for the comfort and convenience that's been engineered into the massive domed stadium.

Here are some of the plusses: The Metrodome is the world's first rectangular domed stadium, so the sightlines are particularly good. The domed ceiling is constructed of translucent material that lets in natural light; the claustrophobia that afflicts fans in other indoor facilities has been avoided here. And there are some technological wonders: a pitcher's mound that appears and disappears at the flip of a switch; a seating system that converts, in practically no time, from football to baseball and back again; and a triply segmented main scoreboard above left center field that transmits multiple messages and instant replays (auxiliary boards, strategically placed above first and third base and above right center field, keep you in touch at all times with messages from the sophisticated scoreboard control room).

Games at the Metrodome tend to be well attended, and especially if it's a Viking game you've got in mind, it's well to order your tickets in advance. More than 80% of seats here go to season ticketholders.

CANTERBURY DOWNS: After initial skepticism concerning the notion of thoroughbred horse-racing in wholesome Minnesota, the "sport of kings" has recently turned out to be just what the commoners were waiting for. Since 1985, when Canterbury Downs first opened its gates at 901 County Road 83 in south-suburban Shakopee (tel. 937-7712), racing fans of all kinds and all ages have been turning out in surprising numbers. Horse-racing is by now a popular part of summertime fun for folks you might not expect to find at a racetrack.

Busloads of senior citizens can be seen arriving every day in the huge parking lot, while moms, dads, and the kids park nearby, then unload their station wagons and proceed to haul gear and provisions over to the trackside picnic area for their day at the races.

Located on nearly 400 acres of what used to be farmland, this facility includes not only stables, starting gates, and paddocks, but also playgrounds where the youngest members of the family can amuse themselves and one another while their elders set out the good things to eat on picnic tables protected by canvas tents. Concession stands nearby can provide anything that somehow or other didn't get packed up and brought along. Parimutuel windows are conveniently close as well.

Actually, the whole day at Canterbury Downs can be spent in Shire Square, in the shadow of the grandstand and close to the railing, which many find the best place for watching the races. Up in the grandstands you'll find most of the 300 mutuel windows that have been conveniently placed on every level of the rambling three-story facility. You'll also find some of the more than 150 closed-circuit TV monitors that keep the action in full view should bettors be delayed in getting back to their seats.

Trackside bench seats are available without extra charge as part of the $3 price of general admission, and lawn chairs are welcome on the apron that separates the grandstand from the track railing.

For $5 you can reserve a seat in either the open-air or the glassed-in section of the grandstand. Reservations must be made by mail or in person. A reserved seat in the Clubhouse can be yours for $7.50. There's no admission charge for youngsters 17 and under, but they must be accompanied by their parents. You'll pay $2 for general parking, $4 for preferred parking, or $6 for valet parking.

All the trappings of any first-class racetrack are on hand here at Canterbury Downs. Before each race begins you can size up the horses in the paddocks garden, get a closer look at them as they parade around the European-style walking ring, and then feel the pressure as the starting gates open to the announcer's cry, "And they're off!"

Reportedly, the most commonly placed bets are $2, so you can have an exciting time for about the same investment as you'd make in many other kinds of mass entertainment. The secret, of course, is to allow yourself no more money at the betting windows than you've set aside for betting before you get to the track.

The Canterbury Downs racing season usually runs from the end of April to the end of September. Post time for the first race is at 4 p.m. Wednesday through Friday (racing until about 8 p.m.) and at 1:30 p.m. on Saturday, Sunday, and holidays (racing until about 6 p.m.). Gates open at 2:30 p.m. on weekdays, at 11:30 a.m. on weekends and holidays.

Getting to Canterbury Downs

Your hotel or motel may have bus transportation available to the track. If you prefer to drive out by yourself, you'll find the going easy, but you should get an early start because the traffic tends to be heavy on weekends and holidays. Here are alternative routes from both Twin Cities.

From Minneapolis: Take I-35W south to Hwy. 13 and then proceed west; Hwy. 13 becomes Hwy. 101 before you complete the five-mile stretch to the Canterbury exits. Or you can take I-494 west to Hwy. 169, then proceed south to Shakopee and go east on Hwy. 101 to the Canterbury exits.

From St. Paul: Take I-35E south to County Road 42 in Burnsville, then proceed west 11 miles to Canterbury Road and turn north to Canterbury Downs. Or take Cedar Avenue south to Hwy. 13 and proceed west; Hwy. 13 will become Hwy. 101 as you drive the five miles to the Canterbury Downs exits.

Recreation

Of course Twin Citians don't spend all their time watching sporting events—they're participants too.

TENNIS: The popularity of tennis in St. Paul and Minneapolis has grown during recent years, along with the growing number of indoor tennis courts. Now it's no longer necessary to pack away the racquet when outdoor courts close for the season.

Private Clubs

Several local clubs offer guest rates to out-of-town visitors, and offer discounts to those who can identify themselves as members of clubs affiliated with the International Racquet Sports Association of America (IRSA).

The tennis club visited by most out-of-towners is likely to be one of the five major facilities operated by **Northwest Racquet, Swim, & Health Clubs,** at 14600 Burnhaven Rd., Burnsville (tel. 435-7127); 6701 W. 78th St., Bloomington (tel. 835-3113); 1001 W. 98th St., Bloomington (tel. 884-1612); 4001 Lake Breeze Ave. North, Brooklyn Center (tel. 535-3571); and 5525 Cedar Lake Rd., St. Louis Park (tel. 546-6554). In addition to tennis courts, you'll find such features as swimming pools, running tracks, Nautilus and Universal weight equipment, and free-weight and aerobics rooms. The $10 admission charge for out-of-towners ($4.25 for those with an IRSA membership card) entitles visitors to full use of the club facilities. Tennis-court time costs an additional $9.35 per hour, and use of tennis-ball machines is free. Hours are 5:45 a.m. to midnight, seven days a week.

The **Eagandale Racquet and Swim Club,** 3330 Pilot Knob Rd., Eagan (tel. 454-8790), offers indoor and outdoor tennis along with a variety of other activities, including swimming, aerobics, Nautilus, whirlpool, and sauna. The admission fee of $6 entitles guests to use the club's assorted facilities. Tennis court-time costs $3.75 per person per hour for doubles, $6.75 per person for singles. Tennis-ball machines are available at no extra charge. The club is open from 6 a.m. until 11:30 p.m. seven days a week.

There's no visitors' admission charge at the indoor courts of the **Nicollet Tennis Center,** 4005 Nicollet Ave., Minneapolis (tel. 825-6844). This privately leased installation stands on city-owned parkland and is therefore open to the public without charge. Court fees here vary according to time of day and time of year, with prices lower during outdoor-tennis months. From April 30 to September 1, you'll pay $5 per hour before 5 p.m., $8 per hour from 5 to 11 p.m. The charge during the rest of the year is $11 per hour from 7 a.m. to midnight. The Nicollet Tennis Center is open seven days a week. Located in Martin Luther King Park, these well-maintained courts are among the most popular in the cities, playing host periodically to public-park tennis tournaments.

Public Courts

The seasonal fee scale at the Nicollet Tennis Center reflects the fact that when Twin Citians are able to play tennis outdoors, they tend to do so—and why not? With more than 200 free courts available, many located in picturesque parkland settings, it's no wonder that tennis is so popular an outdoor recreation in St. Paul and Minneapolis.

With more than 100 of these tennis courts located throughout the city of St. Paul, it would be impossible to list them here, but at **Phalen Park** you'll find popular courts at Johnson Parkway and Maryland Avenue, in a particularly beautiful location adjacent to Lake Phalen. Tennis play is on a first-come, first-served basis; posted signs urge that court time be limited to one hour if others are waiting. Tennis courts here are lit after dark, thanks to a control box that stops functioning at 11 p.m. In Minneapolis, only the Nicollet Tennis Center offers lighted courts.

Among the most beautifully located and popular courts in the Twin Cities are the ones you'll find in Minneapolis' **Kenwood Park,** at the north end of Lake of the Isles. The most centrally located Minneapolis courts may be the ones in **Loring Park,** at Hennepin Avenue and Harmon Place. On the edge of downtown Minneapolis, these courts have a view of Loring Lake and are only a footbridge away from the Guthrie Theater/Walker Art Center complex. For information about municipal courts, call the Park Board (tel. 348-2226 for courts in Minneapolis, 292-7400 for courts in St. Paul).

GOLF: There are more par-3 courses in the Twin Cities than in any other metropolitan area in the country, and visitors are often surprised not only by the number of busy courses in the area, but also by the excellent condition of the public greens. If golf is your game, here are a few courses for you to consider.

Private Clubs

The **Majestic Oaks Golf Course,** 701 Bunker Lake Blvd., Ham Lake (tel. 755-2142)—privately owned but open to the public—was rated among the top 50 American public golf courses by *Golf Digest.* Rates are $8 for 9 holes, $15 for 18 holes. Carts are available at $9 for the 9-hole course, $17 for the 18-hole course, and clubs can be rented for $5.

The **Braemar Golf Course,** 6364 Dewey Hill Rd., Edina (tel. 941-2072), has hosted many national tournaments, and recent-

ly converted its par-3 course into an executive 9-hole course.
Rates are $8 for 9 holes, $12 for 18 holes. Rental carts cost $9
for 9 holes, $17 for 18 holes; club rental is $4.50.

Municipal Courses

The following are three of the area's best 18-hole municipal
golf courses. Facilities include clubhouses, food service, lockers, and showers.

The **Francis A. Gross Golf Course** is at 2201 St. Anthony
Blvd., Minneapolis (tel. 789-2542). Rates are $8 for 9 holes,
$10 for 18 holes. Carts are available at $10 for 9 holes, $17 for
18 holes, and clubs can be rented at $3 for 9 holes, $6 for 18
holes.

At the **Meadowbrook Golf Course**, 300 Meadowbrook Rd.,
Hopkins (tel. 929-2077), rates are $8 for 9 holes and $10 for 18
holes. Rental carts are available at $9 for 9 holes, $17 for 18
holes, and clubs can be rented for $6.

The **Hiawatha Golf Course**, 4553 Longfellow Ave. South,
Minneapolis (tel. 724-7715), charges $8 for 9 holes, $10 for 18
holes. Carts are rented at $10 for 9 holes, $17 for 18 holes, and
clubs are available for $6.

In addition, the 18-hole public course in St. Paul's **Como
Park** was completely renovated in 1986, and the 9-hole Como
Park course remains one of the best around. Phone 488-7291
for information.

Brand-new is the **Edinburgh USA** golf course in Brooklyn
Park, 8600 Edinbrook Crossing (tel. 424-7060). Green fees are
$17.

City and Suburban Parks

Golf is extremely popular in the superb public parks that the
Twin Cities boast, but golf is only a small part of what these
parks have to offer in the way of recreation.

PARK ACTIVITIES: For walkers, joggers, and runners, there are
more than 38 miles of designated bituminous parkland trails,
and for bicyclists, 36 miles of bike paths. If you didn't bring
your bike along, you can rent one, and if you like, a sailboat,
canoe, fishing boat, or windsurfer as well. During the winter
you'll find ice skating, snowshoeing, snowtubing, sledding, and
skiing. In fact, those golf courses that prove so popular during
the spring, summer, and fall, serve in winter as popular cross-country skiing sites.

Each of the Twin Cities' parks deserves a chapter of its own,
but there's room here for just a mention of the fun to be found
in some of them.

Call for further **information** about all the activities in local parks (tel. 348-2243 in Minneapolis, 488-7291 in St. Paul).

Water Sports

Whether they're gliding through Minneapolis' picturesque chain of lakes, skimming the expanses of St. Paul's lovely Lake Phalen, or winding through Minnehaha Creek, boats of all kinds are an everyday sight in many Twin Cities neighborhoods. If you want to go **canoeing**, you can literally paddle your way through these towns. For example, canoeists can start out in Minnetonka, then follow Minnehaha Creek from Gray's Bay through suburban Hopkins, St. Louis Park, and Edina, and then go on to a spot not far from the Mississippi River in Minneapolis. **AARCEE Recreational Rental**, 2900 Lyndale Ave. South, Minneapolis (tel. 827-5746), rents 15-foot Coleman canoes for $30 a day and 17-foot aluminum canoes for $36 a day, including life jackets, paddles, and car-top carriers. Some hardy sportsmen make the round trip in one outing; others arrange for a car to be waiting for them when they reach the end of the route.

Shorter outings are popular at Cedar Lake in Minneapolis, and canoes and rowboats can be rented at **Lake Calhoun** for $4 an hour, $1.25 for each additional 20 minutes. A particularly popular course here leads canoeists through the chain of lakes that extends from Lake Calhoun to Lake of the Isles and then to Cedar Lake. In St. Paul, you can canoe or row on **Lake Phalen** for $4 for the first hour and $2.50 for each additional hour.

Bright-hued sailboats are a familiar part of the summertime scenery in Minneapolis and St. Paul, where the next best thing to **sailing** is watching these graceful boats making their colorful way through local lakes. Sailboat races are a weekend event each summer at **Lake Nokomis,** at Cedar Avenue and 50th Street in South Minneapolis, but more leisurely boaters are welcome to enjoy the facilities as well. In fact, this is one of the three Minneapolis lakes designated for sailing; the other two are **Lake Harriet,** at Lake Harriet Parkway and William Berry Road, and **Lake Calhoun,** at 3000 E. Calhoun Parkway, off Lake Street.

If you'd like to try your own hand at sailboating, or even **windsurfing** on one of the Twin Cities' most beautiful public lakes, head again for **Lake Phalen.** You'll reach the lake from an entrance at Wheelock Parkway and Arcade Street (Hwy. 61), or Maryland Avenue and Johnson Parkway. Awaiting you there at the boathouse will be sailboats and windsurfing boards for rent at $9 for the first hour and $6 for every hour thereafter. (A $25 deposit and a photo ID are required for rentals.) Hours are 10 a.m. to sundown.

Suburban **Lake Minnetonka,** the largest freshwater lake in the metropolitan area, is another favorite spot for sailing. In fact, this lake has been known for centuries as a uniquely beautiful recreational area. Dakota Indians favored it long before wealthy southerners traveled up the Mississippi River to spend their summers here. With the advent of the railroad, summer resorts began to appear. One of them, the Lafayette Hotel, built by railroad magnate James J. Hill, was among the most popular before it fell victim to fire; occupying that lakeside site today is the Lafayette Country Club. The more than 200 miles of shoreline surrounding Lake Minnetonka is the locale of some of the loveliest homes in Minnesota, while the lake plays host to some of the biggest and best recreational craft.

If you're an experienced sailor, you can rent a sailboat at **Windward Marina,** 1444 Shoreline Dr., Wayzata (tel. 473-8249). Weekday rates for a four-hour rental vary according to the length of the boat: a Freedom 21-foot craft is $59; an Ericson 26-footer, $79; a Columbia 29-footer, $99; and a Freedom 32-foot boat, $109. Weekend rates for these same craft are $89, $119, $159, and $179 respectively. This is a bare-boat charter (you supply the captain and crew), though all boats have marine radios, marine toilets, and safety equipment. A $75 damage deposit is refundable after 24 hours. All boats are due back by 6 p.m.

Want something to show for your day on the water? For **fishing,** try the lagoon in St. Paul's ever-popular Lake Phalen. You'll pay $8 to rent a fishing boat for four hours, plus $1.50 for each additional hour (there's a $10 deposit on all boats).

For more passive boating, you might enjoy a ride on an old paddlewheeler, the *Queen of the Lakes,* which will take you on a leisurely ride around Lake Harriet in about 25 minutes. The charge is $1.75 per person.

I'll end this run-down with the most basic water sport of all: **swimming.** In St. Paul, **Phalen Park** offers a lovely sandy beach, adjacent to walking and jogging paths and other park facilities. In Minneapolis, try the beach at **Cedar Lake. Thomas Beach,** at the south end of Lake Calhoun, is a favorite with Twin Cities visitors too. In suburban Eden Prairie, you'll find the popular **Round Lake Park** north of Hwy. 5 and west of Hwy. 4. And in northwest Bloomington, you'll enjoy **Bush Lake.** Exit onto Bush Lake Road from I-494, proceed south on Bush Lake Road for about 1½ miles, and there you are.

Winter Sports

Here in the Twin Cities, the same lovely lakes and golf courses that provide so much fun during summer months become wintertime playgrounds for skiers, skaters, snowtubers, and other hale and hearty folks.

For serious **skiing,** experienced downhill skiers often head north for Duluth's Spirit Mountain during the winter (see Chapter XII, "Twin Cities Getaways"), but for beginning downhill skiers and for absolutely all cross-country skiers, there's a lot of fun to be had right here in the twin towns. At **Como Park** in St. Paul there's downhill skiing, with a ski lift and a chalet featuring light food service. In **Wirth Park,** snow machines are ready to help nature along whenever that turns out to be necessary. Cross-country skiing has long been popular here, but another lovely Twin Cities setting remains something of a secret. At **Crosby Farm Park,** with an entrance off Shepherd Road and Mississippi River Boulevard, cross-country skiers can imagine they're off somewhere in the remote wilderness as they traverse the trails under a canopy of trees, amid shrublined paths—truly an idyllic setting.

One of the big surprises of the past couple of winters was the enthusiastic response to **snowtubing** at Wirth Park, where "Winter at Wirth," a comprehensive program of snow-related activities, has attracted people from throughout the Twin Cities. For $2.50 per day you can rent an innertube large enough to carry two or three daredevils who'll whirl round and round even as they're sliding uncontrollably down the snowy hill.

You'll see **ice skating** on virtually all city and suburban lakes, at most of which warming houses provide a welcome and considerate touch.

SUBURBAN PARKS: By the way, don't overlook the many activities to be enjoyed in suburban parks. For example, you'll find skiing galore in Bloomington's **Hyland Hills** at 8800 Chalet Rd. (tel. 835-4604). Nine downhill runs serve skiers of different abilities; three triple-chair lifts and four rope tows will get you back up so you can start down all over again. The snow-making equipment there keeps the skiing prime, with or without the cooperation of nature. Skis are available at $5, boots at $4, and poles at $2. Lift tickets range from $6 to $14. Seniors can ski for $4 at any time, and preschoolers ski free. The area is lighted for picturesque night skiing too.

WENDING YOUR WAY THROUGH THE PARKS: And then there's the always-popular recreation in walking or jogging or running through the parks of Minneapolis and St. Paul. Each park has its own distinctive attractions, and you'll glimpse them first-hand as you follow their foot and bicycle paths through some of the loveliest settings in any city anywhere. Since this is all new to you, you may find yourself straying from the straight and narrow, taking time to explore more closely some of the picturesque places that you pass.

Lake Harriet, 42nd Street West and Lake Harriet Parkway, is famous hereabouts for its exquisite flower gardens, an All-American Rose Selection Test Bed foremost among them. But there's a beautiful iris garden here too, as well as special areas for seasonal and perennial flowers. And across the street is the fascinating Lake Harriet Rock Garden, which was reconstructed in 1984–1985, more than 50 years after it was first created on that site. It includes a "peace garden" with rocks from Nagasaki, Japan.

In **Wirth Park,** the largest in the Minneapolis park system, you'll see the Eloise Butler Wildflower Garden and Bird Sanctuary. This 20-acre garden features plants native to Minnesota. Exhibits of prairie and woodland plant life are labeled. The serenity of these gardens is enjoyed by a nearly incredible variety of birds that add their own delightful dimension to this lovely setting, just minutes away from busy downtown Minneapolis.

Como Park is the largest park in St. Paul and reportedly the most popular in the entire Twin Cities area. Most frequently visited is its free zoo, which welcomes between 850,000 and 1,000,000 visitors a year. Another stellar attraction is the Como Park Conservatory, an enclosed structure where plants from all over the world are exhibited year round. Many's the wedding that's been conducted here in the most exquisite setting imaginable. Built at the turn of the century, the Conservatory features a succession of flower shows and other events that draw visitors in very great numbers. The recently renovated 18-hole golf course now boasts a brand-new clubhouse, and down by the lake there's a popular pavilion where plays and concerts are presented.

Lake Como is a year-round attraction, of course, with canoes and paddleboats for rent during the summer and both ice-skating and speed-skating programs available during the winter months. Landscaped and lighted bike and walking paths are much used by visitors. Baseball diamonds, swimming pools, and picnic pavilions are busy places too. An amusement area with miniature-golf course, merry-go-round, occasional pony rides, and other delights for the young and the young at heart is located at Como Park.

THE MINNESOTA ZOO: At the Minnesota Zoo, 12101 Johnny Cake Rd., Apple Valley (tel. 432-9000), the terrain has been carefully created to resemble the hilly grasslands and woodlands of the wild animals that now make their home here. What may be the world's most remarkable cross-country skiing takes place in the Minnesota Zoo, where, for the price of admission—$4 for adults, $2 for seniors, $1.50 for ages 6 through 16, plus $1 per car for parking—you glide within full view of camels, Siberian tigers, Asiatic wild horses, moose, snow monkeys, musk oxen, red pandas, and more.

The Minnesota Zoo is, of course, a year-round recreation attraction for Twin Citians and visitors to these parts. It's open daily from 10 a.m. to 6 p.m. Six separate "trails" offer education so entertainingly that you won't even realize how much you've learned until you've left the 480-acre site, approximately half an hour from downtown Minneapolis and St. Paul.

The **Tropics Trail** is one of the most exotic areas of the zoo, an indoor oasis of plants and animals from far-away tropical areas. This is the largest structure in the zoo, with more than 650 animals and 15,000 plants of 500 different varieties—a fascinating environment in which crowds move slowly and thoughtfully through paths alive with the sounds of rushing water and fluttering birds.

The **Minnesota Trail** features animals indigenous to these parts, but they're more clearly visible and accessible here than in the wild, of course. A beaver pond, one of the highlights of this extraordinary zoo, provides amazing evidence of the inborn engineering know-how of these industrious creatures. Other native Minnesotans in indoor, outdoor, daylight, and nocturnal settings include otters, lynx, weasels, and an assortment of creatures hailing from Minnesota's lakes, prairies, and forests.

The **Discovery Trail** will introduce you to some unlikely new friends. Visited with a tarantula lately? Or a sea star? You'll have the opportunity for close encounters with these and other unusual beings in the **Zoo Lab.** And you'll be able to watch an intriguing bird show, ride a camel or an elephant, pet a goat, and enjoy other hands-on experiences in one of the most deservedly popular of all the areas here.

On the three-quarter-mile **Northern Trail,** you'll be surrounded by northern types like tigers, Asian lions, coyotes, musk oxen, camels, wild horses, and moose. And you'll get to meet what may be your first-ever pronghorn, a graceful antelope look-alike.

The **Sky Trail** is an option you can enjoy for an additional $2 per passenger (children under 5 ride free). This monorail weaves in and out of hills and lakelands as you view wild terrain and listen to "nature narratives" provided by knowledgeable guides.

And finally the **Ocean Trail.** I've left this for last, although until recently this was the first place that most visitors headed. Home of two cult figures, the beluga whales Big Mouth and Little Girl, Ocean Trail was the indisputable star among zoo attractions until 1986, when Big Mouth underwent much publicized surgery for an infected jaw. In April 1987, after a succession of watches by mournful children and their elders, Big Mouth and his lady (who'd proved disconsolate when the two were separated) were wrapped and transported by charter plane to the San Diego Zoo so he could receive treatment. At this writing, Big Mouth is showing signs of recovery—the actual seawater in the tank seems to help. The Minnesota Zoo at first announced plans to simply substitute dolphins for the belugas, but public opinion seemed likely to make reconsideration of that stand necessary. By the time you arrive all problems will undoubtedly have been resolved, so head first for Ocean Trail to see what's occupying center stage in the huge indoor/outdoor tank.

Getting to the Zoo

To reach the Minnesota Zoo from Minneapolis by car, take the Cedar Avenue Expressway south to Apple Valley, then follow the signs directing you to the zoo. From St. Paul, take I-35E to the Cedar Avenue Expressway and follow the directions above.

On weekends and on the third Tuesday of every month you can take the no. 57 bus from any bus stop on Marquette Street in downtown Minneapolis. Buses leave at 9:30 and 11:05 a.m., and return back downtown from the zoo at 1:20 and 3 p.m. Fares are $1.50 for adults, 70¢ for children 6 through 17; kids under 6 ride free.

PARKS ENTERTAINMENT: Along with the natural beauty of the parks, an extensive selection of entertainments may be enjoyed there. Let me give you an idea of what will be available to you if you're in the Twin Cities during the summer months. Much of what's being offered each activity-full season comes as a surprise to many locals as well as to visitors.

There's always something new to enjoy here; for example, brand-new in 1987 and 1988 are features at two unique parks on the Mississippi. At **Nicollet Island Park,** adjacent to historic

St. Anthony Falls, a new **picnic area** has been established on a large deck overlooking the Mississippi River. Not far from the bridge that connects the island to Riverplace, the **Durkee Atwood Building,** a historic industrial structure, will house the park system's first **flea market.** (You'll find newer, more expensive items there and at nearby St. Anthony Main!) The Durkee Atwood, whose outer shell was saved while its interior was gutted and remodeled, will serve as a large picnic building when inclement weather makes outdoor picnics impossible.

Boom Island Park, connected to Nicollet Island by a railroad bridge, was dedicated during the summer of 1987 and opens officially in the summer of 1988. It offers a boat-launching dock into the Mississippi and will have a lighthouse as well. Picnic tables are available here too.

As for outdoor summertime entertainment, a glimpse at the past offers a glimpse at the future. During June and July 1987, for example, **Nicollet Island** offered **instrumental music** seven nights a week by groups as diverse as the Latin Jazz Combo and the Minneapolis Pops Orchestra, the singing Sweet Adelines and the Minnesota Dance Alliance. On Sunday, July 26, there was a fireworks salute to the Aquatennial celebration.

At **Lake Harriet,** during the summer of 1987, you could have heard the St. Anthony Civic Orchestra, the Linden Hills Chamber Players, and the Goodtime Gospel Quartet, among many many other talented groups.

And at Lake Harriet, Loring Park, Powderhorn Park, and Minnehaha Park, among others, you'd have been delighted by perennially popular **acting companies.** The Comedy Troupe offered *Off the Wall and Into the Frying Pan,* the Minnesota Shakespeare Company presented *Two Gentlemen of Verona* and *The Winter's Tale,* and the Luminous Theater added another Shakespearean comedy, *Love's Labour's Lost,* to the summer-in-the-parks line-up. And then there were the Commedia Theater's light and delightful selections: *A Servant of Two Masters, The Marriage Proposal,* and an original work in the commedia dell'arte tradition, *Isabella's Strategem.*

Of course, this isn't nearly all that you'll find by way of sports and recreation in the Twin Cities, but it's enough to prove that there's truly something for every taste. What's most exciting about it all is the opportunity to expand your taste by trying new forms of entertainment, thanks to the wide diversity available.

Chapter X

SHOPPING

AN AMERICAN REVOLUTION got under way in the Twin Cities back in October 1956 when the country's first fully enclosed, climate-controlled suburban shopping mall—Southdale—opened its doors to a somewhat skeptical public.

Southdale

There were lots of unanswered questions at the time. Would there really be enough business in the quiet community of Edina to support two of the Twin Cities' largest department stores? At Southdale, Donaldsons and Dayton's, the Twin Cities' version of Macy's and Gimbels, became the first competing department stores in America ever to locate under one roof. In addition to these blockbusters, 64 specialty shops had leased space in the center. Well and good, but after the initial novelty wore off, would customers revert to their long-established shopping patterns, leaving the mall a fully enclosed, climate-controlled suburban ghost town?

Not a bit of it! Today, more than 30 years after that grand opening, Dayton's and Donaldsons still face each other across Southdale's busy courtyard, while since 1972 a third department store, J. C. Penney, has been doing a brisk business elsewhere in the center. And the 64 specialty shops that seemed such a phenomenal number in 1956 have grown to 140.

Located at 66th Street and France Avenue in the southern Minneapolis suburb of Edina, Southdale is south of crosstown Hwy. 62, north of I-494, and between I-35W and Hwy. 100. In addition to the three big-name department-store anchors—Dayton's, Donaldsons, and J. C. Penney—Southdale houses nationally known shops like Peck and Peck, Eddie Bauer, Soldati, Florsheim, and Buster Brown. But what may interest you more are the dozens of specialty shops with less-familiar names that feature fine apparel, jewelry, toys, mementoes, and more. You'll also find a self-service post office here, along with a Northwest Orient Airlines ticket office, and a one-hour photo-processing shop. And should you feel like stopping for something to eat, there are more than a dozen restaurants and snackbars to serve you, in addition to a centrally located sidewalk café.

Southdale's success has been contagious. The undeveloped land that surrounded its 84-acre site now houses a wide variety of medical, commercial, and governmental agencies. Southdale Medical Center and Fairview Southdale Hospital stand just one block away, across busy 66th Street. Southdale Square offers its own shopping features nearby. And a powerful magnet, the bountifully stocked Southdale-Hennepin Area Library of Edina, with its extensive book and audio-visual holdings, is within a short walking distance. So are some of the Twin Cities' most desirable condominium apartment complexes.

One of Southdale's greatest claims to fame is the manner in which it has integrated itself into the surrounding community. For example, at 8 a.m. Monday through Saturday, and at 10:30 a.m. on Sunday, long before the shops open for business, members of the Southdale Walking Program arrive to track their course along designated routes. At 8:30 a.m. on the fourth Tuesday of each month, doctors and other medical personnel from Fairview Southdale Hospital conduct seminars in the Southdale Community Room on subjects of local concern— exercise, diet, cancer awareness, stress reduction, etc.

At other times the center plays host to book fairs, musical programs, symphony balls, and demonstrations of every kind (phone 922-4400 for information).

It's been said that shopping centers are today's version of yesterday's town square. Southdale, the granddaddy of all of America's shopping malls, is that and more. Though not the biggest shopping center in the state (Burnsville Center claims that distinction) or the handsomest (there are many candidates for that laurel), Southdale remains, in fact, the state's most popular shopping destination. But maybe because it was for so long the only mall of its kind here, a whole generation of shoppers grew up wearing the clothes and playing with the toys that came from Southdale. For these and many other Twin Citians, Southdale remains to this day simply the most natural, most comfortable place to go shopping.

Other Shopping Centers

Southdale may be the queen of the malls, but there are nearly 200 other shopping centers hereabouts. And while it's impossible, of course, to tell you about all of them, here are a few of the many popular places that Twin Citians have to choose from.

Shopping hours generally are 10 a.m. to 9 p.m. Monday through Friday, 9:30 a.m. to 6 p.m. on Saturday, and noon to 5 p.m. on Sunday. During holiday periods, shopping hours are usually extended.

GALLERIA: Located at 69th Street and France Avenue, a block south of Southdale (tel. 925-4321), is a fashionable upscale center with 60 shops and restaurants, many of which are run by the people who own them. The setting is picturesque, with lush greenery, soft lighting, and cobblestone walkways. You'll find stores specializing in handbags, books, swimwear, furs, cookware, dolls, gourmet foods, pottery, and a great deal more. When Galleria advertises a sale, *run* do not walk. At other times, be advised that prices—and quality—tend to be high, although as one entrepreneur recently pointed out, you can buy a $9 sweater here as well as a $30,000 mink coat.

RIDGEDALE: Located on Hwy. 12 (Wayzata Boulevard), one mile east of I-494 in the western suburb of Minnetonka (tel. 922-1938), Ridgedale first opened in August 1974 with two anchor department stores, Dayton's and Donaldsons. Five months later J. C. Penney and Sears moved in as well. A cascading fountain stands among sheltering trees in the skylit center court. Four sections extend in a pinwheel pattern that contains more than 130 specialty shops representing national and local retailers. A sidewalk café is one of the 11 restaurants and snackbars here. Unlike many other suburban malls, Ridgedale contains a Woolworth's variety store. There's also a U.S. Post Office and an AT&T phone center, as well as medical and dental offices.

And a program sponsored by Methodist Hospital and Ridgedale Center enables "morning milers" to walk year round without concern for the weather. The center opens its doors to walkers at 7 a.m. Monday through Saturday and at 9 a.m. on Sunday.

BONAVENTURE: This small, picturesque shopping center (tel. 925-4321) is located adjacent to Ridgedale at Plymouth Road and Hwy. 12 (Wayzata Boulevard). There's no anchor department store at Bonaventure, but there is one of Leeann Chin's phenomenally popular Chinese buffets, and that may be just as good. Whatever the reason, this beautifully designed mall is a popular place, with its 40 specialty shops clustered around a fountain and glass elevator. Bonaventure is home to three restaurants, including Good Earth with its much-frequented wooden "pods," circular extensions that jut out over the court-yard of the second-story restaurant and provide prime viewing. The Ediner, famous for its hamburgers and malts, is the third in the trio of Twin Cities favorites that serve diners at Bonaventure.

There's a high concentration of women's fashions and accessories here, along with shops that feature classic and contemporary furnishings, toys, gifts, and artwork. Another popular feature here is the summer dining in the garden court.

BANDANA SQUARE: Situated north of I-94, between Snelling Avenue and Lexington, not far from Como Park and the State Fair Grounds, Bandana Square (tel. 642-1409) is an interesting blend of the old and the new. The buildings that house this St. Paul collection of specialty shops, eating places, and recreational areas are listed on the National Register of Historic Places. That's because these were previously the Como Shops, where Burlington Northern Railroad coaches and locomotives were maintained at the turn of the century, the period when railroading was a dominant force in the Midwest. Exposed beams, skylights, and even railroad tracks are reminders of those times, and serve as an interesting setting for more than 50 retail and dining places, and for the ambitious and highly appropriate project of the Twin City Model Railroad Club. In their own section of the upper level of Bandana Square, railroad-club members are re-creating the railroading era with what eventually will be 1,800 feet of track, accommodating four main lines on which ten model trains can travel at one time. This is, in fact, a popular parking place for fathers and their young, while the women of Twin Cities families make the rounds of shops that feature fashions, furnishings, and gifts, many of them appropriate souvenirs of Minnesota.

Outdoor dining and band concerts are popular warm-weather attractions at Bandana Square, and so is the nearby Children's Museum, also housed in a historic place that used to be a blacksmith shop.

ST. ANTHONY MAIN: The builders of St. Anthony Main, 201 Main St. SE, Minneapolis (tel. 379-4528), a popular shopping complex on the banks of the Mississippi, just five minutes away from downtown Minneapolis, opted for transformation rather than restoration back in 1974. Although the exteriors of these historic buildings look much as they did when they were turn-of-the-century warehouses, the interiors have been gutted and reconstructed. On view within are exposed wooden ceiling beams, sandblasted brick walls, strip maple flooring, and contemporary shops selling everything from sheepskin outerwear to silk underwear. And there's a good selection of truffles and writing paper, both sold by the pound.

There have been three additions to St. Anthony Main since the doors first opened in 1977, and each of the structures is somewhat different from the others. In some areas, shops are connected to one another by narrow, winding walkways, so you often find yourself surprised at what's around the next curve or corner. In the latest phase, though, portions of the interior were carved out to reveal a three-level open space, making it possible for shoppers to see where they're going as well as where they are. More than just a shopping center, St. Anthony Main houses three popular restaurants and plays host to annual events like the Main St. Jazz Festival, a happening that would have astonished Minneapolitans who frequented this part of town when this cobblestone riverfront thoroughfare really was the main street of Minneapolis. Just walking around here is fun, and spending money is fun as well.

RIVERPLACE: This shopping center, at Hennepin Avenue and Main Street (tel. 378-1969), shares the Mississippi banks with St. Anthony Main. Riverplace calls itself the Midwest's first mixed-use development, meaning that besides being a specialty center with restaurants and offices, it contains some of the most elegant and expensive housing in downtown Minneapolis. Condominiums and apartment houses adjoin the beautiful and festive complex where you'll find a succession of year-round events, from a Victorian Christmas to a springtime Mardi Gras and, for the first time during the summer of 1987, a musical theater presenting such favorites as *The Fantastiks, Dames at Sea,* and *Grease.*

Shopping here is varied, with one of the world's great bookstores, **Rizzoli** (tel. 331-2005), occupying three levels. You'll find rare books, fine art, unusual jewelry, foreign magazines, and videocassettes galore. And do take time to visit the **Afton Toy Shop** to see their endearing assortment of dolls and stuffed animals, plus games and a whole lot more.

CALHOUN SQUARE: Elsewhere, in the trendy Uptown section of Minneapolis, (also known as "Yuptown"), you'll find Calhoun Square at the corner of Hennepin Avenue and Lake Street (tel. 824-1240). This is a bustling two-story center where the shopping, dining, and people-watching are among the best anywhere. If the weather's warm, try for a sidewalk table outside **Figlio's,** the popular Italian restaurant recommended in Chapter IV. During recent years there's been a picturesque influx of punkers in this area, making Calhoun Square a place where punk hair is a center of interest among those who wear it and those who wonder why. Expect to see everything from mohawks to multicolored hairdos. But there's more to be found than that. **Hmong Folk Art** (tel. 825-9506) features the intricately fashioned needlework of the mountain people of Laos—expensive but worth it. There's also one of the cities' best bookstores, **Odegard Books** (tel. 825-0336). All in all there are more than 70 shops and restaurants here, including the **Ediner** (an upscale "diner") (tel. 822-6011) and **Tony Roma's** (tel. 824-RIBS). Get it?

Other Shopping Areas

GRAND AVENUE: This St. Paul specialty shopping and ethnic dining area has gained enormous popularity during recent years with young upwardly mobile professional types much like the ones who inhabit the Uptown area of Minneapolis. Turn-of-the-century residences abound here, many of them now serving as condominiums, town houses, and rental apartments.

How specialized are the specialty shops on Grand Avenue? Well, you'll find the **Balloon Bunch** here at 638 Grand Ave. (tel. 292-0289), where you can order balloons sent out singly or by the dozen(s). Or you can come in and pick out the balloon of your choice from a variety of sizes and colors. You can even have it personalized or inscribed with a significant message.

You probably won't be in town long enough to need the **Wedding Shop,** 1196 Grand Ave. (tel. 298-1144), but many local folks find this one-stop service invaluable, with absolutely everything taken care of, from selecting the invitations to videotaping the ceremony.

One of the Twin Cities' favorite markets is here on Grand Avenue too: **Crocus Hill Market,** 674 Grand Ave. (tel. 228-1761), with grocery shelves on one side and a meat showcase on the other. This might be the place to find some picnic provisions before an afternoon or evening at one of St. Paul's delightful parks.

If you'd rather dine out at one of Grand Avenue's many popular restaurants, try the informal **Café Latte,** 850 Grand Ave. (tel. 224-5983), famous for made-from-scratch soups, sandwiches, and desserts. And if it's Greek food you favor, the **Acropol** awaits at 748 Grand Ave. (tel. 298-0151), one of the most popular dining spots in either town.

There are four popular **shopping malls** on Grand Avenue: Victoria Crossing East, West and South, 857 Grand Avenue, and Milton Mall at Milton and Grand. That's where you'll find shops like **Old Mexico Shop** (tel. 293-3907), with lovely imports from across the Rio Grande, and the **Coat of Many Colors,** at 1666 Grand Ave. (tel. 690-5255), with some of the most unusual clothing around.

Whether or not you actually buy anything during your visit to Grand Avenue, the browsing is bound to be memorable.

THE CONSERVATORY: At 808 Nicollet Mall, Minneapolis, this remarkable new shopping center opened in the fall of 1987, and chances are you've never seen anything quite like it. Designed as a "20th-century public square," the Conservatory incorporates the activity outside the block-long building with the activity within. Passersby on the picturesque Nicollet Mall can glimpse two dramatic four-story glass atriums, two gracefully winding staircases, a succession of multistoried waterfalls, an abundance of decorative trees, a ground-floor dining court, and more. And at the same time, of course, the activity taking place on the Nicollet Mall is visible to those within.

Custom-made for the site it occupies, the Conservatory is designed as a conscious contrast with suburban malls, which generally would look out, if they could, on hundreds of cars in crowded parking lots. But here the decorative Nicollet Mall serves as a living mural for those looking out through the imported rose-colored glass walls of the Conservatory.

Connected by skyway and by underground "serpentine" to Dayton's, one of the city's première department stores, the Conservatory offers enticing wares of its own. Among the upscale retailers located here is the fabulous **F.A.O. Schwartz** toy store, a veritable wonderland for children and their elders. Another local firm that chose to locate at the Conservatory is **Frost and Bud,** a specialty gift shop well known to shoppers in fashionable Wayzata on Lake Minnetonka. What souvenirs you'll discover here! Want to take home a set of bocce balls, a sundial, or a personalized birdhouse? The Conservatory can offer you these—and a whole lot more.

OTHER SHOPPING AREAS: The opening of the Conservatory adds to the diversity of fine shops already located in downtown Minneapolis in nearby **City Center** and the **IDS Crystal Court,** as well as on the **Nicollet Mall.** St. Paul has its own array of fine shops at **Town Court, Town Square,** and **Carriage Hill,** where savvy shoppers find a lot to choose from.

And bargain hunters have their own special places, some of them already known beyond these borders. There's **Loehmann's** in suburban Bloomington (tel. 835-2510) for discount designer fashions, and the **Burlington Coat Factory** in St. Louis Park (tel. 929-6850) for a lot more than coats. You'll find a very wide variety of clothing for the whole family here, with periodic arrivals of ultrasuede apparel at very good prices.

A SPECIAL SUPERMARKET: Finally, you won't want to leave the Twin Cities without a visit to **Byerly's,** 3777 Park Center Blvd. in suburban St. Louis Park (tel. 929-2100), one of the world's most unusual supermarkets and, in fact, a self-contained shopping center par excellence.

Retailers from throughout the world travel to the Twin Cities regularly to tour the flagship of Don Byerly's local chain of eight supermarkets. What's all the fuss about? When you've seen one supermarket, haven't you seen them all? Not quite. In contrast with the usual supermarket, which carries 15,000 to 18,000 items, Byerly's carries over 25,000. And that includes everything from catsup for 25¢ to mustard for $25 (it's a French Dijon packaged in a ceramic jar, in case you're curious). That's not the only import here of course. There are some very special items in the Gift Gallery, where collectibles are available at prices ranging from $10 for small hand-carved wooden animals to $75,000 for a gold-plated six-foot-tall bird cage. Laliques and Hummels are sold here too; so are imported women's accessories by Judith Leiber, whose snakeskin belts go for $50 to $300.

Services as well as goods are available at Byerly's. Particularly popular is the on-site cooking school, with classes in everything from ethnic to microwave to couples' cooking. Other services include the opportunity to consult with representatives of the Hummel factory, who arrive from Germany about once each year for a week of demonstrations, with time out to appraise Hummel pieces that customers may already own.

News of these and other classes and services is published in the in-house publication called *Byerly's Bag.* Each month 75,000 of these are printed and left on racks near the entrances of the stores. They go fast.

How this all got started could hardly be a shorter, simpler story. Don Byerly decided in the late 1960s to find out what people liked and didn't like about shopping—and then to do something about it. Hence the 24-hour day at Byerly's, a store that's open at everybody's convenience. And hence the understated but very considerate touches: low lighting, wide carpeted aisles, on-site restaurants, and on-site delicatessens and salad bars for quick and easy food to go.

Whether you're seeking supplies for a lakeside picnic or a souvenir to take home from this visit to the Twin Cities, chances are you'll find just the thing at Byerly's. If not, mention it to a member of the staff. It'll be here by the time you come back.

Chapter XI

FESTIVALS AND FAIRS

WHAT'S SO AMAZING about the fairs and festivals in Minneapolis and St. Paul is the number that are record-breakers of one kind or another.

The Minneapolis Aquatennial, for example, is the largest summertime civic celebration in the United States. And the St. Paul Winter Carnival ranks first among the nation's annual salutes to winter.

The Minnesota State Fair, after more than 100 years, is still the largest 12-day fair in the United States, and after nearly 20 years, the Renaissance Festival is the country's largest.

Taste of Minnesota, born in 1983, is still a fledgling, but it, too, is well on its way to establishing its own national records.

Whatever the season, the fairs and festivals in the Twin Cities are perennially popular with home folks and visitors alike. You'll enjoy them too.

The Minnesota State Fair

For more than 100 years the annual Minnesota State Fairs have been identified with the city of St. Paul, but it wasn't always thus. These gala end-of-summer get-togethers began as Territorial Fairs that used to bring mid–19th-century farm families together to display their prize products and to enjoy final festivities before the long, cold winter set in.

The first official Minnesota State Fair was held in 1859, one year after Minnesota was officially named a state. For the next 25 years this annual event was moved from city to city until the Minnesota Agricultural Society, governing body of the Minnesota State Fair, began considering suggestions that a single permanent site be found.

Not surprisingly, it was the two largest and most influential cities, Minneapolis and St. Paul, that ended as finalists in the ensuing competition. A fierce battle burst out between the Twin

Cities and finally the issue was brought to the legislature, where oratory flourished while action stalled.

But back in those simpler times it was possible for the Ramsey County Board of Commissioners to hold a secret meeting with the State Agricultural Society and to make them an offer they couldn't refuse: St. Paul was willing to make a gift of its 200-acre Poor Farm to the society as a permanent home for the Minnesota State Fair. Of course the cost of maintaining the Poor Farm had become something of a burden, and many of the city fathers welcomed the chance to be rid of this nonproductive land that lay more than two miles from downtown, but these considerations apparently didn't come up during the discussions.

The Agricultural Society accepted St. Paul's offer without great objection from Minneapolis. After all, the Poor Farm was about equidistant from both downtowns, so if Minneapolis wasn't going to get the State Fair within its own city limits, neither was St. Paul—not then, at least.

By now St. Paul has expanded to the very edge of the State Fair site, as those early St. Paul commissioners must have expected it would. What they couldn't have expected is that one century later this would be the largest 12-day state fair in the country, and the model for all other festivals of its kind. Unlike most other fair sites, these grounds now extend over nearly 300 acres of well-kept lawns and trees, with large, spacious permanent buildings on paved streets that offer easy access to a great array of activities. And the fairgrounds offer a varied program of events, not just at Fair time but all year round.

Although any passing Minnesota schoolchild can tell you that the State Fair takes place at the end of summer, just before school vacation ends, had you visited the Twin Cities during the spring and summer of 1987, you could have attended a number of events there.

In May there was a model railroad hobby sale at the State Fairgrounds and a golfers' swap meet, a reining-horse show, a country folk-art show and sale, and a General Motors car display and swap.

June brought a personal electronics show and swap, the North-Central Morgan horse show, and the state Arabian horse show. Later in the month a gem fair attracted craftsmen and spectators in great numbers.

Fourth of July fireworks were featured in July, of course, and on August 21 the 1987 Minnesota State Fair got under way.

Many of the events at the Minnesota State Fair are, of course, farm related, and involve the judging of crops and livestock, but many others are of more general interest to nonfarming types, including those innocents who take it for granted that produce grows in supermarkets. For fair-goers of this type, the live entertainment in the Grandstand is probably one of the greatest attractions.

One of the very biggest changes in the activities at the Minnesota State Fair came about with the turn-of-the-century introduction of gas lighting. Now it was possible to extend events beyond daylight hours. Fireworks, vaudeville, and other forms of evening entertainment became an important part of the program then, and remain so to this day.

There are four stages on the fairgrounds, with daily free shows offering everything from comedy to mime to music to variety shows. And for an extra charge, the Grandstand features a galaxy of nationally known entertainers. Past performers include a *Who's Who* of contemporary entertainment: Bob Hope, Rodney Dangerfield, John Denver, Willie Nelson, Tom Jones, Huey Lewis, Alabama, and the Oak Ridge Boys, among many many others.

But the most consistently popular attractions at the fair involve exhibits. More than $400,000 in cash prizes lures entrants in a wide variety of competitions. The largest juried art show in the state takes place here each year, with winning works exhibited in the Fine Arts Building during the fair. Prizewinning works of needlecraft and carpentry are displayed in the Creative Activities Building, while outstanding school projects and technological exhibits can be seen in the Education Building.

One of the best-attended exhibitions during the past 50 years has been the one established by the Department of Natural Resources, which maintains a display of state minerals and animals in a giant log cabin.

Food is an important part of fair-going, of course—not only the hot dogs, french fries, snowcones, "Tom Thumb" minidonuts, and other goodies you get at busy concession stands, but the down-home meals available at dining halls staffed by various churches, where you can get a full dinner at very nominal cost. Many fair-goers bring their own picnic baskets along and take advantage of picnic facilities on the grounds.

The midway is a must, of course, and so is the chance to watch marching bands, floats, and parades pass by. If you prefer viewing motor sports, you'll enjoy the auto races or the truck-and-tractor pulls. And, of course, rodeos and horse shows are always well attended.

Maybe by now you're getting the idea that there's a lot to be seen and done at the Minnesota State Fair, but it's important to remember that first and foremost this is an event that salutes the agriculture of Minnesota. Take time to visit some of the prize-winning examples of the work being done by present and future farmers of Minnesota. They'll remind you how much we owe to an industry that's too often taken for granted.

The Minnesota State Fair is held midway between the downtowns of St. Paul and Minneapolis; take I-94 from either city to the Snelling Avenue exit and go north about half a mile. The festivities take place around the end of August and the very beginning of September, ending each year on Labor Day. It's traditionally regarded as the official end of summer in Minnesota. Admission to the fair is $3.50 for adults, $2 for children 5 to 15. There's no entrance charge for children under 5. Parking anywhere on the grounds is free. For information, phone 642-2200.

The St. Paul Winter Carnival

The oldest winter carnival in the United States came into being back in 1886 after a New York newspaperman published stories about his visit to the bone-chilling wasteland of wintry Minnesota. Far from dignifying these reports with a defense of the local climate, St. Paulites chose to organize a celebration of the fun to be found amid the snow and ice.

From this defiant beginning, the St. Paul Winter Carnival has grown into an exuberant 12-day annual festival that features more than 100 events including parades, snowtubing, hot-air-balloon rides, ice-carving contests, treasure hunts, and assorted team sports, from volleyball and touch football in the snow to softball, "snow golf," and auto racing on the ice. The specific dates of the frosty gala vary from year to year, but takes place roughly from the end of January through early February. Phone 297-6953 for carnival information.

Not all Winter Carnival events take place outdoors. In the massive St. Paul Civic Center you'll find a four-day event that's come to be called the carnival's "Indoor Fun Fair." A midway offers varied attractions including ferris wheels and tilt-a-wheels, and games of skill and chance, while in Lifestyle Lane browsers can examine a variety of products and services, with demonstrations of everything from computers to chiropractic. And if you're so inclined, you can have your hair cut in the latest fashion. Adults wearing a Winter Carnival button—available for $3 virtually everywhere in St. Paul during this period—pay an additional $3 to enter the Civic Center for this event; children 7 to 12 wearing a carnival button and accompanied by an adult are admitted free (no charge for children 6 and under).

Nearby, at the Roy Wilkins Auditorium, named for the St. Paulite who served as longtime head of the National Association for the Advancement of Colored People, musical entertainment is featured, much of it provided by notable local performers. One locally based artist created something of a stir when he made an unscheduled appearance in 1986. Prince apparently enjoyed what he saw, and remained long enough to greet his fans and play a few pieces for them.

Much of the merriment associated with the Winter Carnival centers around a mythology that's grown up to occupy center stage: the story of arch-enemies King Boreas and Vulcanus, God of Fire. Long ago, it seems, King Boreas, the monarch of the ice and snow, discovered a winter paradise called Minnesota. He made this lovely land his winter playground, but Vulcanus, God of Fire and arch-foe of Boreas, set out to melt the snow and ice that were needed for the joyous winter carnival presided over by Boreas and his lovely Queen of the Snows.

Finally, after ten days of frosty frolic, interrupted from time to time by the mischief-making of Vulcanus and his followers, the Queen prevailed upon Boreas to return to Olympus for a while until the developing warmth of spring and summer passed, and winter fun returned again.

Each year a prominent citizen of St. Paul is chosen to represent King Boreas, while candidates of St. Paul neighborhoods and companies vie to become Queen of the Snows. These royal figures rule over the myriad festivities and then set out to visit other festivals across the country and as far away as London. The announcement and coronation of King Boreas is a highlight of each year's Winter Carnival, and so is the selection of his queen. As well as the machinations of Vulcanus and his red-clad followers, who roar through the city in fire engines when they're not bursting into elegant balls and banquets to leave a spot of soot on the faces of women who fail to elude them.

It's estimated that 1.5 million people take part in the Winter Carnival each year, either as participants or as observers. Ice skaters glide across an illuminated rink in Rice Park or on Harriet Island, while dedicated nonskaters have a fine time in both locations watching the creation of exquisite snow-and-ice sculptures.

Two big parades draw enthusiastic crowds to downtown St. Paul during Winter Festival Week. The King Boreas Grand Day Parade weaves its way through the city accompanied by marching units and colorful floats. Each year a different national celebrity is chosen to serve as Grand Marshall of the parade; after a succession of TV and movie stars, the selection in 1986 was a pleasant change of pace when the parade was led by Ann Bancroft—not the movie star, but the St. Paul native who had recently become the first woman to reach the North Pole by dogsled.

Vulcan's Victory Torchlight Parade takes place on the final Saturday night of the carnival, which ends with a spectacular fireworks display that concludes the festivities until next year.

The Minneapolis Aquatennial

As St. Paul's Winter Carnival celebrates the wintertime fun to be enjoyed in the Twin Cities, the Minneapolis Aquatennial salutes the water-related activities that make summer such a festive time in Minnesota.

The fun gets underway during the third week in July each year with the downtown Grand Day Parade that features the antics of AquaJesters, an assemblage of 70 solid citizens who go into hiding once a year behind the traditional makeup and costumes of clowns. With more than 40 crowd-pleasing years to their credit, these zanies proceed by foot or skates or on bikes or other means of locomotion, delighting kids and their elders, many of whom bring along folding chairs for a comfortable view of the floats, bands, and marching groups.

A sampling of events during the 1987 festivities will give you an idea of the kinds of events that have led to the perennial popularity of this largest of American summer civic festivals.

Family Fun Day is a free ice-cream-and-cake social held on Nicollet Island on the edge of downtown Minneapolis. Musicians, mimes, jugglers, and other entertainers are on hand, and so are arts-and-crafts booths for grownups, and games and contests for children.

Sky of 10,000 Frisbees is a competition at Lake Nokomis among nationally ranked Frisbee players vying for the North American freestyle championship. A special category for novices is open to the rest of us.

Tug O'War, also at Lake Nokomis, is a contest that pits ten-person teams against each other; the danger of a mass dunking in the nearby lake seems not to frighten anyone.

The challenging **Aquatennial Triathlon** is held in a number of city parks and parkways, where 2,000 participants swim and bike and foot-race to the finish line.

The enormously popular **Youth Fishing Clinic** at Lake Calhoun provides children with free tackle and bait, and with instructions from fishing experts on how to keep that big one from getting away.

Elsewhere on Lake Calhoun, the **Sand Castle Sculpture Competition** divides beach sand into plots for teams of up to six people. Some of the castles and shapes and structures are remarkable, constructed with only the use of pails and wood and water.

The **Nicollet Mall Art Fair** generally offers more substantial artifacts—works of blown glass and batik, paintings and sculpture, and other forms displayed by craftspeople from across the nation.

And then there are the ever-popular **boating events**— everything from sailboards to sailboats to rowboats to the 17th annual milk-carton boat races.

And all of it comes to a rousing conclusion each year with a dazzling display of fireworks set off in downtown Minneapolis.

For **information** on Aquatennial events, call The Connection (a local advertiser-supported service) at 922-9000.

The Renaissance Festival

Have you been back to the 17th century recently? Thousands of Midwesterners have traveled back in time since 1971, starting season for the annual Renaissance Festival. By now this is the largest such festival in the country in terms of attendance and number of activities. It's also the largest in area—125 acres of farmland about four miles southwest of suburban Shakopee on Hwy. 169.

You'll be greeted at the banner-bedecked gates by costumed peasants, royals, and members of every social class in between. And you'll find more than 150 booths selling everything from pottery and jewelry to furniture and flowering plants.

When hunger pangs begin to gnaw, you can choose from a grand array of edibles, the most popular of which are enormous turkey legs which may or may not resemble food favorites of that day.

Visitors find themselves mingling with a variety of acrobats, magicians, jugglers, and jousters, and on eight separate stages there's nonstop entertainment by talented comics, musicians, and singers.

You'll see dancers here of all kinds—Scottish country dancers, Morris dancers, belly dancers. Yes, belly dancers are indeed on hand, as they reportedly were in England after the Crusaders returned home from their journey to recover the Holy Land for the faithful. While in the Middle East, these Crusaders encountered a wholly unfamiliar and exotic culture and brought back with them intriguing mementoes and reports of activities, some of which caught on at home.

Arabic numbers went over well in the West. So did falconry, a sport involving the use of specially trained hunting hawks. And so did a new kind of dancing by entertainers adept at moving muscles proper Britons didn't even know they had.

Actually we don't get to meet very many proper Britons at the Renaissance Festival. Most are bawdy Brits who engage in loud harangues with one another and even with modern-day passersby.

There seems to be a parade in progress nearly all the time, in addition to demonstrations and competitions that include such unlikely contests as human chess matches: living forms on a giant chess board, moving from one square to another on direction from wily chess masters.

The American Bus Association recently named Minnesota's Renaissance Festival among the top 100 events in North America, but visitors, performers, and craftspeople from all over the United States didn't need to be told that; they've been making their way here, summer after summer, since the very start of it all. There's truly never a dull moment at this annual celebration that helps wind up the summer season in a very merry way.

The Renaissance Festival takes place on weekends from mid-August through September each year. Gates open at 9 a.m. on Saturday and Sunday and close at 7 p.m. Admission at the gate is $10 for adults, $4 for children 6 to 12. There's no charge for children 5 and under.

Taste of Minnesota

The youngest and most surprising major festival in Minnesota dates back to 1983, when members of the St. Paul Downtown Council came up with an unlikely proposal—a Fourth of July celebration featuring food and fun in the shadow of the beautiful Minnesota State Capitol. It wasn't the setting of this proposed fête that was so surprising—it was the timing. Fourth of July weekend is traditionally the time when roads leading out of the cities are clogged with folks on their way "to the lake." (Somehow locals expect you to know which one of the more than 10,000 Minnesota lakes they're referring to.) Who'd be left to come to a festival in St. Paul? It seemed an impractical idea at best, but the planners went ahead anyway, on the premise that there must be plenty of people without a lake to call their own. How nice for them if the Capital City played host on our national holiday in a truly spectacular setting, when the weather's at its warm and sunny best.

The planners gambled that hundreds of people would be attracted by the prospect of browsing through dozens of crafts booths and would enjoy the chance to buy sample-size portions of specialties from the Twin Cities' most famous restaurants. An added attraction was free musical entertainment every day and evening, culminating in a Fourth of July appearance by the Minnesota Orchestra, whose performance in front of the State Capitol Building would conclude with a spectacular fireworks display.

The gamble paid off in a very big way. Nearly 250,000 people now come to the beautifully landscaped Capitol approach during the Fourth of July weekend to enjoy a down-home celebration that gets more popular year after year. Restaurants vie for the privilege of preparing and selling their samples on the premises in exchange for tickets that are purchased at booths throughout the grounds. Save your cash for the jewelry, leather goods, woodworking, pottery, metalwork, and other crafts you'll find here. To pay for food, you hand over the requisite number of 25¢ tickets from the $5 block you bought earlier at one of the booths on the grounds.

What kind of food will you find at Taste of Minnesota? Everything from gyros sandwiches to barbecued ribs to chicken nuggets on skewers to corn on the cob to cookies and cakes and soft drinks and wine and snowcones and Häagen-Dazs. And much of this is consumed by celebrants sitting on manicured lawns under graceful branches, watching performances on stages set up at strategic locations throughout the grounds. A main stage in front of the Capitol steps features different types of music each day: jazz and contemporary, oldtime rock and roll, country, and finally classical, via the stirring strains of the Minnesota Orchestra.

Children have an area and program of their own, and the number of beaming little faces with flowers, butterflies, and other colorful designs painted on them leaves no question as to which activity they enjoy the most.

What's best about Taste of Minnesota is that there's no after-taste of commercialism here. You can spend a delightful day or evening enjoying the surroundings and the entertainment without spending a penny. And that's particularly nice on this particular holiday. It shouldn't cost money to celebrate our country's birthday and our own good fortune in living here.

Chapter XII

TWIN CITIES GETAWAYS

THERE'S SO MUCH TO SEE and do in the Twin Cities that you could spend your entire Minnesota stay just getting acquainted with Minneapolis and St. Paul. If time permits, though, you might want to see for yourself some of the places that lure local folks out of town for weekend excursions. Actually, historic Stillwater is close enough for a one-day shopping and dining getaway. Rochester, home of the famous Mayo Clinic, is close enough for a 90-minute drive, a bit of sightseeing, and a return on the same day. For the Rivertown rambles, though, or a visit to Duluth, you'll probably want to set aside at least one night, maybe more. In any case, these excursions will give you an idea of the diversity to be found in marvelous Minnesota.

Stillwater

This is where it all began. It was on August 28, 1848, that 61 delegates gathered in Stillwater to draft a petition asking Congress and President James J. Polk for the "early organization of the Territory of Minnesota." On March 3 of the following year, under the sponsorship of Sen. Stephen A. Douglas, the bill was passed and the rest, as they say, is history.

Nestled in the picturesque St. Croix River Valley, Stillwater today is as readily reached by boat as by car, and during the summertime pleasure craft from throughout Minnesota and nearby Wisconsin, just across the St. Croix River, occupy the docks that are located a block or two from the city's main street. The St. Croix River has been an important factor in Stillwater's commercial and recreational well-being since the early 19th century when logs from the area's bountiful forests were floated down the river to distant lumber mills and markets. In 1904,

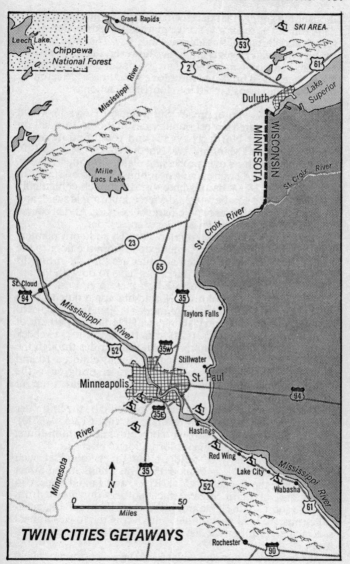

TWIN CITIES GETAWAYS

though, the supply that had seemed virtually inexhaustible finally ran out as the last log drive marked the exhaustion of the forests and the end of this lucrative industry. The spirit of 19th-century Stillwater lives again today, however, thanks to an ambitious restoration program that got under way during the 1970s when aged brick and limestone structures were carefully renovated and transformed into tourist attractions.

ATTRACTIONS: As you approach Stillwater on Hwy. 36, you'll pass one of the area's most popular destinations. Turn left on Manning Avenue North (Hwy. 15) and you'll find **Aamodt's Apple Farm,** 6428 Manning Ave. North (tel. 439-3127), a 180-acre orchard with its own processing plant, gift shops, bakery, and lunchroom. A large carving of Johnny Appleseed stands in the renovated 1800s barn, where visitors munch contentedly on apple-related goodies—apple-cheese soup, apple salad, and most popular of all, giant apple-oatmeal cookies. And of course they're washing it all down with tasty apple cider.

Antique scythes, rakes, wooden shovels, and corn planters hang from the wooden joists that extend from the floor to the beamed ceiling. Apple-related antiques are for sale in the gift shop, but the most popular purchases have to do with the apples that are grown and processed on these premises. Try the popular Haralson, an oldtime Minnesota apple noted for its tart crispiness. At this writing, Aamodt's is open from August to March, with cross-country skiing available through 30 km of groomed tracked ski trails. (Call from the Twin Cities to check on the hours.) Weekend horse-drawn trailer rides through the orchards are popular at $2 for adults, $1 for children 10 and younger. If you're lucky enough to be here in spring, enjoy the visual and aromatic pleasure of apple-blossom time at Aamodt's.

Once you get to town, your first stop should be the **Stillwater Chamber of Commerce,** 423 S. Main St. (tel. 612/439-7700). You'll find maps here, along with brochures about mini-tours, lodgings, antiques, and other information of interest.

There's a diversity of outdoor fun to be found at such Stillwater picnic sites as **Pioneer Park,** on a bluff at 2nd Street overlooking the scenic St. Croix River, and **Lowell Park,** two blocks east of Main Street, which borders downtown from north to south. In the large amphitheater at Pioneer Park, musical events are held all summer, and during the town's annual spectacular, Lumberjack Days, local talent shows are presented too.

At Lowell Park during **Lumberjack Days**—customarily held

the third weekend of each July—you'll be able to watch a variety of lumber-related entertainments including log-rolling, tree climbing, and cross-chop-sawing demonstrations by professional lumberjacks. On Sunday the festivities end with a grand parade that features marching and musical groups from all over the state. Downtown store windows are customarily decorated with historical artifacts during Lumberjack Days.

On July 19, 1987, the **Minnesota Zephyr** made its inaugural run from the old depot at 601 N. Main St. and promptly became one of Stillwater's most popular dining and sightseeing attractions. Passengers board these meticulously restored 1949 dining cars for a three-hour "travel back in time" that carries them through some of the most beautiful landscape in Minnesota. You'll pass the meandering St. Croix River on one side and picturesque limestone river bluffs on the other, then make your way through forests in which maple, ash, oak, walnut, white birch, and other state trees abound. An abundance of sumac, wildflowers, and lacy ferns cover the forest floor.

The taped dinner music and the authentic decor will put you so much in mind of the late 1940s that you may find yourself startled to see an occasional '80s automobile whizzing by or idling near the railroad track, waiting for the *Zephyr* to pass by. (The entire journey proceeds at about five miles per hour and takes about 3¼ hours.)

The delightful four-course dinner service begins with chicken-and-wild-rice soup, followed by green salad, and your choice of prime rib, filet of swordfish, or chicken Kiev, served with vegetable, potato or rice, and hot bread sticks. And finally there's excellent cheesecake along with coffee or tea. You can have pre- and post-dinner libations brought to your table, or you can enjoy them in one of the beautifully restored Vista-Dome club cars, each with its own bar.

The cost of this visit to the past is $42.50 per guest, with one glass of wine included in the price of the meal; cocktails and gratuity are not included. In late summer 1987 a luncheon schedule was introduced, featuring a lighter menu at $36.50 per guest. And by spring 1988 both a new depot and a railroading museum will be on site further to enhance this very welcome addition to the many attractions of historic Stillwater.

For reservations and further information, call 430-3000, a local phone call from Minneapolis and St. Paul.

SHOPPING: Browsing and buying, popular pastimes in Stillwater, are especially enjoyable because so many of the stores are located in historic structures. On Main Street you'll find an assemblage of fine specialty shops in a complex called the **Grand Garage and Gallery,** 324 S. Main St. This was the Stillwater Motors Building when it first opened in the 1880s. Now among its occupants is the charming **Kmitch Girls Shop** (tel. 430-1827), which features not only dolls, but a delightful collection of cats, dogs, and teddy bears as well. At the **Brick Alley Mall,** 423 S. Main St., two 19th-century structures, separated by an old alley, have been connected by an enclosed walkway. Here, among other interesting shops, you'll find **St. Croix Knits,** 423 S. Main St. (tel. 439-9120), which offers the makings of everything from coats and jackets to swing sets and musical instruments.

Elsewhere in town, **Tamarack House Galleries,** 236 S. Main St. (tel. 439-9393), attracts art collectors from throughout the Midwest, while sweater and outerwear collectors have a fine time in another restored building where the **Winona Knitting Mills Factory Outlet,** 215 S. Main St. (tel. 430-1711), offers a wide selection of apparel at prices about 30% to 50% lower than in department and specialty shops. (The only items that aren't made in America are the genuine Icelandic sweaters, jackets, and accessories available here.) At the other end of Main Street you'll find a collectors' delight, **Staples Mill Antiques,** 410 N. Main St. (tel. 439-8674), a complex which accommodates more than 30 dealers and craftspeople in a converted 19th-century sawmill. And at the **Old Post Office Shops,** 220 E. Myrtle St. (tel. 430-1431), across from the famous Lowell Inn, you can browse among a variety of shops for gifts, many of them handcrafted, to bring back home as souvenirs.

WHERE TO STAY: The **Lowell Inn,** 102 N. 2nd St., Stillwater, MN 55082 (tel. 612/439-1100), offers by far the most famous accommodations in Stillwater. A beautiful three-story structure with large white columns, arched windows, and during the summer months, a comfortably furnished veranda, it offers 25 lovely guest rooms. This "Mount Vernon of the West" was first opened in 1930 by a handsome and enterprising theatrical couple, Arthur and Nelle Palmer, whose experiences on tour had taught them a thing or two about how hotels should be run. They envisaged an elegant establishment offering impeccable service, and the reputation of their Lowell Inn has more than fulfilled that dream. Today their son, Art, his wife, Maureen, and a third generation of hoteliers are carrying the tradition forward. Sumptuously furnished with a mixture of French provincial and Victorian reproductions and antiques, these romantic rooms are much in demand by couples who find this the the perfect place for an anniversary celebration. Others favor the Lowell Inn as a relaxed and elegant getaway. In fact the demand is so great that you might have trouble getting a room here, so do call ahead for reservations. Rates range from $79 to $129 per night depending on the room's size, location, and accoutrements. Four of the rooms have Jacuzzis (presumably these don't date back to the 18th century); one room has its own adjoining living room, and one boasts a shower-in-the-round, with fixtures imported from Italy.

Just minutes away from Stillwater, about 12 miles south on Hwy. 95, you'll find the delightful **Afton House,** 3291 S. St. Croix Trail, Afton, MN 55001 (tel. 612/436-8883). On the banks of the St. Croix River, the inn's 12 guest rooms have been furnished individually with antiques that include trundle beds, clipper chairs, and English armoires. Four of the rooms have small private balconies, with a larger one available to all guests. Rates range from $42 to $65 during the winter, $50 to $110 during the summer. Roll-aways are available at $8, and portacribs are provided without charge.

At the **Stillwater Inn Motel,** 1750 W. Frontage Rd., Stillwater, MN 55082 (tel. 612/430-1300), you'll find more modest but very pleasant accommodations ranging in price from $33 to $42, with larger rooms that offer waterbeds and sitting areas ranging from $39 for one to $57 for four. All prices include a free continental breakfast.

WHERE TO DINE: A block off Main Street, overlooking the St. Croix River, you can while away your time at the **Freight House Restaurant,** 435 S. Water St. (tel. 439-5718). This building, listed on the National Register of Historic Places, used to be occupied by an old railroad company, and the large picture windows that now provide diners with a panoramic view of the St. Croix River were guillotine doors back when lumber and mill products were being shipped nationwide from this Stillwater terminal. Prices here are moderate, with lunch ranging from $6 for salads, sandwiches, and hamburgers to $7 for the popular prime rib sandwich. Barbecued ribs at $11 remain a long-time favorite for dinner, with other a la carte entrees ranging from $10 to $13. Wintertime hours, usually from November 1 to March 1, are 11 a.m. to 4 p.m. for lunch, 4 p.m. to 10 p.m. for dinner Friday and Saturday, and 11 a.m. to 8 p.m. on Sunday with the lunch menu in effect the entire time. During the rest of the year, hours are 11 a.m. to 10 p.m. Sunday through Thursday, 11 a.m. to 11 p.m. Friday and Saturday.

Vittorio's, 402 S. Main St. (tel. 439-3588), features tasty northern Italian food in a large restaurant with four dining rooms and a lounge where a 19th-century brewery once stood. In fact, if you dine in the most elegant room of all, the Blue Grotto, you can look through a window in the original limestone wall and see part of a network of storage caves that were dug by hand during the early 1840s. Popular dinner entrees, served here with antipasto salad and garlic toast, include ravioli carne (meat-filled pasta prepared with the house red sauce) at $9.50 and pollo alla cacciatore (chicken sautéed in wine, and served with a portion of baked canelloni rossi) at $11.75. In the front dining room, you can enjoy a wide variety of homemade pizza and pasta specialties ranging from $4.75 for spaghetti with white sauce to $17 for a large Vittorio's special pizza, topped with a mixture of cheese, sausage, pepperoni, green olives, green pepper, and onion. Open for lunch from 11 a.m. to 3 p.m. daily; for dinner, from 3 to 11 p.m. Sunday through Thursday, to midnight on Friday and Saturday.

In what used to be an 1860s general store, **Brine's Old Fashioned Meats,** at 219 S. Main St. (tel. 439-7556), offers first-floor grocery shopping with informal dining on the second floor. Old-world delicatessen items along with hamburgers and milkshakes are the specialties of the house.

But the most celebrated dining in Stillwater is still to be found at the **Lowell Inn,** 102 N. 2nd St. (tel. 439-1100), which attracts diners from throughout the state. In the comfortable cocktail lounge you can await your table in one of the three dining rooms. The George Washington Room is elegant, with its Capi di Monte porcelain, Sheffield silver, Dresden china, and antique sideboards. In the Matterhorn Room, notable for its acid-etched stained-glass windows, you'll find authentic Swiss carvings dominated by a formidable life-size carved eagle. And in the Garden Room, with its indoor trout pool, you can eat your entree just a little while after you fish for it. The Matterhorn Room features a beef-and-shrimp fondue dinner with a European wine-tasting for $75 per couple; the George Washington Room and the Garden Room have the same varied American menu, with dinner ranging from $18 for sautéed chicken livers to $27 for lobster tail. Lunch and dinner hours vary from room to room, so phone ahead for specifics and reservations.

Just minutes away from downtown Stillwater, the **Afton House,** 3291 S. St. Croix Trail, in Afton (tel. 436-8883), with three dining rooms of its own, is accessible by road and by river. Close enough to the Twin Cities to make it a special dinner destination, this beautiful inn, now on the National Register of Historic Places, caters to a wide variety of patrons throughout the year. Skiers from nearby Afton Alps make this a mandatory stop during the winter months. And during the summer, boaters tie up at the on-site dock.

Look for the unique carvings throughout the dining rooms and bar, done by the late Elmo "The Builder" Erickson, whose talent and sense of humor are best expressed in the Erickson Room, where you get an underwater view of the world, with the legs and bare feet of a fisherman extending downward from the ceiling while a wary fish swims by.

Proprietor-manager Gordy Jarvis had been a chef at a number of fine Twin Cities restaurants before he and his wife, Kathy, bought the Afton House in 1976. Three meals a day are available here, with early-bird breakfast specials ranging from $2 for two eggs, toast, and coffee, to $5 for steak, eggs, hashbrowns, and toast. In the elegant Wheel Room, dinner favorites include steak Diane garnished with fresh vegetables, and poached salmon served with champagne sauce. Dinner prices range from $11 to $18; for lunch your tab will be somewhere around $3 to $7. The Catfish Salon features a variety of burgers, sandwiches, and two much-requested soup selections: a thick, rich seafood chowder and a savory chili. Breakfast is served at the Afton House only on Saturday, from 8 a.m. to 11 a.m., and brunch on Sunday from 10 a.m. to 2 p.m. Lunch is served Monday through Saturday from 11:30 a.m. to 2:30 p.m. Dinner is served seven nights a week, from 5 p.m. to 10 p.m. Monday through Thursday; 5 p.m. to 11 p.m. Friday and Saturday; and 3:30 p.m. to 10 p.m. Sunday.

Taylors Falls

For a view of the St. Croix River Valley, follow Hwy. 95 from Stillwater. Drive past lush farmlands, magnificent bluffs, and dramatic waterways until you reach Taylors Falls, nestled on the northern end of the 900-acre Interstate Park that extends from one side of the St. Croix to the other and includes within its scope the towns of St. Croix Falls, Wisconsin, and Taylors Falls, Minnesota. (This was the first interstate park ever established in the United States.)

ATTRACTIONS: Taylors Falls is famous for its hiking, camping, boating, and swimming, as well as for the catfish, smallmouth bass, northerns, and walleyes to be caught here. But perhaps this area's greatest claim to fame derives from potholes and log jams, reputedly the largest in the world. You can see for yourself an enormous pothole, more than 60 feet in depth, which was created out of volcanic rock during the meltdown of ancient glaciers. No remnants of the great Taylors Falls log jam remains, but the memory lingers on of those months in 1886 when lack of rain made it impossible for logging companies to float white pine downriver to the sawmills at Osceola. Huge piles of logs accumulated on the riverbanks and finally, when heavy rains did begin to fall, there was a mad dash by loggers to get the wood on its way. Unfortunately, though, the St. Croix River narrows and then bends just below Taylors Falls; that's where a log jam developed that eventually reached a height of 30 feet and a length of more than two miles. It took until the following spring before the jam was completely cleared, long enough for it to have become a tourist attraction in its own day and a legend in ours.

Another tie with the past is Taylors Falls' famous **historic residential area** where 19th-century homes and churches have been carefully preserved. One of them might be of special interest to you.

WHERE TO STAY: The **Taylors Falls Jail,** 102 Government Rd., Taylors Falls, MN 55084 (tel. 612/465-3112), now a unique two-story guesthouse, started life as the lockup for unruly locals and still has bars on its windows, but in recent years it's welcomed some very estimable citizens indeed. The jail's outside appearance was restored after consultation with the Historic Preservation Office of the Minnesota Historical Society. Its interior has been turned into a comfortably furnished living room, well-equipped modern kitchen and bathroom, and a loft bedroom far cosier than anything oldtime prisoners ever enjoyed. In fact, at certain times of year you'll need a reservation to spend the night in jail. Taylors Falls Jail offers a weekend package for two guests—$110 for two nights, with a third night free. During the week the rate is $55 per night for two guests, with a $5 per night fee for each additional guest. Also, provisions are left for you in the refrigerator so that you can do your own cooking at your convenience.

A pleasant, economical, and centrally located alternative to the hoosegow can be found at the **Springs Inn,** one block west of the junction of Hwys. 8 and 95 (P.O. Box 11) Taylors Falls, MN 55084 (tel. 612/465-6565), which features a popular hot tub and Jacuzzi, housed in an adjoining geodesic dome. Basic rates here range from $32 for a room with one double bed to $38 for a studio kitchenette. There's a $4 surcharge on weekends, a $5 surcharge for a roll-away, and a $3 surcharge for a crib.

Rochester

Rochester, Minnesota, about 80 miles south of the Twin Cities, may be the most cosmopolitan community of its size in the entire country. That's because nearly a quarter of a million visitors from throughout the world arrive here each year to visit the famous Mayo Clinic.

The pleasant drive to Rochester from the Twin Cities takes you along Hwy. 52 through some of the state's loveliest rolling countryside and luxuriant farmland. If you'd prefer to leave the driving to Greyhound (tel. 371-3320 or 222-0509) or Trailways Bus Lines (tel. 332-3273 or 228-0681), the fare each way for the two-hour trip will be about $10. Northwest Airlines (tel. 726-1234) has a 30-minute flight from the Twin Cities to Rochester, with prices ranging from $42 to $90 each way.

THE MAYO CLINIC: With a staff of more than 800 physicians, surgeons, and medical scientists, in addition to 1,500 medical trainees and more than 5,000 paramedical personnel, the Mayo Clinic, 200 1st St. SW (tel. 507/284-2511), is the largest and probably the most prestigious group medical practice in the world. It also maintains the largest graduate school of medicine in the world, with an international student body that adds further to the cosmopolitan atmosphere in Rochester.

How did so famous a medical complex happen to develop in a small midwestern city? The story began back in 1883, when a devastating tornado struck this obscure farming community, leaving 26 people dead and the entire northern part of the town demolished.

Dr. William Worral Mayo was a local English-born physician who had practiced in Rochester for 20 years, after first coming here as an examining surgeon for the Union Army Enrollment Board. After the tornado struck, he worked with other Rochester doctors and with the nuns from the Convent of Saint Francis to treat the injured, but their efforts were severely hampered by the lack of adequate medical facilities.

Shortly after the disaster, the Mother Superior at the convent suggested to Dr. Mayo that he head the medical staff of a hospital which the sisters were planning to build and maintain. At first reluctant, Dr. Mayo agreed, although he knew that hospitals then were frightening to the public, who viewed them as places where people went to die. Physicians were leery of hospitals too, it seems. When St. Mary's Hospital was opened in 1889, other local doctors refused to associate with it, leaving Dr. Mayo and his two physician sons, Will and Charlie, to serve as the entire medical staff.

Both Drs. Will and Charlie had been trained in the antiseptic methods introduced by Joseph Lister, and both began to practice the relatively new field of surgery as staff members of St. Mary's Hospital. Word soon got around that patients suffering from chronic ailments like ulcers, appendicitis, and gallstones were being made well again, quickly and permanently, by these young physicians.

Even as patients in Minnesota helped spread the word about Drs. Will and Charlie Mayo, physicians from around the country and even from Europe began coming to Rochester to see for themselves the kind of work that the young Mayos had described at medical meetings and had written about in medical journals.

By the mid-1890s their growing practice made it necessary for the Drs. Mayo to enlarge their medical staff, and by 1914 they opened a building which they called the Mayo Clinic. The group medical practice they established then was unique in those days because it provided for a sharing of knowledge among a group of medical specialists for the purpose of promoting more comprehensive care for patients. That remains the practice and the purpose of the Mayo Clinic to this day.

WHERE TO STAY: Should you decide to stay the night in Rochester, you'll have a wide choice of accommodations in this city that prides itself on making visitors feel at home.

Some of the most famous names in the world have been registered at Rochester's 720-room **Kahler Hotel,** 20 Second Ave. SW, Rochester, MN 55902 (tel. 507/282-2581, or toll free 800/ 533-1655). Elegant enough for the most festive of getaways, this hotel serves primarily as a comfortable home away from home for those who have come to Rochester to visit the Mayo Clinic.

Accommodations here are comfortable and cheery, nearby medical facilities notwithstanding. Rates range from $40 for a room for one with one double bed to $110 for a room for two with two double beds. Suites are available for $325 to $815 a night. (It was presumably a suite that was occupied by the Saudi Arabian princess who lived at the Kahler for nearly a year.) Along with fine restaurants (see my dining recommendations) and shops, the Kahler offers a domed recreation center with swimming pool, sauna, and whirlpool.

The Mayo Clinic and the Kahler Hotel are very careful to protect the privacy of the hotel's visitors to Rochester, but word does get around town when celebrities like Lady Bird Johnson, Bill Cosby, or Jim Nabors check in. And then there was the genial old gentleman whose daily greeting to fellow patrons in the Kahler Coffee Shop was, "Hi. I'm Johnny Carson's father." And he was.

Another property with connections to the Mayo Clinic is the more modest 142-room **Clinic View Inn,** 9 Third Ave. NW, Rochester, MN 55901 (tel. 507/289-8646). Rates here range from $44 to $54 for rooms with private baths; for accommodations that include kitchenettes, you'll pay $57 for a single, $67 for a double, with a $5 charge for each additional person.

A recent and very welcome addition to available accommodations in Rochester is the city's very first bed-and-breakfast. Located just three blocks from the Mayo Clinic, the **Canterbury Inn,** 723 2nd St. SW, Rochester MN 55902 (tel. 507/289-5553), is a restored three-story Victorian home which offers four double-bedded guest rooms, each of which has a private bath with both shower and tub. A fireplace for wintertime guests and a cool, shady porch for summertime visitors provide a cozy atmosphere, as do the abundance of turn-of-the-century furnishings. Adding to the warmth is the gracious welcome you'll receive from proprietors Mary Martin and Jeffrey Van Sant. Word is spreading too about the gourmet cooking at the Canterbury Inn. Breakfast is likely to include such items as wild-rice waffles, Norwegian fruit soup, Grand Marnier French toast, or fresh pears poached in sherry, served either downstairs in the comfortable dining room or upstairs in the guests' own rooms. King-size, queen-size, and twin beds are available. Rates are $65 per day double occupancy, $55 per day single.

WHERE TO DINE: You won't find a more elegant setting for a memorable dinner than the famous **Elizabethan Room** at the Kahler Hotel, 20 Second Ave. SW (tel. 282-2581). The coats-of-arms on dark paneled walls, the stained-glass panels, red velvet hangings, and large, double-tiered wrought-iron chandeliers give a majestic ambience to this handsome room. A romantic air is provided by the Elizabethan Strings, strolling violinists who make a lovely musical contribution to your dining pleasure. The irresistible blend of impeccable service and fine fare—for example, breast of chicken at $12.25 or rack of lamb for two at $35—make for a terrific evening out. The Elizabethan Room is open for lunch Monday through Friday from 11:30 a.m. to 2 p.m., and for dinner Monday through Friday from 5:30 to 9 p.m., on Saturday from 6 to 10 p.m.; Sunday brunch is on from 10 a.m. to 2:30 p.m.

The adjoining Lord Essex Room is a perfect complement to the Elizabethan Room. Similar in decor but smaller in size, the Lord Essex Room provides a delightfully intimate setting. Primarily a cocktail lounge, the Lord Essex becomes a small dining room during the Elizabethan Room's elaborate Sunday brunch. Overflow brunchers are directed to the Lord Essex Room, a very pleasant alternative indeed!

If you're interested in another cocktail lounge, try the Kahler's Penthouse, a delightful retreat where you can sink into overstuffed chairs amid towering plants with a commanding view of the city. And there's a third bar down on street level in the Greenhouse, with a terrarium, an aquarium, an oversize TV screen, and 2,000 hanging plants, all of them for sale.

A new restaurant here has quickly gained a popular following. Rochester's first Japanese restaurant, **Sakura,** at 848 S. Broadway (tel. 228-2771), is housed in an unprepossessing building at the edge of a small shopping center. A great favorite among Japanese personnel of both the Mayo Clinic and IBM, the city's other major employer, Sakura is decorated with large portraits of Kabuki actors and has adopted the practice of serving complimentary tea, as is the custom in Japan.

A wide assortment of appetizers ranges in price from $1.75 for sliced avocado with green mustard to $4.25 for shrimp-and-vegetable tempura. You'll find tempura listed as an entree too, along with sukiyaki, yosenabe (mixed chunks of seafood and vegetables cooked in a special soup), and specialties like salmon teriyaki, beef teriyaki, and deep-fried pork cutlets. Although there's a separate menu for lunch and dinner, prices and selections are pretty much the same, with entrees ranging from $5 to $10. Lunch boxes are available for $4 to $6.

Sakura is open Tuesday through Friday from 11:30 a.m. to 2 p.m. for lunch, from 5 to 9:30 p.m. for dinner. Hours on Saturday and Sunday are 11:30 a.m. to 9:30 p.m. The restaurant is closed on Monday.

WHAT TO SEE AND DO: Many of the tourist attractions in Rochester are related to the **Mayo Clinic,** a complex of buildings which extends over a seven-block area of downtown Rochester. Free tours of the impressive clinic facilities are available from 10 a.m. to 2 p.m. Monday through Friday.

The **Mayo Medical Museum,** open free to the public, offers a variety of films and videotapes as well as exhibits which enable visitors to examine the human body and its functions, to learn about some of the illnesses and injuries that pose a threat around the world, and to learn about some of the methods by which the medical profession deals with these problems. Hours are Monday through Friday from 9 a.m. to 9 p.m., on Saturday to 5 p.m., and on Sunday from 1 to 5 p.m.

Perhaps the most beloved local attraction in downtown Rochester is the **Rochester Carillon,** in the tower of the Plummer Building. This set of 56 stationary bells of various sizes, sounded with levers pressed by a carillonneur's fist, was bought by Dr. Will Mayo during a trip to Europe in the 1920s. Capable of covering a range of 4½ octaves, it's the most complete carillon in North America. Concerts are offered at 7 p.m. on Monday and at noon on Wednesday and Friday. Additional recitals are held on holidays and for special events.

Mayowood, the splendid home of two generations of the Mayo family, was built in 1911 by Dr. Charles H. Mayo. He and his wife, Edith, brought up four daughters and two sons in this large, gracious home. Later, Dr. Charles (Chuck) W. Mayo, his wife, Alice, and their four sons and two daughters resided here. Perched on 3,000 acres overlooking the Zumbro River Valley, Mayowood has welcomed such famous figures as Helen Keller, Franklin D. Roosevelt, and Adlai Stevenson. Over 38 rooms are furnished in American, English, French, Spanish, and Italian antiques. There are also less imposing evidences of the personal tastes of a family to whom Mayowood was not a showplace but a home. The only way to get to Mayowood is via an Olmstead County Historical Society shuttle bus; phone 282-9447 for information concerning tours.

Another popular home tour is offered at the **Plummer House,** 1091 Plummer Lane (tel. 281-6182), once the residence of Dr. Henry Plummer. Dr. Plummer joined the Mayo Clinic staff in 1901, and he is credited with having devised the pneumatic tube and the clinic's remarkable communication and record-keeping systems. When he and his family moved into this Tudor-style mansion in 1924, they were the first in the area to make use of natural gas and the first to have burglar alarms. It's still notable for its exquisite rose garden and for its 11 acres of parkland, open to the public throughout the year from sunrise to sunset. House tours are available, June through August, on Wednesday from 1 to 7 p.m. at $1 per adult and 50¢ per child or student; children under 5 are admitted without charge.

Perhaps the unlikeliest of all clinic-related attractions in Rochester are the hordes of giant **Canadian geese** that winter here each year. They were first attracted by a flock of 12 large brethren donated by a grateful patient in 1947 and released in Silver Lake Park, at North Broadway and 13th Street. The following year, Rochester's new power plant began using Silver Lake for cooling water, with the result that the lake remained free of ice throughout the winter. The Canadian geese stayed on that winter—and ever since. Now numbering in the tens of thousands, these amiable birds are welcomed in Rochester by human friends of all ages, who bring them breadcrumbs, popcorn, and other goodies. Silver Lake Park has more than geese to offer, though. Paddleboats and canoes can be rented during the warmer months, and picnicking is popular then too.

Other outdoor activities can be enjoyed on the city's six 18-hole golf courses and 30 outdoor tennis courts. There's a popular nine-mile nature trail here as well. For **sports information,** phone 289-7414.

Cultural attractions in Rochester include the fine **Rochester Art Center,** 320 E. Center St. (tel. 282-8629), open Tuesday through Saturday from 10 a.m. to 5 p.m., and the highly regarded **Rochester Symphony Orchestra,** 109 City Hall, 200 First Ave. SW (tel. 285-8976).

River Towns

Follow the Mississippi south from the Twin Cities and you'll find a succession of quaint river towns that retain much of the architecture and atmosphere of bygone days.

Combine the historical interest of this area with the natural beauty of the surrounding Hiawatha Valley, then add the unique attractions each community has to offer, and you'll see why Hastings, Red Wing, Lake City, and Wabasha are popular Twin Cities getaways for a day, an evening, a weekend, or longer.

HASTINGS: Just 25 miles from the Twin Cities, Hastings was one of the earliest river towns in Minnesota. A trading post was established here as early as 1833 and the town was incorporated in 1857. Three rivers—the Mississippi, the St. Croix, and the Vermillion—made Hastings readily accessible to other markets, and the spectacular Vermillion waterfalls provided power for the mills that made this one of the great wheat centers of the Northwest.

Attractions

Today, there are 61 buildings in Hastings that have been listed on the National Register of Historic Places. The newest of these is a contemporary work by Frank Lloyd Wright, who in 1957–1959 built the dramatic **Fasbender Medical Clinic** at the southeast corner of Hwy. 55 and Pine Street. Situated on land that blends into an adjacent park, the clinic, which is largely submerged in the ground, is readily identified by its folded roof.

As part of the National Trust program known as "Main Street," all of downtown Hastings has been designated a historic district. See the helpful **Hastings Chamber of Commerce**, at 220 Sibley St. (tel. 612/437-6775), for a handy guide to use on your own walking-tour of these fascinating buildings, foremost among them the **Le Duc–Simmons Mansion**, 1629 Vermillion St. (Hwy. 61). This imposing limestone structure, with its pointed arched windows, high tower, and intricate scrollwork, dates back to 1856.

The **Alexis Bailly Vineyard**, 18200 Kirby Ave. (tel. 437-1413), was founded in 1973 and has since won more than a dozen awards from Wineries Unlimited, an international competition involving wineries all over the United States and Canada. From June through October the winery is open to the public from noon to 5 p.m. Friday through Sunday. And in fact individuals and small groups are welcome to walk through the vineyards and to sample and purchase wines anytime during working hours. By the way, it was the original Alexis Bailey who selected the site for the trading post that would one day develop into the town of Hasting.

The **Carpenter St. Croix Valley Nature Center**, 12805 St. Croix Trail (tel. 437-4359), conducts a number of programs, including the rehabilitation of raptors (birds of prey such as bald eagles and hawks), the banding of birds, and the maintenance of orchards, in addition to maple syruping in the spring, organic gardening in the summer, and animal tracking in the winter. The center is open to the public on the first and third Sunday of the month.

Food and Lodging

Perhaps the best-known restaurant in Hastings is the **Mississippi Belle**, 101 E. 2nd St. (tel. 437-5694), a replica of the side-wheel packet steamers that traveled the Mississippi during the "golden era of riverboats," from 1855 to 1875. A perennially popular dinner entree here is baked seafood au gratin, which combines shrimp, scallops, crabmeat, and lobster in sherry sauce. A smaller version is available at lunchtime as well. Oven-fried chicken, broiled center-cut pork chops, and Port of Hastings steak (a boneless New York cut) are among the items that have made Mississippi Belle a drawing card. The pies here are by now legendary, with lemon angel, sour cream raisin, and southern pecan pies among the delicious offerings.

Lunches, served daily from 11 a.m. to 2:30 p.m., are in the $5 to $6 price range; dinners, served Monday through Saturday from 4:30 to 9 p.m., run $9 to $15, and Sunday dinners, served from 11:30 a.m. to 6:30 p.m., cost $8.

As an overnight suggestion, **Thorwood Bed and Breakfast,** at 649 W. 3rd St., Hastings, MN 55033 (tel. 612/437-3297), is a reconverted 1880 mansion that's been turned into a delightful accommodation by Pam and Dick Thorsen. There are eight rooms here, some with fireplaces, all with private bath, some with whirlpools, and each with its own distinctive decor. Breakfast, brought to your door in an oversize basket, includes oven omelets, warm pastries, sausages, muffins, coffee or tea, and juice. Reservations are recommended. Prices range from $59 to $99.

RED WING: As you continue your Rivertown ramble southward from the Twin Cities, you'll find Red Wing, a town whose beginnings date back to 1680 when Father Hennepin founded an Indian Village here. The town was later named in honor of the area's Sioux Indian chiefs, whose emblem was a swan's wing that had been dyed red. In 1837 white settlers came to Red Wing, and by the 1870s it had become a primary wheat market.

As railroads assumed an ever-greater role in the transportation of products, Red Wing's importance as a shipping center began to diminish even as the manufacture of two products, pottery and shoes, began to draw widespread attention.

Attractions

The Minnesota Stoneware Company, which began production in the late 1800s and eventually became known as Red Wing Pottery, established a national reputation, making use of local clay sources. In 1967, after nearly a century of operation, this company closed its plant as the result of a prolonged and bitter labor dispute. But the historic factory and salesroom have been turned into a major tourist attraction. At **Red Wing Pottery Sales,** 1995 W. Main St. (tel. 338-3562), you'll be able to find some remaining pieces of the original Red Wing pottery, along with collectibles from around the world. You can also browse among a variety of country items, and in the candy section you'll find such old-fashioned sweets as homemade fudge.

Winona Mills, 1902 W. Main St. (tel. 338-5738), one of a statewide network of factory outlet stores, offers a wide assortment of high-quality, reasonably priced apparel, all of it made in the United States, with one notable exception—the genuine Islandic sweaters that sell for much lower prices here than elsewhere.

And then there's **Loons and Ladyslippers,** 1890 W. Main St. (tel. 388-9418), a delightful shop where you'll find a miscellany of gifts, crafts, and collectibles, all of them related in some way to Minnesota, whose official bird is the loon and whose official flower is the ladyslipper.

At nearby **Pottery Place,** you'll find a two-level mall containing factory outlets, specialty shops, and restaurants.

Where to Stay

After making a national name for itself as the manufacturer of fine leather products, the Red Wing Shoe Company took a step in an entirely different direction in 1977, when it bought the 100-year-old **St. James Hotel,** 406 Main St., Red Wing, MN 55066 (tel. 612/388-2846). Meticulous restoration has turned this into one of the state's proudest examples of respect for historical significance and tasteful adaptation to contemporary needs.

With exacting attention to detail, the 60 original guest rooms were reduced to 41 in order to accommodate private modern baths and facilities. Each room is individually decorated with period wallpaper, period pieces, and coordinated handmade down quilts. In a discreet bow to modernity, the doors of Victorian handcrafted wardrobes open to reveal television sets for contemporary travelers. Delightful examples of Victorian workmanship have been displayed throughout the corridors. Accommodations range from $55 to $99 per room for two.

Where to Dine

Only an hour from the Twin Cities, Red Wing and the St. James Hotel are close enough for an afternoon or overnight getaway, close enough even for a lunch or dinner date. **Port of Red Wing,** the St. James's major restaurant, retains its original limestone walls and a variety of period antiques which have been put to ingenious use. The original safe-deposit vault, for example, serves now as a fine wine cellar. Port of Red Wing offers a traditional American menu, with specials every evening. Entrees range from $12.95 to $22.95. Lunch is served Monday through Saturday, 11 a.m. to 2 p.m., dinner every night from 5 to 9:30 p.m. Another popular gathering place at the St. James is **Jimmy's Pub,** which offers not only a fine fifth-story view of the city, but a warm, friendly ambience, enhanced by antique stained-glass panels, old English hunting scenes in antique frames over the oak bar, and upholstered armchairs facing the massive fireplace. Jimmy's Pub should really be called Jimmy's Bar—no food is served in this otherwise hospitable room. But you can get a bite at breakfast or lunchtime at the delightful **Veranda Coffee Shop,** with its lovely view of the Mississippi. You have your choice here of a table in the cheery informal dining room or on the adjoining enclosed porch.

LAKE CITY: Picturesque bluffs overlook Hwy. 61 as you approach Lake City, situated on Lake Pepin, the widest expanse on the Mississippi River. Lake City takes pride in the fact that the sport of waterskiing was invented here back in 1922, when 18-year-old Ralph Samuelson steamed and then bent into shape two pine boards. His theory was that if people could ski on snow, they could also ski on water, and the corroboration of that theory put Lake City on the map and enabled millions of men, women, and children throughout the world to ski, if not walk, on water.

This small city features a variety of activities that center on its major claim to fame, the largest **marina** on the Mississippi River. Following a recent expansion, 625 sailboats can now be docked here while a 90-foot breakwater enables others to fish from three 60-foot railed fishing platforms. Northerns, walleyes, crappies, and bass are among the varieties most often caught in these waters. But fish are not the only wildlife that draws tourists to Lake City. There are also the majestic **bald eagles** that have made their home in the bluffs overlooking Hwy. 61. These imposing birds can be seen from time to time swooping down onto the open water for food, and as the season progresses they do their ice fishing on the shoreline before it, too, freezes over.

If you decide to spend the night in this pretty river town, try the recently restored **Rahilly House,** 304 Oak St., Lake City, MN 55041 (tel. 612/345-4664). Reservations are highly recommended at this sprawling three-story white frame mansion, a prime example of classic Greek Revival architecture. Built in 1862, the Rahilly House was given new life in 1983–1984 by Dorene and Gary Fechtmeyer, a Twin Cities couple who had grown up in Lake City and long admired the grand old house. Now there are six delightful guest rooms here, all named for previous owners, ranging in price from $60 to $80 per night. The Enz room has French doors which open to an outside deck. The Doughty Room, Russell Room, Rahilly Room, and Enz Room have functioning fireplaces. The Doughty Room is the only one with a private bath; other baths are shared or adjacent.

WABASHA: You'll be visiting the oldest city in Minnesota when you arrive in Wabasha. Named for Indian Chief Wapashaw, a peacemaker during the Sioux Indian uprising of 1862, Wabasha was by the 1880s a center of lumbering, milling, and boatbuilding. Many of the buildings of that period, constructed of brick and other local materials, still stand today. In fact, Wabasha's entire downtown business district has been placed on the National Register of Historic Places.

There are two **marinas** here, offering 400 open slips and 200 closed slips, and the **city dock** provides launching to the public as well. Many sailors take advantage of the shuttle service provided at the docks by the Anderson House, the state's oldest operating hotel.

Food and Lodging

Run by the members of the same family since it first opened in 1896, the **Anderson House,** 333 N. Main St., Wabasha, MN 55981 (tel. 612/565-4524), has received national TV, magazine, and newspaper coverage as the Minnesota hotel which gives new meaning to the term "cat house." Here guests can reserve a complimentary overnight cat when they register for a room; a feline, its food, and even a litter box will be delivered to their door that evening. Daytime visits can also be arranged— usually at naptime for children or their elders.

There are other homey touches at the Anderson House as well. Home-baked cookies are available in a large jar on the front desk 24 hours a day. Heated bricks are provided for those who opt for that sort of bed-warmer. Guests with the sniffles are only one phone call to the desk away from having a mustard plaster delivered to the door. And those who remember to leave their shoes outside the door at night will find them there brightly shined the next morning.

Rates are $30 to $50 for single and double rooms, $65 to $69 for suites. Most of the rooms do not have private bath, and there are no elevators in this 1856 three-story hotel.

But the Anderson House is as famous for its home-cooking as it is for its overnight services. Grandma Ida Hoffman Anderson brought her Pennsylvania Dutch recipes from Lancaster, Pennsylvania, at the turn of the century, and the family has been using them ever since. Today Ida's granddaughter, Jeanne Hall, and Jeanne's son, John, share the operation of the Anderson House. They've also shared authorship of a number of cookbooks for those who want to try their hand at the kind of fare that's been described as not only the best, but the biggest: cinnamon and praline breakfast rolls at the Anderson House are massive, and so is the selection of home-baked breads and rolls that waitresses bring to your table at dinnertime.

Entrees include Dutch oven steak, Pennsylvania Dutch beef rolls, and batter-fried cod, as well as such standbys as roast turkey and dressing, baked ham, and barbecued ribs. And then there's the Friday-night seafood buffet, an all-you-can-eat selection of seafood gumbo, shrimp, deep-fried pike, crab sections, oven-baked cod and white fish, along with potato and vegetable and, of course, the bread tray, all for $6.

Never mind that the river recreation is top-notch in Wabasha. The Anderson House itself is reason enough to visit this historic river town.

Duluth

About halfway between the Twin Cities and the Canadian border is Duluth, third in size among the state's major cities, but second to none in its importance as an international inland port. Ships from all over the world arrive and depart each day from April to December, flying foreign flags and imparting a truly cosmopolitan air to this northern Minnesota city.

Like Minneapolis and St. Paul, Duluth is linked to a "sister" —in this case one that resides in a different state. Superior, Wisconsin, and Duluth, Minnesota, have always shared a natural harbor on Lake Superior, the huge inland sea that Henry Wadsworth Longfellow immortalized in 1855 as the birthplace of Hiawatha: "By the shores of Gitche Gumee, By the shining big-sea water. . . ."

Like any sisters, these cities have disagreed at times, most memorably perhaps one April weekend in 1871, after Duluth had decided to do something about the 6½-mile sandbar, Minnesota Point, around which its fishing ships had to travel before reaching open water. The city of Superior enjoyed a natural advantage because Wisconsin Point, less than three miles long, gave its boats readier access to the lake.

On this April day in 1871, Duluth officials authorized the digging of an artificial channel through Minnesota Point. A steam shovel had already started work when Superior officials contacted Washington, D.C., with a request that the excavation be halted. Word reached Duluth on a Friday afternoon that an army engineer was on his way with an injunction to halt the excavation. By the time he actually arrived early on Monday, the entire town had bent to the task, working ceaselessly throughout the weekend and finishing the entryway in time for a little tugboat, *Fero,* to toot its way through while Duluthians cheered.

In 1873 the federal government assumed control of the canal

and the harbor, and ten years later named it the Duluth-Superior Harbor. Today an aerial lift bridge oversees the nearly 40 million tons of domestic and international cargo that passes through each year.

These international ships carry grain to Europe and beyond, while long, flat-bottomed ore boats take on taconite for shipment to cities in the American east. And of course the presence here of ships from all over the world has become a prime tourist attraction for the city of Duluth. There are other attractions as well.

ATTRACTIONS: One of the "musts" in any visit to Duluth is a drive along **Skyline Parkway,** a 26-mile strip of city that hugs the crest of a hillside at the western end of town. Day or night, winter or summer, this is a beautiful drive, looking out on Lake Superior, St. Louis Bay, and many residential areas. Part of the route goes through another sightseeing attraction, **Hawks Ridge Nature Reserve,** a place where birdwatchers gather each fall to watch enormous flocks of migrating hawks and eagles.

At the other end of town, **Spirit Mountain** (tel. toll free 800/247-0146) has been bringing ever-increasing numbers of skiers to Duluth during the past decade to enjoy such innovations as the 444 Express, a chair lift that raises four skiers in a bubble-domed quad to a height of 4,000 feet in just four minutes. The first of its kind in Minnesota, the 444 Express is one of only three or four similar chair lifts in the entire country. Work is constantly under way not only on lengthening and improving existing runs, but developing programs for individual skiers and for families. One of the most notable events at Spirit Mountain takes place each New Year's Eve when instructors and members of the ski patrol lead a torchlight parade down the slopes before fireworks erupt into the cold, clear winter sky.

One of the long-range development plans here is to extend runs as far as the **Lake Superior Zoological Garden,** at Seventh Avenue West and Grand Avenue (Hwy. 23), which maintains more than 500 animals from around the world, including a variety of "night animals" which recently took up residence in their own newly constructed nocturnal building. Another popular spot here is the **Children's Zoo Contact Building,** where children, under staff supervision, are invited to touch and pet a variety of animals. Admission to the zoo from April 15 to October 15 is $1.50 for adults, 75¢ for children 6 to 12. Zoo hours during this period are 9 a.m. to 6 p.m. seven days a week. There's no entrance fee during the rest of the year, when the zoo is open from 9 a.m. to 4 p.m. Closed Thanksgiving, Christmas, and New Year's Days. For further information, phone 624-1502.

Another favorite sightseeing attraction, for children and grownups alike, is the **Depot,** 506 W. Michigan St. (tel. 727-8025). An interesting series of exhibits and museums leads visitors through two centuries of local history, with an early stop at the Immigrants' Waiting Room. Elsewhere along the way, children enjoy the two-story walk-through Habitat Tree, and visitors of all ages admire the wonderful mid–19th-century collection of Ojibwe Indian portraits by Eastman Johnson. Elsewhere at the Depot you'll find a fascinating assortment of antique trains, dolls, and furnishings. Hours here are 10 a.m. to 5 p.m. during the summer months, Monday through Saturday from 10 a.m. to 5 p.m. and on Sunday from 1 to 5 p.m. during the winter.

And then there's **Glensheen,** a runaway favorite among tourist attractions here during the past several years, but maybe for the wrong reason. This magnificent mansion, at 3300 London Rd. (Hwy. 61 North), was donated by the wealthy Congdon family to the University of Minnesota at Duluth and stands in the lakeside neighborhood where logging and mining barons built lavish homes nearly a century ago. The much-publicized murder in this mansion of a member of the Congdon family and the subsequent trial and acquittal of an adopted daughter may have something to do with the renewed interest in the property, but tourists should know in advance that the Junior League docents who lead the tours avoid any reference whatever to the crime—so don't visit Glensheen on that account. If, on the other hand, you'd like to see for yourself a dazzling array of exquisite architecture, interior design, art, and horticulture, you'll find your visit to this 39-room Jacobean manor house one of the highlights of your visit to Duluth. Call 724-8863 for recorded information regarding hours, tours, and admission charges, or 724-8864 for reservations and additional information.

The land-and-sea **Discover Duluth tour** combines sightseeing from the deck of the *Vista Queen* excursion boat with a bus ride along the Skyline Drive and a visit to Glensheen. Tickets and tour pickup service are available at selected hotels and motels. Prices are $18 for adults, $10 for children 3 to 11 years old; there's no charge for children under 3.

For further information about this and other attractions, call or write the **Duluth Convention and Visitors Bureau Information Center,** Fifth Avenue West and the Waterfront, Duluth, MN

55802 (tel. 218/722-6024, or toll free 800/862-1172 in Minnesota).

ACCOMMODATIONS: Theoretically you could make a one-day excursion to Duluth, but since the drive takes about three hours each way, I strongly suggest that you plan to spend the night. There's a lot to see and do in this lovely city. There's also a lot of choice so far as accommodations are concerned, everything from small independent motels to large, nationally known hotels. And there's one very special bed-and-breakfast spot that has gained statewide recognition and admiration, although it's only been open to the public since 1983 and just for limited periods each year at that.

The Mansion, 3600 London Rd., Duluth, MN 55804 (tel. 218/724-0739), located just two doors away from Glensheen, was from 1928 to 1932 the ten-bedroom home of another member of the Congdon family, Marjorie Congdon Dudley, and her husband, Harry C. Dudley. Accommodations here are named for the color of the rooms and the view they command. You'll pay $65 per night for the Yellow Pondside bedroom with a queen-size bed and a shared bath, and $95 per night for the Green Lakeside bedroom with a king-size bed and a private bath. Top of the line are two lakeside rooms with king-size beds at $130 per night.

A hearty country breakfast, served in the formal dining room, is included in the rates. So is access to the oak-paneled library, the pine-paneled living room, and the sun porch and dining room. As of this writing the Mansion is open to overnight guests only from May 15 to October 15, with certain other periods available by special arrangement. The doctor's family that runs this beautiful and gracious home has made a labor of love out of the project, and you'll find all manner of delightful reasons to come back again.

Another notable overnight can be found at **Fitger's Inn,** 600 E. Superior St., Duluth, MN 55802 (tel. 218/722-8826, collect). Listed on the National Register of Historic Places, this restored 19th-century structure offers 48 individually styled rooms, some of them with a view of Lake Superior, some with original stone walls from the days when the building served as a famous Duluth brewery. Rates range from $70 to $84 for individual rooms and $135 to $260 for deluxe suites.

Less expensive but very comfortable accommodations are available at the **Edgewater Inn,** with two locations: Edgewater West, at 2211 London Rd., Duluth, MN 55804 (tel. 218/728-5141), and Edgewater East, 2330 London Rd., Duluth, MN

55804 (tel. 218/728-3601). Rates for a room with continental breakfast delivered to your door range from $65 to $71 in season (May 22 through September 22) and $51 to $57 off-season. The more expensive rooms, not surprisingly, are those that look out on Lake Superior. Edgewater East, the original lakeside complex, faces Edgewater West, located on the other side of busy London Road.

You'll find an interesting variation on the usual increased desirability of lake-view rooms at the **Holiday Inn**, 207 W. Superior St., Duluth, MN 55802 (tel. 218/722-1202, or toll free 800/232-0070). Here during the autumn of the year, when many Twin Citians drive up to see the splendid fall colors in Duluth, the hillside rooms that are less expensive than lakeside ones are considered more desirable because you look out on a living mural of bright fall colors. Rates at the Holiday Inn vary according to the season, ranging from $62 to $70 for one person, $70 to $78 for two from November through May, about $8 more per room during the rest of the year.

WHERE TO DINE: There are some really wonderful and famous restaurants in Duluth. I'll give you a quick introduction to a few of them.

Grandma's Saloon and Deli, 522 Lake Ave. South (tel. 727-4192), is something of an institution throughout the state, not so much because of its food, which is very good, or its decor, which is very imaginative, but because of its marathon, which is very famous and getting more so year after year. In 1977 Grandma's agreed to sponsor a North Shore run that attracted about 150 participants. One decade later the same route from Two Harbours to Duluth attracted 8,000-plus runners. By now there's a pre-race $5 all-you-can-eat spaghetti fest to fortify the runners with carbohydrates, and $50,000 worth of prize money awaiting the winners. Please note that Grandma's Marathon, which attracts runners from throughout the country, is the only race on record that ends at a bar. Tents, bands, and vendors with balloons, T-shirts, and other memorabilia are also on hand for the occasion.

Oh yes, the food and decor. You'll find absolutely everything hanging on the wall or from the ceiling at Grandma's. That means antique neon signs, stained-glass windows, brass beds and cribs, and even a stuffed black bear (the one, supposedly, that ran into the Hotel Duluth some years ago and thereby achieved immortality). The food is Italian-American—equal proportions of each, actually—and all of it well prepared and reasonable in cost. Pasta ranges from $6 to $10; steaks, from $7 to $15. Grandma's is open Sunday through Thursday, 11:30 to 1 a.m., and Friday and Saturday, 11 to 1 a.m.

The family-owned **Pickwick,** 508 E. Superior St. (tel. 727-8901), has been serving fine food at reasonable prices since 1914. The decor here is 19th-century German, the cuisine is primarily American, and the beer is imported from a number of European countries. Lunch items range from $1.75 to $11.50. Dinner features T-bone steak, broiled or fried walleyed pike, and more, ranging from $8.25 to $25.50. The Pickwick is open Monday through Saturday from 11 to 1 a.m. It's closed on Sunday.

The service will make you think of an earlier, more gracious time; so will the across-the-board senior citizens' 10% discount, which may account for the somewhat advanced average age here. Or the explanation may be that older folks know value when they run into it and return because of it. At any rate, the Pickwick is a beautiful, unique, and very popular Duluth tradition.

The **Chinese Lantern,** 402 W. 1st St. (tel. 722-7486), was the first Cantonese restaurant in the history of Duluth when it opened in 1965. By now, as photos on the walls attest, diners have included Bob Hope, Loretta Lynn, Pearl Bailey, Barry Manilow, and Tom Jones. The only restaurant north of Minneapolis to be listed in *Who's Who of American Restaurants,* the Chinese Lantern is owned by Wing Y. Huie, whose family fled China in the mid-1930s. His father, Joe Huie, ran a famous 24-hour Duluth café for many years, asserting that it was open all day and all night because he'd lost the key. He questioned Wing's decision to offer Chinese cuisine to a primarily blue-collar clientele, but lived long enough to admit with enormous pride that his son's judgment in that regard was better than his own. Prices here range from $6 for beef chop suey to $15 for lobster tail Cantonese. After dinner, climb the stairs to the second-story Brass Phoenix Night Club, another gamble that paid off handsomely for the enterprising Wing Huie. The Chinese Lantern is open weekdays from 11 to 1 a.m., Saturday from noon to 10 p.m., and Sunday from noon to 10 p.m.

Chapter XIII

FAMILY FUN

THE TWIN CITIES ARE A MECCA for family fun. Some prime entertainment spots have already been covered in earlier chapters, but for those of you with restless youngsters on your hands, this quick, comprehensive alphabetical listing should head off any threats of boredom at the pass. And lest the weather report put you in a quandary, I've divided this chapter into "rain-or-shine" and "better-in-the-sun" activities.

Admittedly this is something of a judgment call. For example, I've listed the Minnesota Zoo as a rain-or-shine attraction because so many of the animals, birds, and other residents here live in huge, beautifully landscaped, but totally sheltered areas that will keep you as comfortable as they are throughout the year, and should provide hours and hours of fascination. You're in the best position to know which activities will be of most interest to your particular cast of characters, but there's a lot to choose from, as you'll see from the sampling below. Have fun!

Family Fun, Rain or Shine

The **American Swedish Institute**, 2600 Park Ave., Minneapolis (tel. 871-4907). This extravagantly beautiful mansion looks like something out of a fairytale. Families have a fine time here admiring the beautifully wrought woodcarvings of griffins (half eagle, half lion) and other fantastical beings. Upstairs, on the third floor visitors enjoy seeing turn-of-the-century clothing, tools, and toys, including an exquisitely furnished dollhouse. The Swedish Institute is open Tuesday through Saturday from noon to 4 p.m. and on Sunday from 1 to 5 p.m.; closed Monday. Admission is $2 for adults, $1 for students and senior citizens.

The **Children's Museum**, 1217 Bandana Blvd., St. Paul (tel. 644-3818). Children get to do all sorts of grownup things here, from operating a crane to driving a bus to playing banker, dentist, grocery-store clerk, or computer whiz. There are two floors of fun here, and parents seem as intrigued by it all as youngsters are. Hours Tuesday through Thursday from 2 to 5 p.m., on Friday from 10 a.m. to 8 p.m., on Saturday from 10 a.m. to 5 p.m., and on Sunday from 11 a.m. to 5 p.m. The museum is closed on Monday. Admission is $2.50 for adults, $2 for children (no charge for children under 2).

The **Children's Theatre,** 2400 Third Ave. South, Minneapolis (tel. 874-0400). This theater is known throughout the world for its imaginative productions of plays for children. Characters like Babar and the Little Match Girl have come to life on this stage in an immense auditorium with wonderful sightlines. Prices are $10 to $16 for adults, $7 to $12 for children under the age of 17 and for senior citizens.

The **Festival of Nations,** at the International Institute of Minnesota, 1694 Como Ave., St. Paul (tel. 647-0191). This is an exciting celebration of the diversity of nationalities to be found in Minnesota. Dozens of countries are represented by costumed Twin Citians, who demonstrate the food, crafts, costumes of their respective countries. Music, dance, and entertainment make this a truly lively event. Admission is $6 for adults, $4 for children 5 to 16 (no charge for children under 5).

The **Indian God of Peace,** located in the St. Paul City Hall and Courthouse at 4th and Wabasha, is a truly majestic figure of white onyx. A good many of the grownups who bring their children here these days first saw this magnificent work of art when they themselves were children. There's no charge for admission of course, but the courthouse is open Monday through Friday from 8 a.m. to 4:30 p.m.

The **James Ford Bell Museum of Natural History,** on the Minneapolis Campus of the University of Minnesota, University Avenue and 17th Avenue SE (tel. 624-7083). Enjoy wonderful re-creations of animals, birds, and fish in their natural habitat, and on the third floor, visit the popular "Touch and See" room, where children can encounter prehistoric monsters, try on antlers, and consider—usually from a respectful distance—a grinning skeleton. There's no admission charge. Hours are 9 a.m. to 5 p.m. Tuesday through Saturday, from 1 to 5 p.m. on Sunday.

The **Minnesota State Capitol Building,** Aurora and Park Avenues, St. Paul (tel. 297-3521). This magnificent building is a memorable sight for families; also memorable are the free tours that take you past beautiful Minnesota-related paintings and statues and up sweeping marble stairways to official government chambers. Tours are conducted every day, leaving from the Information Desk, every hour on the hour from 9 a.m. to 4 p.m. Monday through Friday, 10 a.m. to 3 p.m. on Saturday, and 1 to 3 p.m. on Sunday.

The **Minnesota State Fair,** at Como and Snelling Avenues in St. Paul (tel. 642-2251), has something for everybody. There's a lot to see, a lot to eat, a lot to do during the end-of-summer State Fair celebration each year, and the fact that these are permanent installations means that your good time won't be rained out. The daily newspapers carry full listings of each day's special events. Admission is $3.50 for adults, $1.50 for children 6 to 12. There's no charge for children under 6, and no charge for parking. This largest 12-day fair in the country always ends on Labor Day.

The **Minnesota Zoo,** 12101 Johnny Cake Ridge Rd., Apple Valley (tel. 432-9000). You'll meet all manner of wild animals and birds here, existing in their natural habitats. Wintertime brings superb cross-country skiing opportunities to outdoorsy families who enjoy sharing their trails with creatures of the wild. Others will find plenty to entertain and educate them in a succession of indoor exhibitions. There's a petting barn here for the youngest members of your group. Admission is $4 for adults, $1.50 for ages 6 through 16; children under 6 are free. If you're in town from October through February and can get here on a Tuesday, there's no entrance charge at all.

The **Omnitheater,** in the Science Museum of Minnesota, 30 E. 10th St., St. Paul (221-9400), is popular with audiences of all ages. The huge curved screen and the world's largest film projector literally propel you out into space, down to the ocean's floor, or to places in between. You can go to the Omnitheater early and wait in line, or phone 221-9456 and pay an extra 50¢ per ticket for advance reservations. Ticket prices are $4.50 for adults, $3.50 for senior citizens and children 12 and under.

The **Science Museum of Minnesota,** 30 E. 10th St., St. Paul (tel. 221-9495), is a participatory museum that encourages children to try their hand at everything from grinding grain to operating a computer. Exhibits here cover a wide range of times and places, and one visit may well lead to another. If you attend the Omnitheater on the second floor, your admission to the rest of the Science Museum will be only $1; otherwise the cost of entering the museum is $3 for adults, $2 for children ages 4 to 12; children under 4 are admitted free. Hours October through March are Tuesday through Saturday from 9:30 a.m. to 9 p.m., on Sunday from 11 a.m. to 9 p.m.; closed Monday. Hours April through October are Monday through Saturday from 9:30 a.m. to 9 p.m., on Sunday from 11 a.m. to 9 p.m.

Sibley House, Sibley Memorial Hwy. near Hwys. 55 and 13,

Mendota (tel. 452-1596). Henry Hastings Sibley was a prosperous fur trader before he became the first governor of Minnesota. His gracious home has been restored to the mid–19th-century period, with furnishings of that time and also with a remarkable collection of Indian carvings and peace pipes. Visiting hours May through October are 10 a.m. to 5 p.m. Tuesday through Saturday, from 1 to 6 p.m. on Sunday and holidays. Admission is $2 for adults, 50¢ for children 6 through 15; children under 6, free.

Town Square Park, on the top levels of the Town Square shopping, dining, and office complex at 445 Minnesota St. in St. Paul (tel. 227-3307), is the world's largest indoor park. There's a small playground for children, lots of cozy seating for adults, and a picturesque setting of shrubs, trees, and waterfalls. Come at noon any weekday and you'll hear a musical recital.

The **Twin Cities Model Railroad Club** at Bandana Square, 1021 Bandana Blvd. East, St. Paul (tel. 647-9628), offers children and their elders the chance to see a remarkable exhibit in the process of becoming. Club members are still assembling historic tracks and artifacts that trace the history of railroading in this area during the past 50 years. The exhibit can be seen every day from noon to 9 p.m., but if you want to be able to walk all the way around the layout, plan to visit on Tuesday or Friday evening from 6 to 9 p.m. and on Sunday from noon to 5 p.m.

The **St. Paul Winter Carnival** (tel. 222-4416). The whole city of St. Paul is the setting for this annual late-January to early-February event. What's being celebrated here is not only the variety of wintertime fun, but the fact that by this time of year winter is about to be displaced by spring. Snow sculpture, ice carvings, and piped-in music make a fairyland of inner-city parks. There are parades and contests, and even a treasure hunt. Children can try their hand at ice fishing, and they'll enjoy the food and the fun at the "indoor midway" in the massive St. Paul Civic Center. Daily newspaper listings will keep you informed about what each day's and evening's events and activities will be.

Fair-Weather Family Fun

The **Como Park Zoo,** Midwest Parkway and Kaufman Drive, St. Paul (tel. 488-5572). Sparky, the performing seal, is everybody's favorite here, but there are lots of other animals to meet in the Primate and Aquatic Buildings, and in Wolf Woods. The buildings are open daily, from 10 a.m. to 4 p.m. during the winter months, to 6 p.m. during the summer months. There's no admission charge.

Gibbs Farm, 2097 W. Larpenteur Ave., Falcon Heights (tel. 646-8629), is a turn-of-the-century family homesite which enables children to experience for themselves the surroundings of the girls and boys who lived long ago. In addition to the farmhouse, the seven-acre site holds a red barn with tools of that day and a white barn with domestic animals. If reservations are made early enough in the season, first- through sixth-grade schoolchildren who visit Gibbs Farm during July or August can spend a full day attending the farm's old-style school, at a cost of $7.50. Gibbs Farm is open to the public from late April through mid-December. Admission is $1.75 for adults, 75¢ for children.

Historic Fort Snelling, Hwy. 5 at Hwy. 55, one mile east of the Minneapolis–St. Paul airport (tel. 726-9430). This faithful restoration of the military post that brought the first settlers to these parts is now one of the most popular of all Twin Cities tourist attractions. Costumed guides encourage visitors to take part in the activities that kept soldiers and their families busy during those early days. Children particularly seem to enjoy the Round Tower that provided a lookout up and down the Minnesota and Mississippi Rivers. The schoolhouse, the blacksmith shop, and the hospital are just some of the sources of fascination and education here. Historic Fort Snelling is open from May through October. Admission is $2 for adults, $1 for senior citizens and children 5 to 16; no charge for children under 5. Hours vary according to the season, so phone in advance for specific information.

The *Jonathon Padelford* Sternwheeler, Harriet Island, St. Paul (tel. 227-1100). Passengers board this authentic 19th-century riverboat on Harriet Island, located on the edge of downtown St. Paul, and sail the Mississippi for a two-hour round trip to within sight of Historic Fort Snelling. A taped narration points out special places and facts of interest—a wonderful way to learn more about Twin Cities history. There are four sailings each day from June through August, and one sailing on Saturday, Sunday, and holidays during May and September. Phone for specific details. Prices are $5.50 for adults, $3.50 for children under 12.

The **Lake Harriet Trolley,** 42nd Street and Queen Avenue South, Minneapolis (tel. 522-7417). Many Twin Cities parents and grandparents can remember riding on old-fashioned streetcars, but most children have never had the experience, and so they have a great time on the mile-long ride between Lake Harriet and Lake Calhoun. Just as in the old days, children buy tokens for the ride and a conductor collects them. This line is manned by volunteers, hence the abbreviated hours: Memorial Day through Labor Day, from 6:30 p.m. to dusk Monday through Friday, 3:30 p.m. to dusk on Saturday, and 12:30 p.m. to dusk on Sunday and holidays. After Labor Day, trolley rides continue through October, weather permitting, from 3:30 p.m. to dusk on Saturday and 12:30 p.m. to dusk on Sunday.

Minnehaha Falls / Statue of Hiawatha and Minnehaha, in Minnehaha Park, near the Mississippi River. It was reportedly a description of Minnehaha Falls that inspired Henry Wadsworth Longfellow to write his immortal story-poem about the Indian brave Hiawatha and the Indian maiden Minnehaha. The two are reunited here in a graceful statue near the falls that bear her name. This whole area is a popular picnicking place for families. It's also the site of many large ethnic picnics, so you may run into costumed Scandinavians of all ages if you get there at the right time.

To get to the statue and falls from Minneapolis, take Hwy. 55 for about five miles; turn left on Minnehaha Parkway and enter the parking lot on the right. From St. Paul it's a lot less complex than it sounds: take Hwy. 94 west and get off at the Cretin-Vandalia exit; at the stop sign, turn left and proceed about three miles, turning right onto the Ford Parkway, which becomes a bridge that crosses the Mississippi River; one block beyond the Ford Bridge, turn left on 46th Street, proceed one block to Godfrey, turn right on Godfrey, drive about a block, and turn left into the parking lot.

Unlike other living-history restorations in the area, **Murphy's Landing,** Hwy. 101 near Shakopee (tel. 445-6900), doesn't confine itself to a relatively narrow point in time. Instead, 50 years of Minnesota Valley history unfolds before visitors as they proceed from the 1840s fur trader's cabin to the 1850 timber farm, and ultimately to a village of the 1890s. The costumes of the guides in each of the settings are consistent with the time period they represent. City children in particular enjoy seeing the farm animals roaming through the lanes; they also enjoy watching the churning, spinning, weaving, and other chores being carried on much as they were in the 19th century. Murphy's Landing, located about 11 miles west of the intersection of I-35W and Hwy. 13, about 2 miles past Valleyfair, is open to the public from May through October. Admission is $4 for adults, $3 for students and seniors; children under 6 are admitted free.

Valleyfair, Hwy. 101 near Shakopee (tel. 445-7600). If you're bringing children to the Twin Cities, you might want to consider spending a day at Valleyfair, an enormously popular theme park which occupies 60 acres of land and offers attractions for children and grownups alike. Many Twin Cities parents appreciate the presence here of the beautiful merry-go-round rescued from the now-demolished Excelsior Amusement Park out near Lake Minnetonka. This is reportedly the most popular theme amusement park in the entire Midwest. Come early and stay late. Valley Fair is open from the middle of May through Labor Day and then on weekends until the end of September. Admission for anyone 48 inches tall or over is $13. If you're less than 48 inches tall or if you're a senior citizen, your ticket will cost $8. There's no admission charge for children under 3. Parking costs $2.50. Valleyfair is located about nine miles west of the intersection of I-35W and Hwy. 13, about two miles from Murphy's Landing.

Finally, check Chapter XI, "Festivals and Fairs," to see if one may be under way during your visit. They're a sure-fire source of family fun in these parts and will provide you with lots of local color in addition. And consider a family outing at one of the local parks and lakes that have been providing family fun for such a long time. You'll find more information about them in Chapter IX, "Sports and Recreation."

Chapter XIV

TWIN CITIES ABC's

A QUICK RUN-DOWN OF INFORMATION that should prove helpful to you while you're in the Twin Cities follows. The listings are alphabetical, but you might want to turn first to "Tourist Information," where you'll find how very welcome a guest you'll be.

The local tourism offices have put together a really impressive array of guides and services for you, and have made them readily accessible through toll-free "800" phone numbers. In fact, the Minnesota Office of Tourism also maintains a database which will identify for you, before you leave home, accommodations that offer the special amenities you're interested in, everything from babysitting services to honeymoon packages to senior's rates. They touch virtually all bases! You can even have a personalized printout mailed to you. Now that's hospitality, Minnesota style.

Of course, the concierge and front-desk personnel of your hotel will be helpful too, once you've settled in. They know the area and can point you in the right direction, whether you're looking for a local place of worship or a place to have your hair cut, your shoes shined, or your photos processed.

AIRPORT: The Minneapolis–St. Paul International Airport is about a 15-minute drive from both downtown Minneapolis and downtown St. Paul. With more than 500 flights arriving and departing each day, this is the 19th-busiest airport in the country.

AREA CODE: The telephone area code throughout the Twin Cities area is 612.

CALENDAR OF EVENTS: You'll find upcoming events listed weekly in the daily newspapers, on Thursday in the *St. Paul Dispatch* and *Pioneer Press,* and on Friday in the *Minneapolis Star and Tribune.* See "Tourist Information," below, for offices in the Twin Cities that offer useful brochures on daily events.

In Chapter XI you'll find the approximate dates for annual events like the Minnesota State Fair, the Minneapolis Aquatennial, the St. Paul Winter Carnival, and the Renaissance Festival. The dates vary from year to year, so once again the daily newspapers, tourist information offices, and hotel personnel will be able to give you timely specifics.

CAR RENTALS: Most national car-rental companies have offices in the Twin Cities, including **National Car Rental** (tel. 726-5600), **Hertz Rent a Car** (tel. 726-1600), **Dollar Rent a Car** (tel. 726-9494), and **Avis Rent a Car** (tel. 726-1723).

CLIMATE: During an average year in the Twin Cities, there are four distinct seasons, with average monthly temperatures (in degrees Fahrenheit) as follows:

January	12°	July	72°
February	17°	August	70°
March	28°	September	60°
April	45°	October	50°
May	57°	November	32°
June	67°	December	19°

Of course the actual temperature on any given day can vary quite a bit from these averages, but you probably won't feel uncomfortable here for several reasons. And whatever the weather, you'll be comfortable downtown because of the extensive skyway system.

If you're visiting during the summertime, the shade trees and the lakes serve as natural air conditioners, so unless the weather's humid, you'll find that ordinary summer clothing will keep you quite comfortable. And should the temperature soar, you're only a step away from climate-controlled comfort. All public buildings are air-conditioned, of course.

During the wintertime, the temperature may sound more frigid than it feels. Generally it's a still, dry cold, unlike what you've experienced in windy cities like Chicago or oceanside cities like New York. On days when the temperature really dips, the temptation is to stay indoors, but as often as not, proper clothing will enable you to enjoy the clean, crisp invigorating outdoors.

The number of the **weather bureau** is 725-6090.

CLOTHING: Twin Citians tend to dress for the season, so during the summertime don't be surprised to see shorts worn by men, women, and children in many city locations as well as suburban ones. Of course you'll dress more formally if you're going to a restaurant or to an office, but by and large, dress tends to be informal in these parts. Light clothing will see you through every warm-weather occasion, but remember that evenings tend to be cool and so do some air-conditioned buildings, so bring along a light jacket or sweater.

During the wintertime you'll certainly want to bring a pair of boots to keep your feet dry in case of snow. In fact here, as in metropolitan centers around the world, women's boots have become a fashionable wardrobe accessory, and you'll see certain styles indoors day and evening. What you probably won't see, except maybe on the slopes or the rinks or the cross-country ski trails, is earmuffs. You really should bring a woolen hat, though, and of course warm gloves and coat or jacket. Then you'll be ready for anything that might be on the bill during what is called the "theater of seasons."

CREDIT CARDS: Most establishments, with the exception of a few restaurants, accept all major credit cards and, with proper identification, personal checks.

DRINKING AGE: The legal drinking age in Minnesota is 21. Identification is required in nightclubs and bars.

EMERGENCIES: Here, as in so many other areas of the country, a phone call to 911 will bring help for **fire, police, or ambulance emergencies.** There's another number you should know, as well. **Abbott Northwestern Hospital** (tel. 863-4095) offers 24-hour-a-day telephone consultations. Prescription medicine, emergency-room visits, or hospital care can be provided as needed, and specialist referrals can also be arranged at competitive fees. VISA, MasterCard, and personal checks are accepted, and insurance forms will be completed if requested.

FILM DEVELOPING: There are now several one-hour color-print developing and printing companies in the Twin Cities. Many of them operate seven days a week in shopping centers. Proex, one of the first and still one of the best of the lot, prides itself on redoing without charge any prints that customers find unsatisfactory.

HOTEL TAX: The hotel tax in downtown St. Paul and on the Bloomington "strip" is 11%; in downtown Minneapolis, 12%.

OFFICE BY THE DAY: If you're here on business, you might want to know that **Control Data,** 511 11th Ave. South, Minneapolis (tel. 375-8100), or 245 E. 6th St., St. Paul (tel. 202-2693), can make the following services available to you: word processing, duplicating, business library, audio-visual equipment, meeting rooms, and local telephone service. The basic service charge is $25.

POST OFFICE: The main U.S. Post Office in Minneapolis is located at South 1st Street and Marquette (tel. 349-4970); in St. Paul it's at Kellogg Boulevard and Jackson Street (tel. 293-3011). There's 24-hour postal service available at the airport.

SALES TAX: The 6% Minnesota state sales tax does not apply to clothing, prescription drugs that are not available over the counter, and food that is purchased in stores. Within the city limits of Minneapolis you'll pay an additional ½% sales tax on the same items that are subject to the state 6% sales tax.

TELEVISION: You'll find all the major TV networks in the Twin Cities, but here's a reminder that may keep you from missing your favorite show: unless you hail from the same time zone (Central Time), the program you want to watch may be aired one or two hours earlier or later than what you're used to. Just check the TV pages in one of the local newspapers. There are six TV channels available here: Channels 2 (PBS), 4 (CBS), 5 (ABC), 9 (Independent), 11 (NBC), and 17 (PBS).

TIME: Minnesota is in the Central Time zone, one hour behind the East Coast and two hours ahead of the West Coast (if it's 8 p.m. in New York, it's 7 p.m. in the Twin Cities, 6 p.m. in Denver, and 5 p.m. in San Francisco). It observes Central Standard Time in the fall, winter, and spring, and Central Daylight Time (daylight savings) in summer.

TIPPING: The usual tip for service well rendered is 15%.

TOURIST INFORMATION: The **Minnesota Office of Tourism** (tel.

612/296-5029, or toll free 800/328-1461, 800/652-9747 in Minnesota) is unique in the services it provides to tourists even before they arrive in the Twin Cities. A toll-free phone call will put you in touch with a travel counselor who can answer your questions and, with regard to accommodations, can key into a database listing the hotels, motels, resorts, and campgrounds that offer the specific amenities and options you desire. Here's a list of some of the specific information available to you by phone, and if you like, can be mailed to you as a computer printout: accommodations with no charge for children, week-end packages, senior citizen rates, honeymoon packages, AAA recommendations, pets permitted, babysitting and day care available, indoor pool, whirlpool, indoor tennis, waterbeds, limousine and shuttle service, and scheduled entertainment. Also, a seasonal travel newspaper, the *Minnesota Explorer,* and a variety of informational brochures will be sent to you free of charge, at your request.

The **St. Paul Convention and Visitors Bureau** (tel. toll free 800/328-8322) maintains a comprehensively stocked Visitor Information Booth on the street level of Town Square, at 7th Street and Cedar Avenue, with brochures and guides designed to make it easier for tourists to make their choice among the diversity of attractions available. Hours are 8:30 a.m. to 5:30 p.m. Monday through Friday.

The **Minneapolis Convention and Visitors Commission** (tel. 612/348-4313, or toll free 800/445-7412) has information for you at their booth in the IDS Crystal Court, 7th Street on the Nicollet Mall, open 8 a.m. to 5 p.m. Monday through Friday.

Among the many useful free guides awaiting you at both these offices are brochures (published quarterly) providing day-by-day listings of dance, music, sports, and theater presentations.

Minnesota Miscellany

And now, a few facts I'd like you to know about this Land of 10,000 Lakes:

The **state bird** is the loon, a sleek black-and-white bird whose haunting call is a memorable part of visits to the lakes of northern Minnesota.

The **state fish** is the walleye pike. Although it's little known beyond state borders, walleye makes delicious, delicately flavored seafood. Try it—chances are you'll discover a new favorite.

The **state tree** is the Norway Pine, named not for the country of Norway, but for the city in Maine where it grows profusely and where many of our early lumberjacks lived before heading west.

The **state flower** is the pink-and-white ladyslipper, a large, lovely wildflower that flourishes in northern and eastern Minnesota. You mustn't pick one, though—that's against the law.

The **state gemstone** is the Lake Superior agate, a reddish stone with white stripes that's found in central and northern Minnesota. It polishes up into all sorts of distinctive jewelry that you'll find in souvenir shops throughout Minneapolis and St. Paul.

The **state grain** is wild rice, a staple among Ojibway Indians for centuries and presently a gourmet delight among diners in Minneapolis, St. Paul, and far beyond.

And finally, the **state motto,** "L'Étoile du Nord," is expressed in the language of those hardy French explorers who first discovered these shores back in the 17th century. "Star of the North" is what Minnesota was then and what it remains to this day.

Come and see for yourself.

NOW!
ARTHUR FROMMER LAUNCHES HIS SECOND TRAVEL REVOLUTION with

The New World of Travel

The hottest news and latest trends in travel today—heretofore the closely guarded secrets of the travel trade—are revealed in this new sourcebook by the dean of American travel. Here, collected in one book that is updated every year, are the most exciting, challenging, and money-saving ideas in travel today.

You'll find out about hundreds of alternative new modes of travel—and the many organizations that sponsor them—that will lead you to vacations that cater to your mind, your spirit, and your sense of thrift.

Learn how to fly for free as an air courier; travel for free as a tour escort; live for free on a hospitality exchange; add earnings as a part-time travel agent; pay less for air tickets, cruises, and hotels; enhance your life through cooperative camping, political tours, and adventure trips; change your life at utopian communities, low-cost spas, and yoga retreats; pursue low-cost studies and language training; travel comfortably while single or over 60; sail on passenger freighters; and vacation in the cheapest places on earth.

And in every yearly edition, Arthur Frommer spotlights the 10 GREAT-EST TRAVEL VALUES for the coming year. 384 pages, large-format with many, many illustrations. All for $12.95!

ORDER NOW
TURN TO THE LAST PAGE OF THIS BOOK FOR ORDER FORM.

NOW, SAVE MONEY ON ALL YOUR TRAVELS!
Join Arthur Frommer's $35-A-Day Travel Club™

Saving money while traveling is never a simple matter, which is why, over 26 years ago, the **$35-A-Day Travel Club** was formed. Actually, the idea came from readers of the Arthur Frommer Publications who felt that such an organization could bring financial benefits, continuing travel information, and a sense of community to economy-minded travelers all over the world.

In keeping with the money-saving concept, the annual membership fee is low—$18 (U.S. residents) or $20 U.S. (Canadian, Mexican, and foreign residents)—and is immediately exceeded by the value of your benefits which include:

(1) The latest edition of any TWO of the books listed on the following pages.

(2) An annual subscription to an 8-page quarterly newspaper *The Wonderful World of Budget Travel* which keeps you up-to-date on fastbreaking developments in low-cost travel in all parts of the world—bringing you the kind of information you'd have to pay over $35 a year to obtain elsewhere. This consumer-conscious publication also includes the following columns:

   Hospitality Exchange—members all over the world who are willing to provide hospitality to other members as they pass through their home cities.

   Share-a-Trip—requests from members for travel companions who can share costs and help avoid the burdensome single supplement.

   Readers Ask . . . Readers Reply—travel questions from members to which other members reply with authentic firsthand information.

(3) A copy of *Arthur Frommer's Guide to New York*.

(4) Your personal membership card which entitles you to purchase through the Club all Arthur Frommer Publications for a third to a half off their regular retail prices during the term of your membership.

So why not join this hardy band of international budgeteers NOW and participate in its exchange of information and hospitality? Simply send $18 (U.S. residents) or $20 U.S. (Canadian, Mexican, and other foreign residents) along with your name and address to: $35-A-Day Travel Club, Inc., Gulf + Western Building, One Gulf + Western Plaza, New York, NY 10023. Remember to specify which *two* of the books in section (1) above you wish to receive in your initial package of member's benefits. Or tear out the next page, check off any two of the books listed on either side, and send it to us with your membership fee.

Date_____

FROMMER BOOKS
PRENTICE HALL PRESS
ONE GULF + WESTERN PLAZA
NEW YORK, NY 10023

Friends:

Please send me the books checked below:

FROMMER'S $-A-DAY GUIDES™

(In-depth guides to sightseeing and low-cost tourist accommodations and facilities.)

☐ Europe on $30 a Day $13.95	☐ New Zealand on $40 a Day $10.95
☐ Australia on $25 a Day $10.95	☐ New York on $50 a Day............ $10.95
☐ Eastern Europe on $25 a Day $10.95	☐ Scandinavia on $50 a Day.......... $10.95
☐ England on $40 a Day.............. $11.95	☐ Scotland and Wales on $40 a Day..... $11.95
☐ Greece on $30 a Day............... $11.95	☐ South America on $30 a Day $10.95
☐ Hawaii on $50 a Day............... $11.95	☐ Spain and Morocco (plus the Canary
☐ India on $25 a Day $10.95	Is.) on $40 a Day $10.95
☐ Ireland on $30 a Day $10.95	☐ Turkey on $25 a Day $10.95
☐ Israel on $30 & $35 a Day $11.95	☐ Washington, D.C., & Historic Va. on
☐ Mexico on $20 a Day $10.95	$40 a Day $11.95

FROMMER'S DOLLARWISE GUIDES™

(Guides to sightseeing and tourist accommodations and facilities from budget to deluxe, with emphasis on the medium-priced.)

☐ Alaska $12.95	☐ Cruises (incl. Alaska, Carib, Mex,
☐ Austria & Hungary $11.95	Hawaii, Panama, Canada, & US) $12.95
☐ Belgium, Holland, Luxembourg $11.95	☐ California & Las Vegas $11.95
☐ Egypt.......................... $11.95	☐ Florida......................... $11.95
☐ England & Scotland $11.95	☐ Mid-Atlantic States $12.95
☐ France......................... $11.95	☐ New England $12.95
☐ Germany $12.95	☐ New York State $12.95
☐ Italy........................... $11.95	☐ Northwest $11.95
☐ Japan & Hong Kong $12.95	☐ Skiing in Europe $12.95
☐ Portugal (incl. Madeira & the Azores) . $12.95	☐ Skiing USA—East................. $11.95
☐ South Pacific.................... $12.95	☐ Skiing USA—West $11.95
☐ Switzerland & Liechtenstein $12.95	☐ Southeast & New Orleans........... $11.95
☐ Bermuda & The Bahamas........... $11.95	☐ Southwest....................... $11.95
☐ Canada $12.95	☐ Texas.......................... $11.95
☐ Caribbean $13.95	

TURN PAGE FOR ADDITIONAL BOOKS AND ORDER FORM.

THE ARTHUR FROMMER GUIDES™

(Pocket-size guides to sightseeing and tourist accommodations and facilities in all price ranges.)

☐ Amsterdam/Holland	$5.95	☐ Mexico City/Acapulco	$5.95
☐ Athens	$5.95	☐ Minneapolis/St. Paul	$5.95
☐ Atlantic City/Cape May	$5.95	☐ Montreal/Quebec City	$5.95
☐ Boston	$5.95	☐ New Orleans	$5.95
☐ Cancún/Cozumel/Yucatán	$5.95	☐ New York	$5.95
☐ Dublin/Ireland	$5.95	☐ Orlando/Disney World/EPCOT	$5.95
☐ Hawaii	$5.95	☐ Paris	$5.95
☐ Las Vegas	$5.95	☐ Philadelphia	$5.95
☐ Lisbon/Madrid/Costa del Sol	$5.95	☐ Rome	$5.95
☐ London	$5.95	☐ San Francisco	$5.95
☐ Los Angeles	$5.95	☐ Washington, D.C.	$5.95

FROMMER'S TOURING GUIDES™

(Color illustrated guides that include walking tours, cultural & historic sites, and other vital travel information.)

☐ Egypt	$8.95	☐ Paris	$8.95
☐ Florence	$8.95	☐ Venice	$8.95
☐ London	$8.95		

SPECIAL EDITIONS

☐ A Shopper's Guide to the Caribbean	$12.95	☐ Motorist's Phrase Book (Fr/Ger/Sp)	$4.95
☐ Bed & Breakfast—N. America	$8.95	☐ Swap and Go (Home Exchanging)	$10.95
☐ Guide to Honeymoons (US, Canada, Mexico, & Carib)	$12.95	☐ The Candy Apple (NY for Kids)	$11.95
☐ How to Beat the High Cost of Travel	$4.95	☐ Travel Diary and Record Book	$5.95
☐ Marilyn Wood's Wonderful Weekends (NY, Conn, Mass, RI, Vt, NH, NJ, Del, Pa)	$11.95	☐ Where to Stay USA (Lodging from $3 to $30 a night)	$9.95

☐ Arthur Frommer's New World of Travel (Annual sourcebook previewing: new travel trends, new modes of travel, and the latest cost-cutting strategies for savvy travelers) $12.95

ORDER NOW!

In U.S. include $1.50 shipping UPS for 1st book; 50¢ ea. add'l book. Outside U.S. $2 and 50¢, respectively.

Enclosed is my check or money order for $ _____

NAME _____

ADDRESS _____

CITY _____ STATE _____ ZIP _____